SAFETY FIRST—ALWAYS!

Tackling home improvement projects and repairs can be endlessly rewarding. But as most of us know, with the rewards come risks. DIYers use chain saws, climb ladders and tear into walls that can contain big, hazardous surprises.

The good news is that armed with the right knowledge, tools and procedures, homeowners can minimize risk. As you go about your projects and repairs, stay alert for these hazards:

Aluminum wiring

Aluminum wiring, installed in millions of homes between 1965 and 1973, requires special techniques and materials to make safe connections. This wiring is dull gray, not the dull orange characteristic of copper. Hire a licensed electrician certified to work with it. For more information, go to cpsc.gov and search for "aluminum wiring."

Spontaneous combustion

Rags saturated with oil finishes, such as Danish oil and linseed oil, as well as oil-based paints and stains, can spontaneously combust if left bunched up. Always dry them outdoors, spread out loosely. When the oil has thoroughly dried, you can safely throw the rags in the trash.

Vision and hearing protection

Safety glasses or goggles should be worn whenever you're working on DIY projects that involve chemicals, dust or anything that could shatter or chip off and hit your eye. Also, sounds louder than 80 decibels (dB) are considered potentially dangerous. For instance, sound levels from a lawn mower can be 90 dB and from shop tools and chain saws can be 90 to 100 dB.

Lead paint

If your home was built before 1979, it may contain lead paint, which is a serious health hazard, especially for children 6 years old or under. Take precautions when you scrape or remove it. Contact your public health department for detailed safety information or call (800) 424-LEAD (5323) to receive an information pamphlet. Or visit epa.gov/lead.

Buried utilities

A few days before you dig in your yard, have your underground water, gas and electrical lines marked. Just call 811 or go to call811.com.

Smoke and carbon monoxide (CO) alarms

The risk of dying in a reported home-structure fire is cut in half in homes with working smoke alarms. Test your smoke alarms every month, replace batteries as necessary and replace units that are more than 10 years old. As you make your home more energy efficient and airtight, existing ducts and chimneys can't always successfully vent combustion gases, including potentially deadly carbon monoxide (CO). Install a UL-listed CO detector, and test your CO and smoke alarms at the same time.

Five-gallon buckets and window-covering cords

Anywhere from 10 to 40 children a year drown in 5-gallon buckets, according to the U.S. Consumer Products Safety Commission. Always store empty buckets upside down and ones containing liquid with the covers securely snapped.

According to Parents for Window Blind Safety, hundreds of children in the United States are injured every year after becoming entangled in looped window-treatment cords. For more information, visit pfwbs.org.

Working up high

If you have to get up on your roof to do a repair or installation, always install roof brackets and wear a roof harness.

Asbestos

Texture sprayed on ceilings before 1978, adhesives and tiles for vinyl and asphalt floors before 1980, and vermiculite insulation (with gray granules) all may contain asbestos. Other building materials made between 1940 and 1980 could also contain asbestos. If you suspect that materials you're removing or working around contain asbestos, contact your health department or visit epa.gov/asbestos for information.

T0054459

CONTENTS

Chapter one
KITCHEN & BATHROOM

Chapter two
GARAGE & OUTDOORS

family handyman

WHOLE HOUSE
STORAGE &
ORGANIZING

family handyman

A FAMILY HANDYMAN BOOK

Copyright © 2022 Home Services Publications, a subsidiary of Trusted Media Brands, Inc.

2915 Commers Drive, Suite 700
Eagan, MN 55121

Family Handyman is a registered trademark of Trusted Media Brands, Inc.

Hardcover ISBN: 978-1-62145-789-3
Paperback ISBN: 978-1-62145-804-3
Component Number: 116400106H
ePub ISBN: 978-1-62145-805-0

We are committed to both the quality of our products and the service we provide to our customers. We value your comments, so please feel free to contact us at TMBBookTeam@TrustedMediaBrands.com.

For more *Family Handyman* products and information, visit our website:

www.familyhandyman.com

Printed in the United States of America

10 9 8 7 6 5 4 3 2 1

Text, photography and illustrations for *Whole House Storage & Organizing* are based on articles previously published in *Family Handyman* magazine (familyhandyman.com).

A NOTE TO OUR READERS: All do-it-yourself activities involve a degree of risk. Skills, materials, tools and site conditions vary widely. Although the editors have made every effort to ensure accuracy, the reader remains responsible for the selection and use of tools, materials and methods. Always obey local codes and laws, follow manufacturer's operating instructions, and observe safety precautions

Image Credits

24 br Rev-A-Shelf **58** cr Dean Tenner **58** br Kenneth Snow **59** tl Scott Beverly **59** b Art Gay **140** b **141** tr, b **142** b AMES Companies **266** Roy Velardi **268** Eric Schleppenbach **269** l Tim Hausman

All other photographs by Tom Fenenga, Jeff Gorton, Mike Krivit and Bill Zuehlke.

All other illustrations and tech art by Mario Ferro, Jeff Gorton, Susan Jensen, Bruce Kieffer, David Munkittrick, David Radtke, Frank Rohrbach III and Eugene Thompson.

Chapter **three**
LAUNDRY ROOM, CLOSETS & CLOTHES

Chapter **four**
AROUND THE HOUSE

Chapter **five**
WORKSHOP

Special **Section**
STORING SPORTS GEAR

Project Index

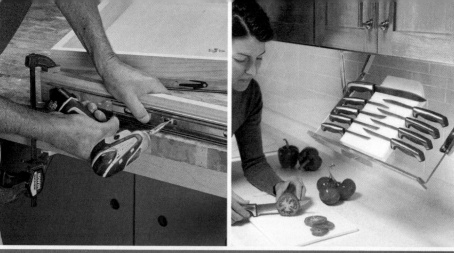

CHAPTER **ONE**

KITCHEN & BATHROOM

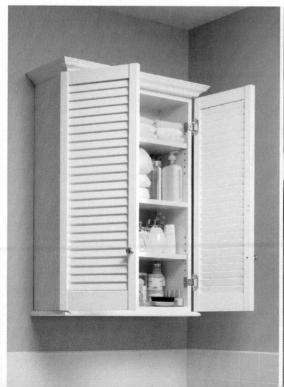

SPACER

Hidden Knife Rack

A knife block takes up valuable countertop space. This insert puts all your cutlery inside a drawer in a safe, tidy, flat rack. Your drawer might be large enough to store all of your sharpening supplies as well.

To make the blocks, glue up two layers of 3/4-in.-thick hardwood. A single thickness would set the knife handles too close together. Size the length and height of the blocks to fit your largest blade. When the glue dries, sand the blocks and then glue them to a piece of 1/4-in. plywood properly sized to fit your drawer.

Cut 1/8-in.-thick strips of wood to space the blocks while the glue dries. Pull out the spacers as soon as the glue starts to hold so they don't get glued in place. A support strip under the handles makes them easier to grab. We added two more 1/2-in. dividers to make compartments for other supplies.

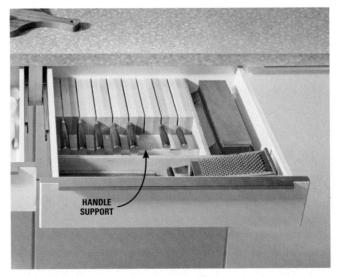

HANDLE SUPPORT

WHAT IT TAKES	
TIME 1-2 hours	**SKILL LEVEL** Beginner

TOOLS & MATERIALS
Handsaw (or power saw), wood glue, sanding paper

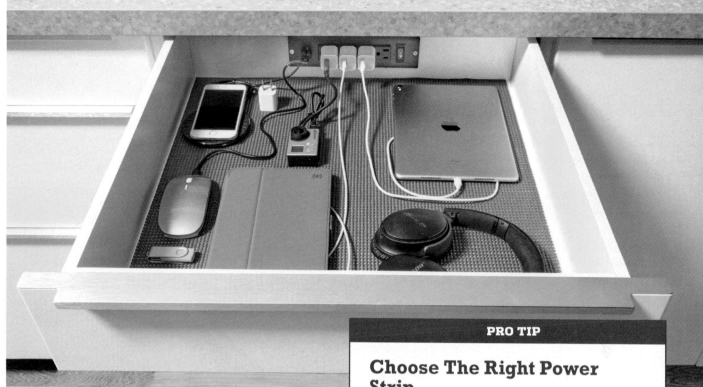

Charging Drawer

Turn your kitchen's eyesore junk drawer into a valuable station for charging your favorite, and most-used, electronics.

Here's another way to remove clutter from the countertop. These power strips don't require any electrical wiring; they just plug into an outlet. If your kitchen is up to current code, it will have an outlet for your sink's disposal. All you need to do is route the cord to the outlet.

1 Cut the opening. Measure the power strip and mark the cutout on the back of the drawer. Drill a hole near each corner and use a jigsaw to cut the opening. Check the fit of the power strip, and then use the jigsaw, a file or a sanding block to adjust the opening as needed.

PRO TIP

Choose The Right Power Strip

The power strip you choose should be UL-listed for this specific purpose. We used a furniture power strip that has a switch to cut the power when the appliances aren't in use. It's UL-listed to be attached to furniture and plugged into a permanent receptacle. We found it online.

2 Install the power strip. Insert the power strip into the hole and secure it with screws through the mounting holes. Use a zip tie or cable staple to attach the cord to the cabinet's back, allowing 2 to 3 in. of slack. Route the cord to your disposal outlet by drilling through cabinet sides as needed.

WHAT IT TAKES

TIME	SKILL LEVEL
1-2 hours	Beginner

TOOLS & MATERIALS
Jigsaw, sanding block or file, zip tie or cable staple

Custom Egg Crate Compartments

It's easy to keep your plastic containers and lids organized with this super-simple divider.

Egg crate compartments are excellent for storing plastic food containers and other stackable items. The partitions aren't fastened to the drawer, so you can easily customize compartments for different containers. All you need is a way to cut slots. We'll show you an easy method using a table saw and a custom spacer. Determine the thickness of the spacer by subtracting the width of the saw's kerf from the thickness of your material.

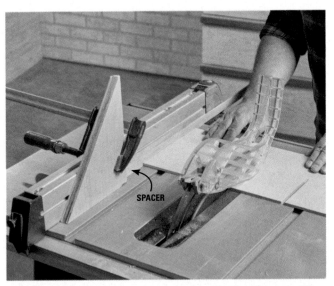

2 Second cut. Slip your spacer between the fence and the partition and make the second pass. This cut defines the right-hand side of the slot. If there's waste left between the cuts, knock it out with a chisel or a utility knife.

1 First cut. Use your containers to figure out the bin size, then lay out the slots on each partition. The first cut defines the left-hand side of the slot. Set the fence for the first cut and clamp a stop block to the fence so you cut only halfway through the partition's height. Push the partition up to the block, and then back it out.

3 Slip in the partitions. After sanding and finishing, stand up the bottom partitions in the drawer with the slots facing up. Then add the top partitions, sliding them into the slots in the bottom partitions.

WHAT IT TAKES

TIME
1-2 hours

SKILL LEVEL
Beginner

TOOLS & MATERIALS
Table saw, clamps, sanding paper

Diagonal Dividers

Diagonal partitions not only optimize drawer space but also allow the drawer to accommodate longer items.

Rip stock to match the drawer's interior height, and then mark the drawer where you'd like the partitions. Use the marks on the drawer to figure the partition lengths, then cut each partition with opposing 45-degree angles on their ends. Check their fit and screw them into place, starting with the short pieces, then the long.

When you get to the last one, you'll probably need a stubby screwdriver to get between the partitions. To make that installation easier, we installed one long piece, removed it and then installed the second long piece. This way, when we reinstalled the first piece, the holes were already threaded, making hand-driving the screws much easier.

WHAT IT TAKES	
TIME 1-2 hours	**SKILL LEVEL** Beginner

TOOLS & MATERIALS
Saw (hand miter box or power saw able to cut 45°-angle), driver/drill, screwdriver

Adjustable Dividers

No more sorting through drawers to get the pots and pans you need with these dividers. They keep everything organized and well within reach—all you need to do is decide what recipe you're cooking up for dinner.

The most efficient way to store your pots and pans is to stack them up, with the largest one on the bottom and the smallest on the top. But that creates its own issues—it's annoying and noisy to dig out the pan you need. Instead of rummaging around and creating a commotion throughout the house, install these adjustable dividers in a deep drawer to provide easy access.

WHAT IT TAKES	
TIME Half a day	**SKILL LEVEL** Beginner

TOOLS & MATERIALS
Table saw, driver/drill, sanding paper

SPACER

1 Create slots. Cut strips to the width that best suits your drawer and pans; these are 1-1/2 in. wide. Sand, finish and attach the strips on opposite sides (front to back or side to side) inside the drawer. Use a piece of 1/4-in. plywood as a spacer between the strips, creating slots for 1/4-in. plywood partitions.

2 Slip in the partitions. Cut, sand and finish the partitions. Slide them into the slots created by the spaced strips to accommodate your pots, pans and lids.

Custom Silverware Tray

Don't go to the department store for your silverware trays! Instead, take a little time and build your own—the results are well worth it.

Store-bought silverware trays get the job done, but they never quite fit your drawers perfectly and are bound to cause frustration the longer you have them. They shift and slide around within the drawer, and they leave all kinds of awkward space around the tray.

Instead of getting your trays from the store, take the time to make them yourself. You can get it done in an afternoon, and you likely already have all the necessary tools you need for the job. You'll be happy with the maximized storage space and minimized annoying sliding—and you'll wonder why you ever had store-bought trays.

WHAT IT TAKES	
TIME 3 hours	**SKILL LEVEL** Beginner

TOOLS & MATERIALS
Handsaw (or power saw), driver/drill, wood glue, sanding paper

1 Start with the main dividers. We sectioned a big drawer with a T-shaped divider made from 1/2-in. plywood. We screwed it into place through one side and the back. If we ever want to change the configuration, it'll be easy to do. Because these drawers are melamine, we sanded and finished all the parts before adding them to the drawer.

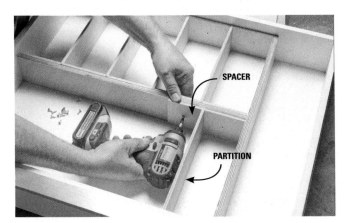

SPACER

PARTITION

2 Add the partitions. Divide the large sections using 1/4-in. partitions. Since the parts are prefinished, we attached the spacers with countersunk 1/2-in. wood screws instead of glue.

Deep Drawer Slider

Deep drawers are ideal for large or tall items, but when they're filled with lots of smaller items, they're just a mess. Adding a horizontal sliding tray on rails neatly divides that depth into much more efficient space.

Build a simple tray to keep your stuff neat and tidy. The tray can be whatever depth you want. The width, however, should be less than half the width of the drawer so that you can easily access everything below. Attach the front and back rails level with each other using screws, and set the tray on the rails. The partitions in the bottom of this drawer are optional. They're just pieces of 1/2-in. plywood assembled with glue and 1-in. wood screws.

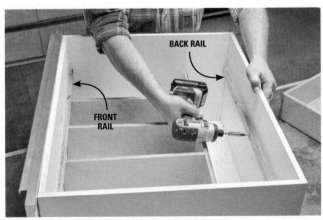

BACK RAIL

FRONT RAIL

WHAT IT TAKES	
TIME Half a day	**SKILL LEVEL** Beginner

TOOLS & MATERIALS
Handsaw (or power saw), driver/drill, wood glue, sanding paper

From Clutter To Clear

Here's how to get gleaming, organized kitchen counters you can be proud of.

A. EXPAND THE COUNTER WITH A KITCHEN CART

A rolling kitchen cart is the next best thing to adding new cabinets and countertop space. The top provides extra work space when you're preparing that big Thanksgiving dinner, and the sliding shelves below hold items that might otherwise clutter surfaces.

If you plan to use a cart for food preparation, choose one with a tough top, such as butcher block, stainless steel or plastic laminate. Carts come in a variety of wood finishes, so there's a good chance you can get one to match your existing cabinets. Or you can go for an eclectic look with a shiny metal or painted cart.

B. TIDY FILE CENTER

Countertops are a landing pad for papers, and once they're there the piles only seem to get bigger. Get that mess off your counter with folders and a file holder. The one shown here mounts with screws or double-sided foam tape. If you don't have suitable vertical surface, get a file holder. It will still take up less space than a stack of papers.

C. UNDER-CABINET STORAGE RACKS

Pull-down racks give you instant access to kitchen essentials without the clutter of spice racks or knife holders on the counter. When the cooking is done, the rack swings up against the underside of the cabinet. You can find a few options for pull-down knife racks online, but your best bet might be to make your own. If you purchase hinges, you can create a storage rack that holds knives and other small knick-knacks, too. Go to www.wwhardware.com and search for items KVUCKR or KVUCCB (cook-book rack).

D. OFF-THE-COUNTER MICROWAVE

Microwave ovens are the biggest space hogs on most countertops. To find a cabinet-mountable microwave and mounting hardware (which will come with an additional cost), search for "under cabinet microwave" online. Before purchasing any brackets, be sure to measure the height of both the microwave and the space above the countertop. If you have a smaller microwave, this solution might work

A.

B.

C.

D.

for you. But if you have a larger microwave, the space under it might end up being too small to be useful.

E. CONCEALED MESSAGE CENTER

Don't let shopping lists, phone messages, to-do notes and various other useful reminders take up your valuable counter space. Instead, mount a dry-erase board and a plastic desk organizer on the inside of a cabinet door with double-sided foam mounting tape. The bin will protrude into the cabinet, so you'll need to be sure to position it where it won't collide with shelves or the stuff inside. Get the board, bin and tape online or at a discount or office supply store.

F. COOKING CADDY FOR QUICK CLEAR-OFF

You always want salt, cooking oils and your favorite spices next to the stove if you use them frequently. But as necessary as they are to a great meal, they really don't have to take up precious space on your counter. Place them all in a caddy that you can instantly stow in a cabinet after cooking—then they're always right where you need them, but they're not in the way. You'll find caddies in various shapes, sizes and prices at any store that sells kitchenware.

G. SUPER SIMPLE WOODEN TABLET STAND

In today's culinary world, life happens on technology—it's where you find your recipes, your ingredient lists and even your helper when things don't go according to plan. Who wants to be bothered with walking around the house to find your tablet when you're in the middle of dinner? Solve the problem with this super simple tablet stand. It looks great, and chances are that you already have the power tools you need to build it. Best of all, when it's not in use it can be disassembled and stored in a drawer. For instructions on how to build it, visit familyhandyman.com and search for "simple tablet stand."

H. DECORATIVE BACKSPLASH RACK

Backsplash racks offer easy access and stylish storage. Most versions take just a few minutes to install. Search for "backsplash rack" online to find a range of styles. You'll find that they're available at a range of prices from a variety of different retailers.

Backsplash racks have a few disadvantages, though. All your kitchen utensils have to look good, since they're on display. And if you ever decide to remove the rack, you'll be left with screw holes in the backsplash; not a big problem with drywall, but unfixable in tile. So before you go ahead and install it, be sure you'll be happy with it for years to come.

E.

F.

G.

H.

Kitchen Rollouts

They changed our lives—and they'll change yours, too!

It may sound like hype, but adding rollouts to your kitchen cabinets can be life-changing. We speak from personal experience. We've added roll-outs to our entire kitchen, and this is what happened:

- The kids have complete access to everything they need—from cereal to the recycling. Now they can get their own breakfast and take the cans to the curb—no excuses!
- Sore backs and bum knees are less of an issue since we no longer have to stoop to find things in our base cabinets.
- Dinner prep goes a lot faster now that we're not hunting for pot lids and baking pans piled on top of one another on our jumbled, dark shelves.
- We're saving money by not buying things we already had, but had been lost in the recesses of our cabinets. We can pull our shelves into the light and see everything, including the rancid oil and three boxes of cornstarch we somehow acquired.
- The kitchen feels larger and works better. The rollouts maximize every cubic inch of storage space, so we can store rarely used appliances in our cabinets instead of on the counters.

Are you a convert yet?

This article will give you a wide range of tips for planning, buying and building kitchen rollouts so they can change your life, too. You can build a simple rollout drawer, like the ones shown here, in a couple of hours and for around $50. But I have to warn you—once you see that rollout in action, you'll want to retrofit all your kitchen cabinets. What are you waiting for?

A. AVOID MISTAKES WITH A STORY STICK

The most obvious way to size rollout parts is to measure the opening of the cabinet and then do the math. But that's a recipe for mistakes. It's easy to forget to subtract one of the components (like the width of the slides or the drawers) from the overall measurement. Try making a story stick instead. You can forget the math and just mark your measurements on a piece of scrap wood. It's a great visual aid that helps you prevent mistakes and having to walk between your kitchen and your shop constantly to double-check measurements. Mark the exact widths of your rollout parts on a stick. It eliminates the math—and the mistakes.

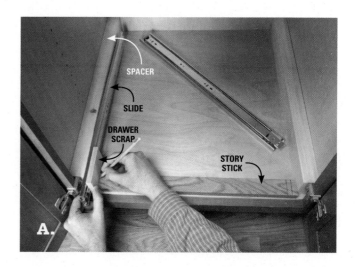

A.

B.

B. KEEP DRAWER BOXES SIMPLE

All the drawer boxes in our shop are super simple: butt-joint corners and glued-on bottoms. No rabbets, dadoes or dovetails. They don't look very impressive, but they've held up for years. So we built our kitchen rollouts the same way. If simple boxes can carry tools and hardware, we figure they can stand up to kitchen use, too.

Field editor tip: Consider having drawer boxes made to your exact specs and then install them yourself. The average cost to order a single solid maple dovetailed drawer is about $35. Compared with buying material and finishing it yourself—not to mention the dovetail joints—you can't beat it. And it looks much nicer.

— Steve Zubik, Nest Woodworking, Northfield, MN

C.

D.

E.

C-E. THINK INSIDE THE BOX

Building a slew of identical drawer boxes is easier, but having a variety gives you more versatility. Think about what you're going to store and build the boxes to suit your needs. **(C)** Rollout drawers with sloping sides keep tall things stable, yet still let you see all the way to the back of the shelf. These are good for nesting pots and pans or storing different-size items on the same shelf. **(D)** Lower sides (3 in. is typical) work well for smaller items such as canned goods and spices. The low sides make reading labels easier. **(E)** Shelves with higher sides all around (6 in. rather than the typical 3 in.) are ideal for tippy plastic storage containers or stacks of plates.

F. WATCH FOR OBSTACLES

Every cabinetmaker has a story about the rollout that just wouldn't roll out. Instead, it collided with something (oops). When you're measuring for the spacer width, watch out for protruding hinges and doors that don't open fully or that protrude into the cabinet opening. Make drawer boxes about 1/32 in. smaller than you need. It's easy to shim behind a slide with layers of masking tape to make up for a too-small drawer. It's a lot harder to deal with a drawer that's too wide.

H. MAKE THE MOST OF SKINNY SPACES

Kitchen designer Mary Jane Pappas typically recommends 18- to 30-in.-wide rollout drawers for cabinets: "Any larger and they're too clumsy. Any smaller and too much of the space is used by the rollouts themselves." But there is one type of rollout that makes good use of narrow spaces, even those only 3 to 6 in. wide. Pappas says that pullout pantries—single tall, narrow drawers with long shelves, drawers, baskets or even pegboard—can be an efficient way to put skinny spaces to work. In a small kitchen with little storage space, you can make even narrow filler spaces work harder by installing a vertical pegboard rollout. Shown is the 434 Series 6-in. Base Filler with stainless steel panel, about $450, from Rev-A-Shelf.com.

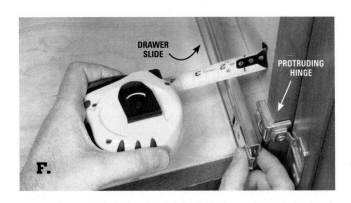

DRAWER SLIDE

PROTRUDING HINGE

F.

H.

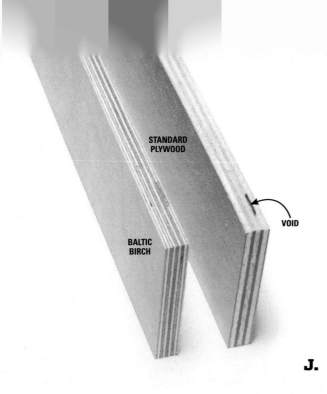

STANDARD
PLYWOOD

VOID

BALTIC
BIRCH

J.

J. BALTIC BIRCH IS BEST

Cabinetmakers love Baltic birch plywood for roll-outs
because the edges look great. Unlike standard hardwood
plywood, Baltic birch never has voids in the inner core. It
may not be labeled "Baltic birch" at home centers, but you'll
be able to identify it by comparing it with other hardwood
plywood in the racks. Baltic birch will have more and thinner
laminations in the plywood core.

The biggest disadvantages of using Baltic birch are that
it costs more than standard hardwood plywood and can be
harder to find. If your home center doesn't carry it, try a
traditional lumberyard.

K. USE THE RIGHT SLIDES

There are a dozen kinds of drawer slides out there, but if you
want to keep shopping and installation simple, stick to these
two types: roller slides and ball-bearing slides. Roller slides
glide on plastic wheels. They're inexpensive, a cinch to install
(it takes about two minutes) and nearly impossible to screw
up. You'll find them at home centers under various names,
including side mount, under mount and bottom mount.
Most are rated to carry 35 to 100 lbs. For heavy-duty rollouts
holding items such as canned goods, use slides rated for at
least 100 lbs. The big disadvantage: Most roller slides extend
only three-quarters of their length—the back of the drawer
stays in the cabinet.

Ball-bearing slides glide on tiny bearings. The big
advantage of these slides is that they extend fully, giving you
complete access to everything in the drawer. They're about
three times the cost of roller slides and they're usually rated
to carry 75 to 100 lbs. Home centers carry ball-bearing slides,
but you'll find a wider variety at various online woodworking
retailers. The big disadvantage: They're fussy to install. If
your drawer is a hair too big or small, these slides won't glide.

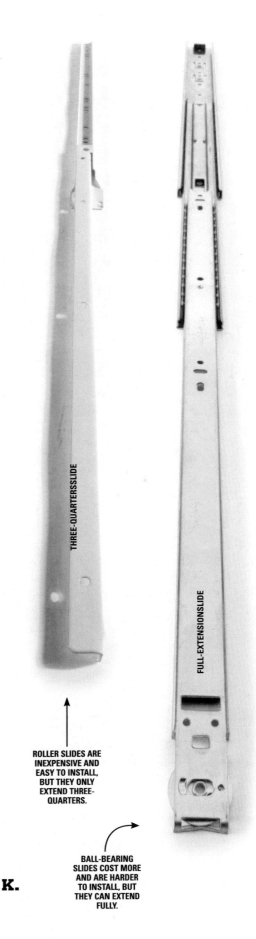

THREE-QUARTERS SLIDE

FULL-EXTENSION SLIDE

ROLLER SLIDES ARE
INEXPENSIVE AND
EASY TO INSTALL,
BUT THEY ONLY
EXTEND THREE-
QUARTERS.

BALL-BEARING
SLIDES COST MORE
AND ARE HARDER
TO INSTALL, BUT
THEY CAN EXTEND
FULLY.

K.

Easy-Build Rollouts

You can build one in an hour, even if you're a beginner!

If you're tired of getting down on all fours and rooting through dark, jumbled base cabinets to find what you need, this project is for you. Rollouts make it easy to organize and access everything from your pantry items and cookware in the kitchen to the power tools and finish cans in your shop.

We've built many rollouts for our houses and workshops, and believe us, the conventional way of building rollouts is tricky, time-consuming and frustrating. With the easier method shown here, you can build the rollouts on your workbench using just a few measurements taken from each cabinet.

PLAN THE ROLLOUTS

Before you build anything, decide what you'll be storing in each rollout. We lay out the items to determine the height of the drawer sides and to plan for clearance at the top **(Photo 1)**. That will let you know how many rollouts are possible in each cabinet and exactly how high to place the cleats **(Photo 10)**.

BUYING THE MATERIALS

Study **Figure A** to understand the construction. Since each cabinet is unique, the quantities of each material will vary. You'll have to measure your cabinets and plan your rollouts to figure out a materials list before you go to the home center. But the basic recipe is the same no matter what size you're building. Each unit requires a pair of 22-in. side-mount drawer slides **(Photos 6 and 7)**. And each one will need 1/4-in. plywood for the bottom **(Photo 5)**, 1/2-in. plywood for the rollout base **(Photos 8 and 9)** and of course, either 1x6s or 1x3s for the rollout frames. (We used clear pine for these, but you can use any wood as long as it's straight.)

Choose a 1x6 frame to corral bulky items like pans, linens or cereal boxes and a 1x3 frame for shorter items like canned goods, spices or utensils. (You can substitute 1x2s or 1x4s if you wish.) Both frames get mounted on a 1/2-in. plywood base, which rests either on the cabinet bottom or on cleats that attach to the cabinet sides for elevated units. For each elevated rollout, you'll need 40 in. of 1x2s for support cleats

1 Plan around your typical contents. Stage the items you wish to store on rollouts until you're satisfied with the heights and the quantity of the drawers. Note the clearance heights needed to get the spacing and positioning correct in the cabinet.

2 Measure the opening. Open the door(s) on the cabinet and measure the space between the narrowest part of the opening (including projecting hinge hardware) to size the rollouts. After measuring, remove the doors to make it easier to work and to prevent damage.

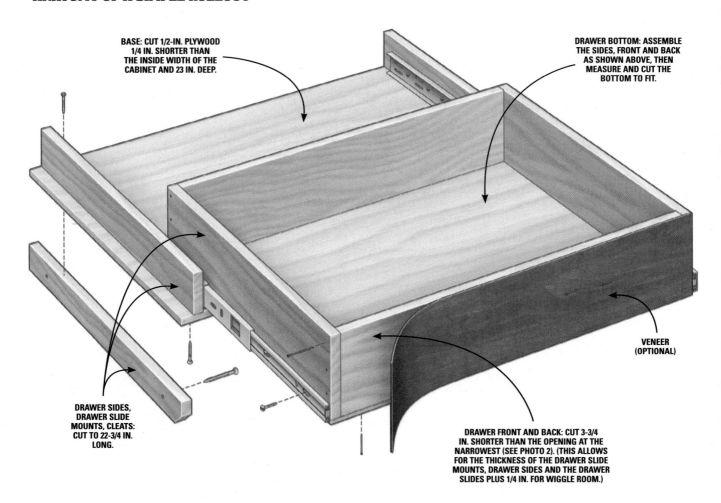

BASE: CUT 1/2-IN. PLYWOOD 1/4 IN. SHORTER THAN THE INSIDE WIDTH OF THE CABINET AND 23 IN. DEEP.

DRAWER BOTTOM: ASSEMBLE THE SIDES, FRONT AND BACK AS SHOWN ABOVE, THEN MEASURE AND CUT THE BOTTOM TO FIT.

VENEER (OPTIONAL)

DRAWER SIDES, DRAWER SLIDE MOUNTS, CLEATS: CUT TO 22-3/4 IN. LONG.

DRAWER FRONT AND BACK: CUT 3-3/4 IN. SHORTER THAN THE OPENING AT THE NARROWEST (SEE PHOTO 2). (THIS ALLOWS FOR THE THICKNESS OF THE DRAWER SLIDE MOUNTS, DRAWER SIDES AND THE DRAWER SLIDES PLUS 1/4 IN. FOR WIGGLE ROOM.)

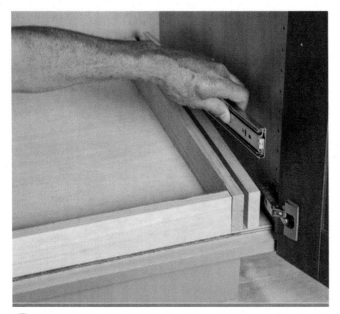

3 Test-fit before assembly. Cut the rollout base, drawer sides, front and back, and drawer slide mounts following Figure A. Loosely assemble the parts in the cabinet to ensure everything will fit before moving on to assembly.

(Photo 10). Each rollout will also require 4 ft. of 1x3, which is used for drawer slide mounts **(Photo 7)**. Rollouts need to be anchored to prevent tipping. Just screw bottom rollout bases to the bottom of the cabinet. Anchor upper rollouts with angle brackets **(Photo 11)**.

ASSEMBLY AND FINISHING

After you cut all the parts, dry-fit everything inside the cabinet to make sure it will fit and allow enough clearance to operate **(Photo 3)**. We can't tell you how many times we've forgotten to account for the width of drawer sides, the thickness of slides or something else, and had to knock everything apart and start over. Plus, dry-fitting will force you to think through the assembly so you can avoid making a mistake.

After you cut the parts and assemble the rollout drawer, apply your choice of finish before you put the drawer slides on and install the unit in the cabinet. We covered the front of our rollouts with a self-adhesive veneer to help them blend in with the cabinets. You can find some veneer options at home centers and woodworking stores, and many more online by searching for "self-sticking veneer."

DRAWER SIDE

DRAWER FRONT

4 Assemble the parts. Glue and nail together the drawer with 2-in. brads. (Remember: The front and back go between the sides, not the other way around!)

DRAWER BOTTOM

5 Add the bottom. Use the bottom to square up the frame when you glue and pin it to the underside with 1-in. brads.

FLUSH

6 Add the drawer slides. Clamp the drawer down to a flat surface, rest the drawer slide flush with the front of the drawer and then predrill the holes into the non-slotted holes with a self-centering drill. Then anchor the slides to the drawer with the included screws.

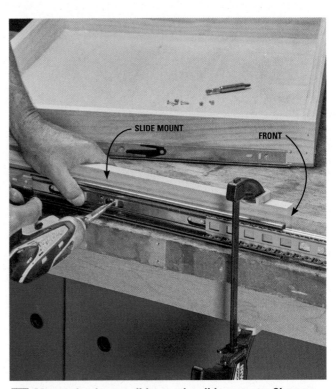

SLIDE MOUNT

FRONT

7 Mount the drawer slides on the slide mounts. Clamp the drawer slide mounts to the bench. Place the drawer slides flush with the end and then screw them to the drawer slide mounts.

8 Clamp drawer assembly to the base. Engage the slides, and then center the rollout drawer on the plywood base and clamp the drawer mounts in place at all four corners.

9 Screw the drawer mounts to the base. Flip over the assembly and predrill and anchor the slide mounts through the base with 1-5/8-in. screws.

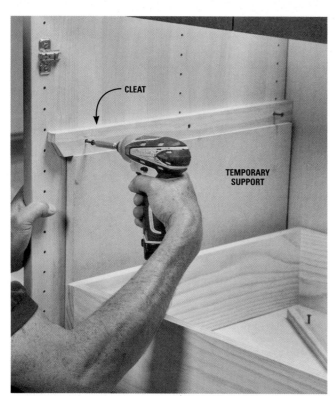

10 Fasten the cleats to the cabinet. Support elevated rollouts on cleats. Rest the cleats on squares of plywood cut to the right width while you screw the cleats to the cabinet sides with 1-1/4-in. screws.

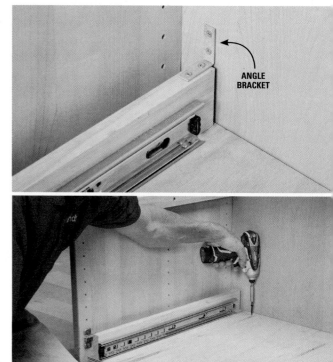

11 Secure the rollouts. Anchor elevated rollouts with angle brackets screwed to the cabinet back and drawer slide mounts (top photo). Anchor bottom rollouts by sinking a couple of 1-1/4-in. screws through the rollout base into the cabinet bottom, as shown in the bottom photo.

Under-Sink Storage

Build these handy rollout trays in a weekend.

Have you finally had it with that dark and dingy, *I'm-not-sure-what's-there* storage space under the kitchen sink? Well, these two types of roll-out trays, which ride on smooth-action ball-bearing drawer slides, will get everything out in the open and let you find exactly what you need at a glance.

This project isn't difficult at all. In fact, there aren't even any miter joints. All the parts are glued together and then nailed or screwed. You can make all the trays in an afternoon using building products from your local home center or hardware store.

You can build everything with simple carpentry tools and some careful measuring. You don't really need a table saw for this project, but it will help you zero in on more exact measurements, especially for the lower tray bases where accuracy is important for the ball-bearing drawer slides. The nail gun shown in the photos is also optional, but

it makes assembly faster and less tedious. It shoots thin 18-gauge nails.

Here, you'll learn how to measure your sink base and custom-size and assemble the wood trays. You'll also get some tips for installing the drawer slides. You'll probably have to adapt the project dimensions to fit your space. For example, you may have a bulky garbage disposal that won't allow you to install both upper slide-out trays. In that case,

WHAT IT TAKES	
TIME 2 days	**SKILL LEVEL** Intermediate
TOOLS & MATERIALS Circular saw (or table saw) driver/drill, wood glue, framing square, clamps (optional: 18-gauge nailer)	

FIGURE A.
SINK CABINET TRAY DETAILS

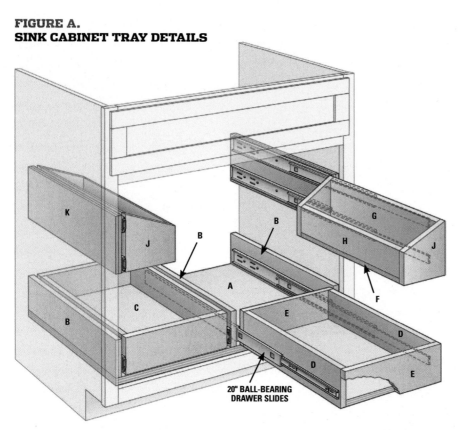

20" BALL-BEARING
DRAWER SLIDES

Materials List

ITEM	QTY.
3/4" x 4' x 8' hardwood plywood	1
1x4 x16' maple	1
1/2" x 2' x 2' hardwood plywood	1
1x6 x 2' maple	1
20" ball-bearing drawer slides	4 prs.
Wood glue	1 pt.
Construction adhesive	1 pt.
6d finish nails, small box	1
1-5/8" wood screws, small box	1

(This list applies to the rollout trays shown; your quantities may vary.)

Cutting List

KEY	QTY, SIZE & DESCRIPTION
A	1x 3/4" x 32-3/4" x 20" plywood base
B	3x 3/4" x 3-1/2" x 20" base partitions
C	2x 3/4" x 12-3/4" x 18-1/2" plywood tray bottom
D	4x 3/4" x 3-1/2" x 18-1/2" tray sides
E	4x 3/4" x 3-1/2" x 14-1/4" tray fronts and backs
F	2x 1/2" x 5-1/2" x 18-1/2" upper tray bottoms
G	2x 3/4" x 5" x 18-1/2" upper tray (high side)
H	2x 3/4" x 3" x 18-1/2" upper tray (low side)
J	4x 3/4" x 5-1/2" x 5-1/2" upper tray front and back
K	4x 1/2" x 5-1/2" x 20" side cleats (double layer)

just make one tray instead. If you have plumbing that comes up through the floor of your sink cabinet, you may need to shorten the lower trays to fit in front of the plumbing. In any case, this project will help you organize this black hole once and for all.

GETTING THE RIGHT STUFF

Before you get the materials, determine if you can build all the trays or only a few of them. At a home center or lumber-yard, look for hardwood plywood. You can often buy 2 x 4-ft. pieces instead of a whole sheet. The hardwood plywood has two good sides and is smoother and flatter than exterior-grade softwood plywood. It costs more too.

In the hardware department, look for ball-bearing side-mount drawer slides. The pairs of the brand shown here are exactly the same—there's no specific right or left, which makes things easier if you misplace a part. Shown are 20-in.-long side-mount slides to fit 20-in.-long trays. This gives you some wiggle room in the back and a bit of extra space to get the pieces into place. If you have plumbing coming up through the bottom of the cabinet, you may need to shorten the trays and buy shorter drawer slides.

Then follow the photos for the step-by-step measuring and assembly instructions. Here are a few specifics to consider:

■ If the opening between the open doors is narrower than the opening between the sides of the frame, use the shorter dimension to make the base.

FACE FRAME

1 Measure the width of your kitchen base cabinet inside the frame. Then cut the base (A) 1/4 in. narrower than the opening.

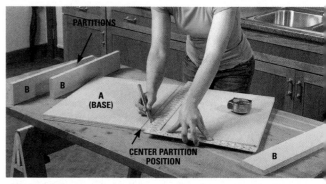

PARTITIONS

B B

A (BASE)

CENTER PARTITION POSITION

B

2 Find the center of the base (A) and mark it for the center partition. Cut the 20-in.-long partitions (B) from 1x4.

- If you have a center stile or partition between the doors, you may need to make two separate bases for each side and a tray for each.
- Make sure the base and the tray parts are cut square and accurately so the trays slide smoothly.

A WORD ABOUT DRAWER SLIDES

The ball-bearing slides are designed to mount on the sides of the trays **(Photos 6 and 7)**. The slides require 1/2 in. of space between the partition and drawer on each side to work properly, so make the trays exactly 1 in. narrower than the distance between the partitions. If the trays are too wide, they'll bind and be tough to open, in which case, you'll have to take them apart and recut the tray bottom. If the trays are too narrow, the slides will not engage. Fixing this is a bit

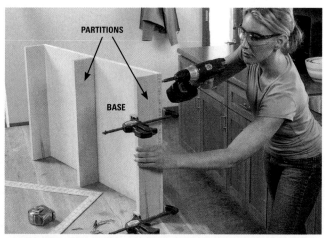

3 Clamp the partitions to the base, drill pilot holes, and then glue and screw the partitions to the base with No. 8 x 2-in. screws.

4 Measure the exact distance between the partitions. Make the outer dimension of the tray 1 in. narrower than this measurement to allow for the slides.

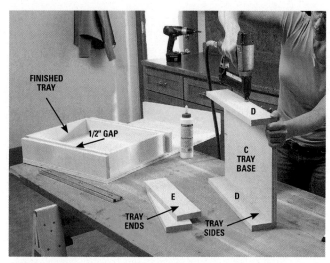

5 Cut the parts for the trays and glue and nail them together. Cut the bases perfectly square to keep the trays square.

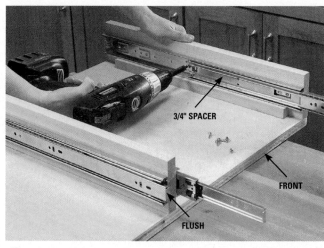

6 Set the drawer slides on 3/4-in. spacers, holding them flush with the front. Open them to expose the mounting holes and screw them to the partitions.

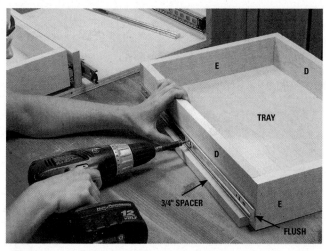

7 Remove the inner sections of the slides and screw them to the sides of the trays. Reassemble the slides and make sure they glide smoothly.

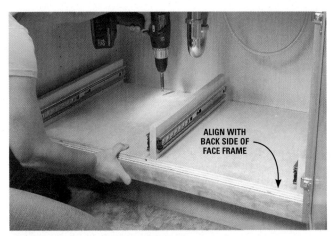

ALIGN WITH BACK SIDE OF FACE FRAME

8 Insert the base assembly into the floor of the cabinet. Align the front of the base flush with the back side of the face frame. Screw the base to the floor of the cabinet.

easier. You can just shim behind the slides with thin washers. Watch for protruding hinges and other obstructions when you mount the lower or upper trays. You may need to adjust the height or placement of the trays to accommodate them.

SEAL THE TRAYS WITH POLYURETHANE

You never know what kind of spill or leak will happen under the sink, so it's best to seal the wood. Once you've finished the project, remove the trays and slides, sand them with 150-grit sandpaper and brush on two coats of polyurethane. Let the trays dry thoroughly, then look through all that stuff you had stored under the sink. Toss out old stuff and combine duplicate products—and enjoy your reclaimed and now easily accessible space.

G
H
G
F
H
J
F

FINISHED UPPER TRAY
J

9 Cut the parts for the upper trays, drill pilot holes, and glue and screw them together. Cut two thicknesses of plywood and glue them together to make the 1-in.-thick side cleats (K, Photo 10).

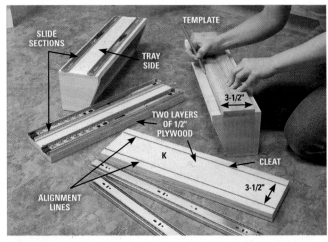

SLIDE SECTIONS
TEMPLATE
TRAY SIDE
3-1/2"
TWO LAYERS OF 1/2" PLYWOOD
K
CLEAT
3-1/2"
ALIGNMENT LINES

10 Cut a 3-1/2-in.-wide template, center it on the cleats and the tall side of each tray and trace the edges. Center the mounting holes of the slides on these lines and screw them to the cleats (outer sections) and tray sides (inner sections).

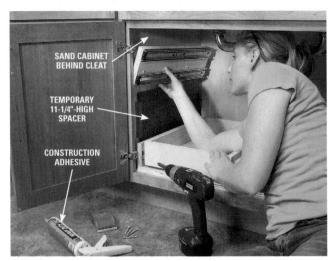

SAND CABINET BEHIND CLEAT

TEMPORARY 11-1/4"-HIGH SPACER

CONSTRUCTION ADHESIVE

11 Sand the side of the cabinet to increase the adhesion, then glue and screw the cleats to the sides of the cabinet. Cut a plywood spacer to hold the cleat even.

12 Slide the upper trays into position and test the fit. Seal the trays with two coats of polyurethane to make cleaning easier.

Double Your Bathroom Storage

Two easy projects add storage and display space to a small bathroom.

Bathrooms never have enough storage or shelf space. Finding a home for all your blow dryers, curling irons, toilet paper, and cans, soaps and bottles can be a challenge. Once you've filled your vanity, how do you squeeze more storage into a small bath? And what do you do with your knick-knacks? Here are two super simple projects to help you get the space you need.

INSTALL GLASS SHELVES

Most bathrooms have one area you can usually count on for additional storage, and that's over the toilet. Open glass shelving is a great way to display decorative bathroom bottles or knick-knacks. There are zillions of glass shelving systems on the market. Follow the directions that come with the system for the installation, but read on for help anchoring the shelves to the wall because you probably won't have studs exactly where you need them. We used painter's tape to avoid marking the walls.

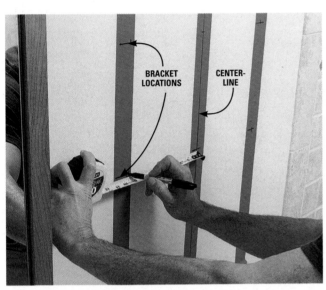

1 Find location for brackets. Apply a strip of 2-in.-wide painter's tape above the center of the toilet and on both sides where the shelf brackets will be mounted. Draw a centerline with a level and mark the heights of the shelves on the center tape. Transfer the heights to the bracket tape with a 2-ft. level. Then measure from the centerline to mark the exact left and right locations for the brackets.

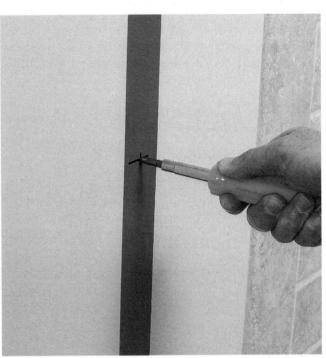

2 Mark with a screwdriver. Indent the drywall at the pen marks with a Phillips head screwdriver. Remove tape.

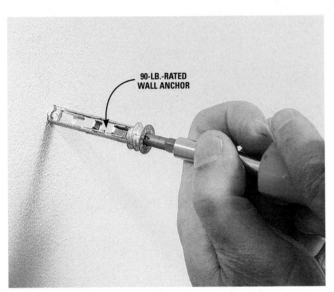

3 Install anchors. Drive hollow wall anchors through the drywall.

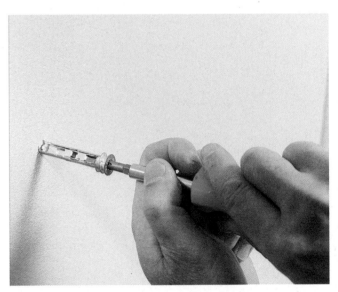

4 Fasten the brackets. Screw the brackets to the wall using the screws included with the anchors.

TIME	SKILL LEVEL
1-2 Hours	Beginner

TOOLS & MATERIALS
Driver/drill, tape measure, level, ladder (optional: 1x2 board)

INSTALL A LARGER MEDICINE CABINET

You can find a wide variety of medicine cabinets and shelves at home centers and kitchen and bath stores. When sizing a medicine cabinet, measure the space you have available behind your sink, both height and width. Keep a few inches away from existing light fixtures (unless you want to move them). Buy a cabinet that fits within those dimensions.

Surface-mounting a large medicine cabinet is just a matter of centering it, leveling it and screwing it to the wall studs. Your old cabinet may be surface-mounted or recessed into the wall cavity between the framing. Remove a recessed unit by opening the door, backing out the screws in the side of the cabinet and pulling it out of the recess. You may need to cut around it with a utility knife if it's caulked or painted in around the edges.

Have a helper support surface-mounted cabinets while you back out the screws, or if you're alone, screw a temporary 1x2 support ledger under the cabinet as shown in **Photo 1** to hold it while you unscrew it from the wall. You may need to move or replace the lighting beside or above the old cabinet. Now's the time to do it.

Hold the new medicine cabinet against the wall and then adjust it up and down until the height is a good compromise for your family members, then mark the bottom and set the cabinet aside. Use the mark to draw a level line for positioning the 1x2 ledger **(Photo 1)**. Then follow the photo series for installation details.

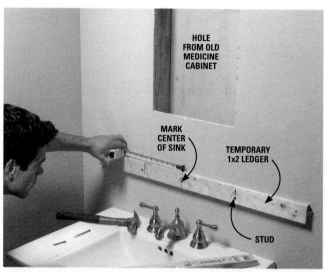

1 Mark the studs. Mark the height of the bottom of the cabinet and draw a line with a 2-ft. level. Find the studs by probing with a nail and mark the stud positions above the level line. Screw a temporary 1x2 ledger board through the drywall into the studs. Mark the center of the sink on the ledger, and then measure over from the center mark to the left and right studs.

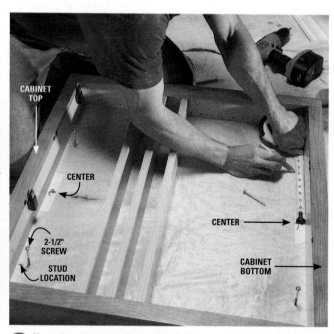

2 Transfer stud locations. Mark the center of the cabinet at the top and bottom and transfer the center-to-stud locations to the inside of the cabinet. Start 2-1/2-in. screws at those marks.

3 Fasten the cabinet. Set the cabinet on the ledger and line up the center of the cabinet with the center mark on the ledger. Drive the screws into the studs, then remove the ledger. Fill the screw holes with spackling compound and touch up the paint.

Sink Cabinet Shelf

Don't let the area under your sink become a magnet for clutter—instead, build this simple shelf to give everything a place.

All that wide-open space under the sink is a black hole for cleaning products, shoe polish, trash bags—you name it. If you're tired of exploring its depths every time you need something, build this handy door-mounted shelf. Better than store-bought wire racks, it mounts securely, has the same wood finish as your cabinet and maximizes space because you custom-fit it for your cabinet.

The shelf is made from standard 1x4 lumber (which is 3/4 in. x 3-1/2 in.). If you have access to a table saw and have a drill, screwdriver, some wood glue and a tape measure, you can build this project. It takes only a few hours. You can also modify this design to work in other cabinets for holding spices, canned goods or craft supplies.

The shelf has a unique built-in system **(Photos 6 and 7)** to make mounting it to the back side of a cabinet door a snap. The shelf gets screwed into the solid wood stiles of the door (not into the panel).

WHAT IT TAKES	
TIME 3-4 hours	**SKILL LEVEL** Beginner

TOOLS & MATERIALS
Table saw, driver/drill, screwdriver, wood glue

SIZING TIPS

Because there's no standard size for sink base cabinets, here are a few tips to help you size your door-mounted shelf. Measure the height and width of the cabinet opening (**Photo 1**). The shelf unit must be 1/2 in. shorter and 2 in. narrower (not including the mounting ears shown in **Photo 6**). These measurements ensure that the shelf unit will clear the frame by 1/4 in. on all sides as you close the cabinet door. Here's how to size each part:

- The height of the 3-1/2-in.-deep sides (A) must be 1/2 in. shorter than the height of the opening.
- The 3-1/4-in.-deep shelves (B) are cut 3 in. narrower than the width of the opening. These pieces are ripped 1/4 in. thinner than the side in order to allow space for gluing the mounting strips (C) to the back side of the shelves (**Photo 4**).
- The 1/4-in. x 3/4-in. mounting strips must be 2-1/2 in. longer than B or 1/2 in. shorter than the width of the door opening.

PREPARING THE SIDES

After measuring the opening's height and width, cut the sides (A) to length. Then cut a 45-degree taper on the tops of each piece, leaving 3/4 in. at the top as shown in **Photo 2**. Label the inside of each side so you don't cut the dado (groove) for each shelf on the wrong side. Notice that there are two 1/4-in. notches on the back edge of each side (**Photo 2**) to accept the mounting strips (C).

To cut the dadoes, set your table saw blade so it's 1/4 in. high. Mark the locations of each dado. The lower dado is on the bottom of the sides, and the top of the upper shelf is 13-1/2 in. from the bottom of the sides.

Cut the dadoes in the inner sides of A using your miter gauge as a guide to push the workpiece through the saw. Our table saw has an extra-wide miter gauge for stability. If your table saw has a small miter gauge, screw a piece of wood to its front edge to extend it to within 1/4 in. of the saw blade. You could make the dado cut in one pass with a special dado blade, but if you don't have one, just make repeated cuts (**Photo 2**) with a standard blade .

1 Measure the cabinet opening (height and width) to size the shelf system.

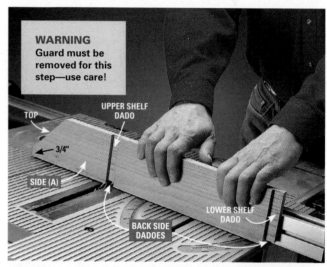

2 Cut the sides (A) to length, then cut the dadoes in the sides and back of each side. See text for dimensions.

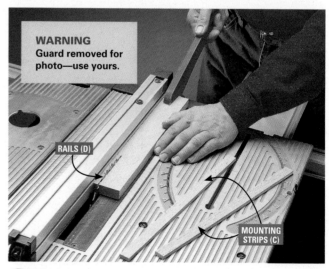

3 Rip the mounting strips (C) and the rails (D) from 1x4 lumber.

MAKING THE SHELVES

Cut the shelves (B) to length from 1x4, then rip them to a width of 3-1/4 in. Make the 1/4-in. x 3/4-in. mounting strips (C) and front rails (D) by ripping them from a wider piece as shown in **Photo 3**.

Before you glue these pieces to the backs of the shelves **(Photo 4)**, drill a 3/16-in. hole 3/8 in. from each end. You'll use these holes later to mount the shelf to the door stiles.

ASSEMBLY

Lay out the sides face down as shown in **Photo 5**. Now, slip the shelves with the mounting strips attached into the dadoes and make sure they fit snugly. Drill pilot holes for the screws (3/4 in. from the front and back of A) through the sides into the shelves. Use 1-1/4-in. wood screws with finish washers to secure the shelves to the sides.

To finish the assembly, flip the shelves and sides face-up. Cut the 1/4-in. x 3/4-in. front rails (D) to length, drill pilot holes and fasten them **(Photo 6)** to the front of the sides. We chose to put the lower rail 2 in. up from the bottom shelf and the upper rail 1-1/2 in. up from the upper shelf. These heights work fine for most products and allow you to pull things out instead of lifting them each time. You can always add a second rail just above if needed.

MOUNTING TO THE DOOR

Before mounting the unit to the door, apply masking tape to the inside of the door as shown in **Photo 7**. Close the door and mark the cabinet opening on the tape with a pencil from the inside. This will guide you when you're mounting the shelf to the door.

Mount the shelf 1/4 in. from the top mark you made on the tape, and align the ear of the mounting strip 1/4 in. from the opening mark on the door. Mark the holes from the mounting strips onto the door and drill pilot holes for the screws. Be careful not to drill through the door! Screw the assembly to the door **(Photo 7)** using No. 8 x 1-in. screws and finish washers.

Because of the added weight of the shelf and the products, some doors with self-closing hinges may not snap closed as easily as before. To remedy this, you may need to install an extra hinge centered between the other two, or add a magnetic catch at the top of the door.

Remove the shelf from the door, sand it with 150-grit sandpaper, then apply varnish. Shown here are several coats of a clear lacquer spray available at hardware stores. Always be sure to apply lacquer in a well-ventilated area away from any pilot flames.

NOTE: If you have small children, make sure that any cabinets containing cleaning products have child-proof latches attached.

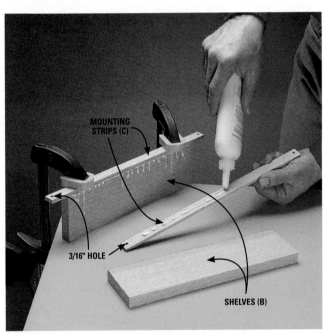

4 Glue the mounting strips (C) to the back side of the shelves. Drill holes in the mounting strips before assembling.

MOUNTING STRIPS (C)
3/16" HOLE
SHELVES (B)

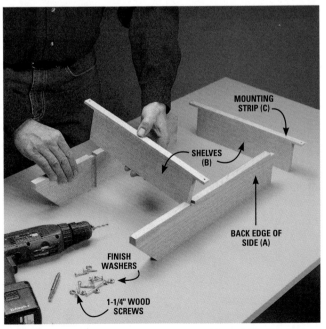

5 Slip the shelves into the dado cuts. Then drill pilot holes into the sides of A and screw the shelves in place with 1-1/4-in. wood screws and finish washers.

MOUNTING STRIP (C)
SHELVES (B)
BACK EDGE OF SIDE (A)
FINISH WASHERS
1-1/4" WOOD SCREWS

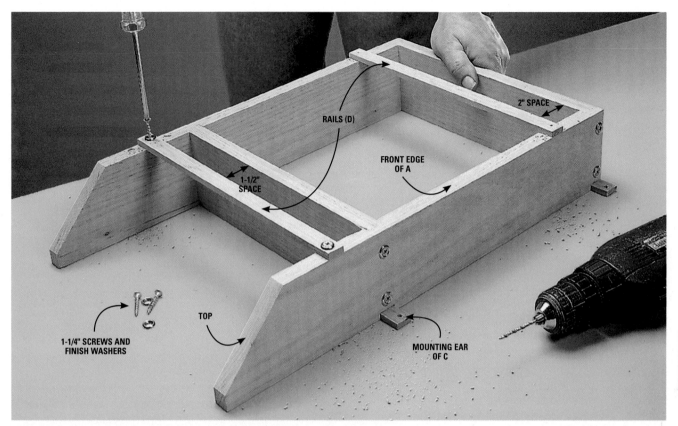

RAILS (D)

2" SPACE

FRONT EDGE
OF A

1-1/2"
SPACE

1-1/4" SCREWS AND
FINISH WASHERS

TOP

MOUNTING EAR
OF C

6 Fasten the rails (D) to the front of the shelf assembly. Drill pilot holes and use 1-1/4-in. wood screws and finish washers.

1" WOOD
SCREWS
AND FINISH
WASHERS

MARK
DOOR
OPENING
ON
MASKING
TAPE

MOUNTING EAR
OF C

7 Clamp and screw the assembly to the door stiles using 1-in. wood screws and finish washers.

Materials List

ITEM	QTY.
4' x 8' x 3/4" birch plywood	1
2-1/4"-wide crown molding	5'
3/4"-tall base cap molding	5'
1-1/4" screws	1 box
1-5/8" screws	1 box
5/16" or 3/8" dowels	16
1-1/2" finish nails	1 box
Inset ball tip hinges	4
Shelf supports	8
Spray primer	1 can
Spray paint	2 cans
Wood glue	
Wood filler	

Cutting List

KEY	QTY, SIZE, & DESCRIPTION
A	2x 8" x 32-5/8" sides
B	3x 8" x 22-1/2" top, bottom and middle shelf
C	2x 3" x 22-1/2" top and bottom cleats
D	2x 8" x 22-1/4" adjustable shelves
E	2x 11-15/16" x 32-3/8" doors
F	2x 9" x 24" crown and base frames
G	3x 2-1/4"-wide crown molding (cut to fit)
H	3x 3/4"-tall base molding (cut to fit)

Except for moldings, all parts are 3/4" plywood.

WHAT IT TAKES

TIME	SKILL LEVEL
1 day	Beginner

TOOLS & MATERIALS
Circular saw (or table saw), miter saw, (optional: brad nailer), [NOTE: louvered closet doors should be on Materials list]

Simple Bathroom Cabinet

Getting more space to store stuff in your bathroom is as simple as building this nifty cabinet.

In most bathrooms, a picture or small shelf hangs above the toilet. But you can make better use of that space with an attractive cabinet that offers about three times as much storage as a typical medicine cabinet.

This article will show you how to build it. The simple joinery and store-bought doors make this a great project for the woodworking novice. Assembling the crown and base is a bit trickier, but this article shows that process, too. You'll need a miter saw to cut the trim. A table saw and a brad nailer will save time, but you can make all the cuts with a circular saw and drive the nails by hand.

The height and width of your cabinet may differ slightly from this one, depending on the bifold doors available at your home center. So choose your doors first and then alter the lengths of the sides, top, bottom and middle shelves if necessary. Bifold closet doors are sold as a pair, usually joined by hinges. Each of the doors shown here measured

11-15/16 in. wide, and were cut to length as shown in the photo on Page 43.

The easy-to-install inset, ball tip hinges used here are available online. All the other tools and materials are available at home centers. You may not find the exact same crown and base moldings used here, but most home centers carry a similar profile. Any 2-1/4-in. crown molding is appropriate for this project. For a more contemporary look, you can skip the crown and base altogether since they're purely decorative.

BUILD A BASIC BOX

Cut the plywood parts to size. The dimensions used here are given in the Cutting List. To make the short-end cuts, use the homemade guide shown in **Photo 3** and described below.

Assemble the cabinet box with glue and screws, followed by wood dowels for extra strength **(Photo 1)**. You can buy long dowels and cut them into short pieces, but dowels

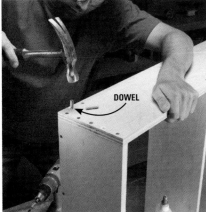

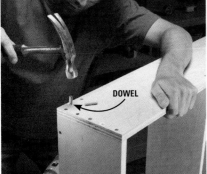

1 Assemble the cabinet box with glue and wood screws. Then add glued dowels for rock-solid joints. Drill splinter-free dowel holes with a brad-point bit.

2 Drill shelf-support holes using a scrap of pegboard to position the holes. Wrap masking tape around the drill bit so that you don't drill all the way through.

BATHROOM CABINET

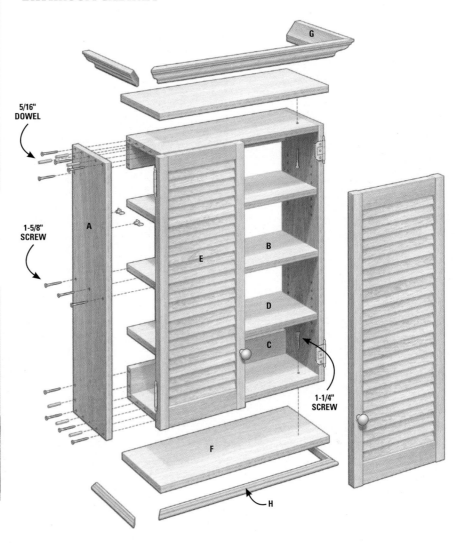

5/16" DOWEL

1-5/8" SCREW

1-1/4" SCREW

3 Cut the doors using a homemade saw guide to ensure a straight cut. Lay the door face down so any splintering takes place on the back of the door.

SAW GUIDE

CLOSET DOOR

4 Mount the hinges on the doors. A self-centering drill bit is great for positioning the screw holes for perfectly placed hinges.

SELF-CENTERING BIT

5 Position the doors carefully and clamp them to the cabinet. Then screw the hinges to the cabinet from inside for a foolproof, exact fit.

6 Cut the crown molding upside down and leaning against the fence. Clamp a block to the saw's fence so you can hold the molding firmly against the fence.

HOLD-DOWN BLOCK

7 Nail the crown to the frame. Nail the mitered corners only if necessary. If they fit tight and are perfectly aligned, let the glue alone hold them together.

CROWN

BASE

8 Center the crown on the cabinet and fasten it with screws driven from inside. Center the cabinet on the base; attach it the same way.

precut and fluted for woodworking are easier to work with. This assembly method is quick, easy and strong. But because it requires lots of wood filler to hide the fasteners, it's for painted work only. If you want to use stain and a clear finish, biscuits or pocket screws are a better choice.

Drill 1/8-in. pilot and countersink holes for the screws using a drill bit that does both at once. Attach the top, bottom and cleats to one side, then add the other side. Mark the middle shelf position on the sides, slip it into place and fasten it (there's no need for glue).

Before you drill the dowel holes, make sure that the box is square by taking diagonal measurements; equal measurements mean the box is square. If necessary, screw a strip of plywood diagonally across the back of the box to hold it square. For clean, splinter-free holes, drill the dowel holes with a 3/8-in. brad-point drill bit, making the holes 1/8 in. deeper than the length of the dowels. That way, you can sink the dowels below the surface of the plywood and fill the holes with wood filler. With the box completed, drill holes for the adjustable shelf supports **(Photo 2)** using a brad-point bit. Most shelf supports require a 1/4-in. hole.

CUT AND HANG THE DOORS

Cut the doors using a saw guide **(Photo 3)**. To make a guide, screw a straight 1x3 to a 14 x 18-in. scrap of 3/4-in. plywood. Run your saw along the 1x3 to cut off the excess plywood and create a guide that steers your saw perfectly straight and indicates the exact path of the cut. Simply mark the doors, align the guide with the marks, clamp it in place and cut.

Screw the hinges to the doors 3 in. from the ends **(Photo 4)**. The fronts and backs of louvered doors look similar, so check twice before you drill. Stand the doors against the cabinet, setting them on spacers to create a 1/8-in. gap at the bottom. The gap between the doors should also be about 1/8 in. Clamp each door in position and screw the hinges in place **(Photo 5)**. If the doors don't align perfectly because

the box is slightly out-of-square, don't worry. You can square the box when you hang it. The hinges also adjust up or down 1/16 in.

ADD THE CROWN AND BASE

Measure the top of the cabinet (including the doors) and cut the plywood crown and base frames to that size. Set your miter saw to 45 degrees and cut the crown molding upside down, leaning against the fence **(Photo 6)**. Also miter a "tester" section of molding to help you position the sidepieces when you nail them in place. To avoid splitting, be sure to predrill nail holes. With the sides in place, add the front piece of crown molding. Cut it slightly long and then "shave" one end with your miter saw until it fits perfectly. Add the molding to the base frame the same way. Screw both the crown and base to the cabinet **(Photo 8)**.

A QUICK FINISH

Brushing paint onto louvered doors is pretty slow, fussy work, but you can avoid that hassle by using aerosol-can primer and paint. First, remove the doors and hinges. Cover the dowels, nails and screw heads with wood filler and sand the filler smooth. Also fill any voids in the plywood's edges.

Sand the cabinet box, crown, base and doors with 120-grit paper. Spray all the parts with a white stain-blocking primer. When the primer dries, sand it lightly with a fine sanding sponge. Finally, spray on at least two coats of spray paint. High-gloss paint will accentuate every tiny surface flaw, so consider using satin or matte.

To hang the cabinet, locate studs and drive two 3-in. screws through the top cleat. Then rehang the doors. Close the doors to check their fit. Nudge the bottom of the cabinet left or right to square it and align the doors. Then drive screws through the bottom cleat.

You've gained plenty of space in your bathroom to store everything you need. Next step—decluttering those counters!

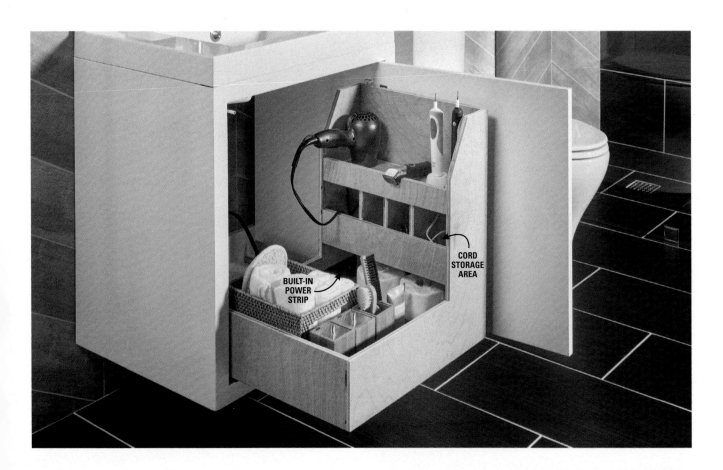

BUILT-IN POWER STRIP

CORD STORAGE AREA

Bathroom Storage Plugged In

Your gear is always ready to go!

We step into our bathrooms every morning to get ready for the day. We pull out hair dryers, curling irons and trimmers, untangle their cords and fumble around for the outlet to plug them in. Then we unplug them and stuff them in a drawer, just to untangle them all again the next morning. What a waste of time! But this cabinet rollout has built-in outlets to eliminate those hassles and get you on your way.

WHAT IT TAKES	
TIME 1 day	**SKILL LEVEL** Intermediate

TOOLS & MATERIALS
Table saw, handsaw, jigsaw, drill, 18-gauge brad nailer

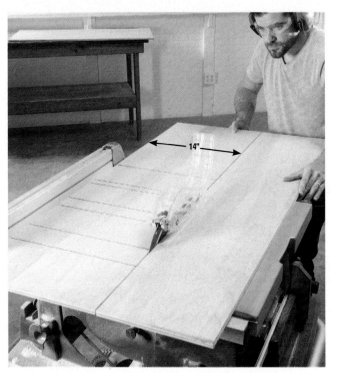

14"

1 Start with two rip cuts. Set the table-saw fence to 19 in. to cut the width of the drawer front and back pieces. Then make another rip at 14 in. for the drawer sides and shelf parts. This approach keeps similar parts the exact same length and helps keep the drawer square and easy to assemble. Crosscut the front, back and tall side at 20 in., then crosscut the remaining parts.

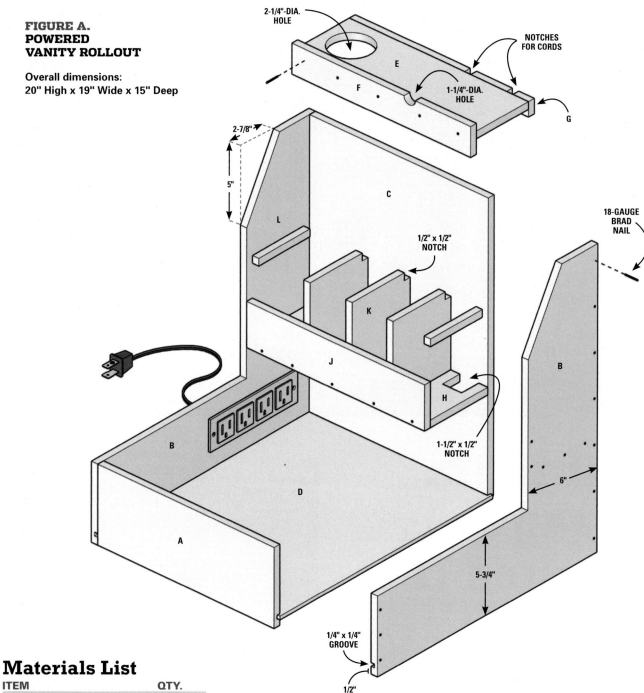

FIGURE A.
**POWERED
VANITY ROLLOUT**

Overall dimensions:
20" High x 19" Wide x 15" Deep

2-1/4"-DIA.
HOLE

NOTCHES
FOR CORDS

1-1/4"-DIA.
HOLE

G

E

F

2-7/8"

5"

C

L

1/2" x 1/2"
NOTCH

K

18-GAUGE
BRAD
NAIL

B

J

H

1-1/2" x 1/2"
NOTCH

B

D

6"

A

5-3/4"

1/4" x 1/4"
GROOVE

1/2"

Materials List

ITEM	QTY.
Pressure-treated 2x8 x 14'	10
Pressure-treated 2x8 x 20'	1
Pressure-treated 2x10 x 20'	3
Pressure-treated 2x10 x 10'	7
Pressure-treated 4x6 posts	5
Pressure-treated 2x4 x 8'	5
Pressure-treated 2x6 x 8'	3
Skewed hangers (left)	22
Skewed hangers (right)	22
Post bases	5
Double 2x8 concealed hangers	2
Triple 2x8 hangers	2
2x8 joist hangers	19
90-degree framing angle	4
Cedar 1x2 x 8'	31
Cedar 1x2 x 10'	142
Cedar 1x12 x 16'	4
Wedge anchors	15
Hanger nails, stainless steel	
15-gauge nails and construction screws	

Cutting List

KEY	PART
A	2x8 ledger board
B	4x6 post
C	3-ply 2x10 main beam
D	2x8 fascia blocks
E	2-ply 2x10 side beam
F	3-ply 2x10 center beam
G	2x8 angled rafters
H	2x6 wall frame
J	2x4 wall frame
K	1x2 horizontal cedar cladding
L	1x2 ceiling cedar cladding
M	Cladding nailer
N	1x10 cedar fascia

STOP HERE

FRONT   SIDES

BOTTOM

2 Cut the front and back. You can cut the front and back of the L-shaped drawer with a jigsaw or circular saw. But here's how to make straighter cuts using a table saw: Mark the cutouts on both sides of the front and back. Set the fence to 6 in. to make the first cut for the depth of the shelf. When you're 3 in. from the end of the cut, stop, turn the saw off and wait for the blade to stop. Do the same with the second part, then flip both parts, set your fence to 5-3/4 in. and make the second cut the same way. Finish the cuts with a handsaw or jigsaw.

3 Size the bottom. Cut the grooves as shown in Figure A. Glue and nail the front and one side together. Slide the bottom into the grooves and mark 5/16 in. inside the front of the drawer and 3/16 in. beyond the side. Then adjust the fence to the marks and cut the bottom to size. Glue and nail the sides, front and back together, leaving the bottom panel floating in the grooves.

POWER STRIP

4 Fit the power strip. Find a spot where there will be enough room for the drawer to close once the power strip is installed. Trace the power strip on your drawer, and then drill a 1/4-in.-diameter hole in each corner. Fit a jigsaw blade into one of them and connect the holes. Insert the power strip and secure it with two screws.

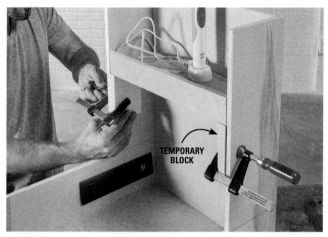

TEMPORARY BLOCK

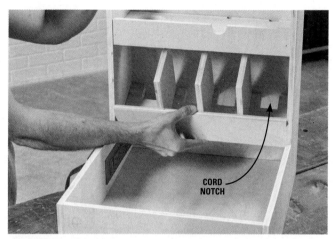

CORD NOTCH

5 Customize the shelf. Determine the height of the shelf by placing the tallest appliance on it and adjusting it up and down to fit. Clamp blocks against the drawer to hold it in place, then mark its position and glue and nail the shelf cleats into place. Use the appliances to map out where and how they will be held. We used a 2-1/4-in. hole saw to make a hair dryer holster and a 1-1/4-in. Forstner bit to cut a half-moon shape for a beard trimmer. We made notches for the charging cords with a pull saw and a chisel.

6 Build storage for your cords. The cord storage shelf separates each set of cords so they don't get tangled. The dividers are spaced between the appliances and fastened with glue and 18-gauge brad nails. For the plugs, we cut 1-1/2-in. square notches with a jigsaw to provide a path to get to the power strip. The removable appliance shelf allows easy access to cords when needed, and the opening in front lets you shove cords in when they're not in use.

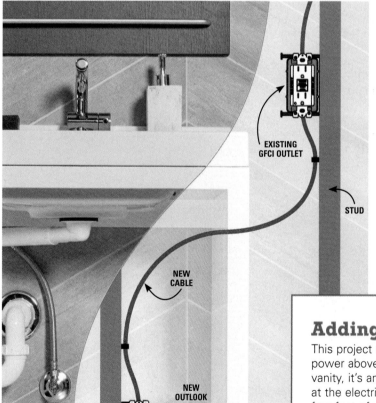

EXISTING GFCI OUTLET

STUD

NEW CABLE

NEW OUTLOOK

STUD

PRO TIP

Don't Fear Fancy Drawer Slides

We used Blum Tandem Plus drawer slides, which can be mounted to the side or bottom of a cabinet. They're hidden when the drawer is open, which gives it a high-end look. They're easier to install than they look. You'll need to build the drawer to match the length of the slides, which require a 1/2-in. recess underneath the drawer. We chose the 15-in. slides to fit into the 18-in.-deep vanity and allow room for the inset door and the power strip.

Adding an Outlet Under The Sink

This project requires an outlet inside the vanity. If there's power above your sink that shares a stud bay inside your vanity, it's an easy job. First switch off the power to the circuit at the electrical panel. Remove the existing outlet and send a few feet of cable to a new single-gang box behind the vanity and make the connections to a new outlet. If there's a stud between the old outlet and the spot for the new one, the job becomes more complicated. To learn more about this, search for "add an outlet" at familyhandyman.com.

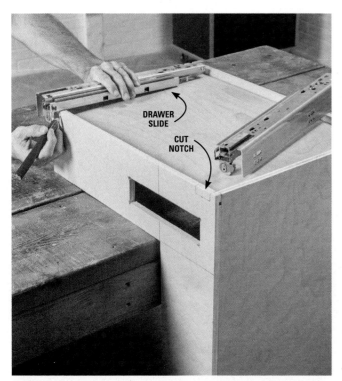

7 Cut notches for the slides. Flip the drawer over, hook the slides over the side lip on the bottom and mark where each slide meets the back. Use a handsaw, a coping saw or a jigsaw to cut the notches to fit the slides. The notches should be 1/2 in. deep and flush with the inside edge of the drawer.

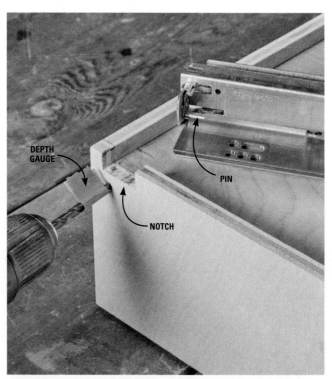

8 Drill the pin hole. The pin that keeps the drawer slide in place requires a 1/4-in.-diameter hole. Put the slide in place and mark the back of the drawer where the pin hits. Drill a hole just deep enough to fit the pin without going through the back, and then apply your choice of finish to the drawer.

9 Fasten the locking devices. Fit the locking devices into the front corners on the underside of the drawer. Drill angled pilot holes for the screws and fasten the devices in place. The locking devices hold the drawer on the slides and allow you to easily remove the drawer.

10 Attach the slides. Screw the first slide to the side of the cabinet opposite the hinges, then measure the inside of the drawer and add 1-5/8 in. to determine the location of the second slide. Draw a parallel line and screw the slide to the bottom of the cabinet inside the line.

CHAPTER **TWO**

GARAGE & OUTDOORS

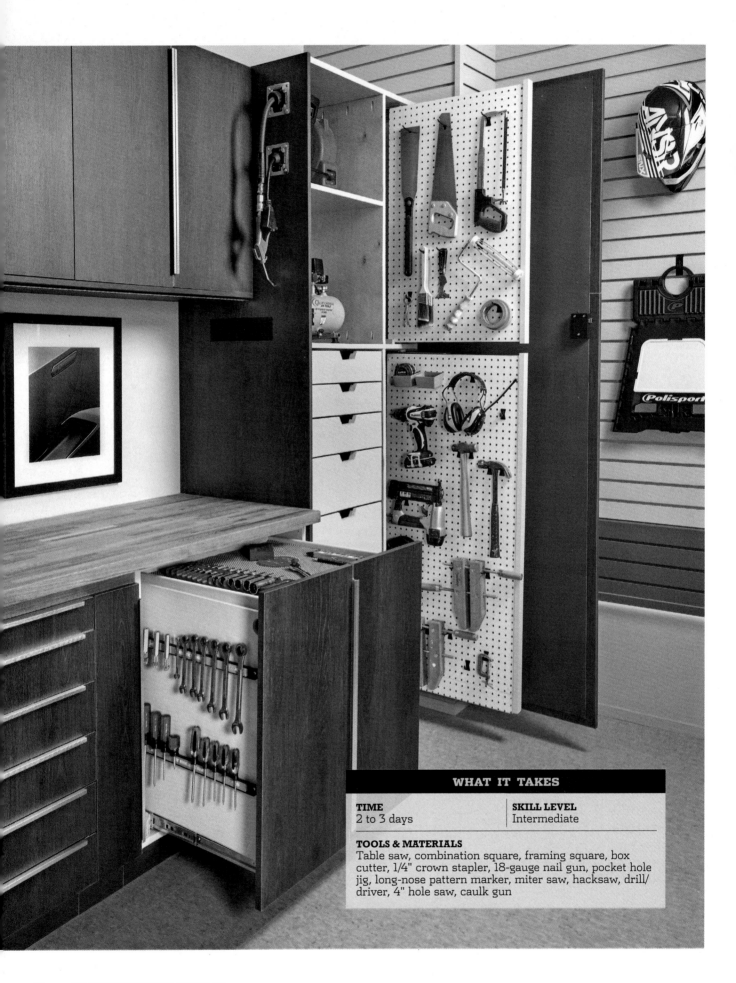

WHAT IT TAKES

TIME
2 to 3 days

SKILL LEVEL
Intermediate

TOOLS & MATERIALS
Table saw, combination square, framing square, box cutter, 1/4" crown stapler, 18-gauge nail gun, pocket hole jig, long-nose pattern marker, miter saw, hacksaw, drill/driver, 4" hole saw, caulk gun

Ultra-Organized Garage Cabinets

Modify your cabinets for greater storage and convenience.

Our garages are multitaskers: vehicle storage, workshop, tool organizer and hangout space for friends and family. For a garage to serve all those purposes, it must be highly organized. We customized two typical kitchen cabinets for maximum storage. Think Swiss Army Knife-caliber organization and convenience.

2 Install the divider panels. Using the upper shelf (D) to serve as a spacer, attach the top and bottom of the lower panel. Repeat the process for the upper divider panel (A), then install the upper shelf. Use pocket screws for all of these connections.

UPPER SHELF (D) USED AS SPACER

PRO TIP

Steps to Staple

Staple horizontally to attach the sides, front and back to the base. Staple vertically to connect the sides to the front and back. Keep the staples slightly away from the outer edge to avoid splintering the plywood's veneer.

CLAMP

LOWER DIVIDER PANEL

1 Install shelves. Use a clamp to temporarily support the middle shelf (C) in its approximate location, and use the lower divider panel (B) as a support and spacer. Attach the shelf with pocket screws. After attaching one side of the shelf, slide the divider to the other side, remove the clamp and attach that side. You'll repeat this process for the upper shelf (D) once the upper divider panel (A) is in place.

VERTICAL STAPLES

HORIZONTAL STAPLES

3 Assemble drawer boxes. After completing the Cutting List, assemble the drawer boxes (N–W) using crown staples and wood glue. Do this on a flat table to ensure the parts stay flush on the bottom.

4 Build pegboard panels. Make a pullout pegboard panel sandwich (J and K) using nails for the mitered corners of the frame (E–H), crown staples and construction adhesive for the panels.

DRAWER SLIDE SUPPORT

GUIDE CLEATS

5 Install the pullout panels. Attach the drawer slide inner rails to the panels and the slides to the supports (L). Install supports and the guide cleats (M) with adhesive and brad nails, centering each panel in its space.

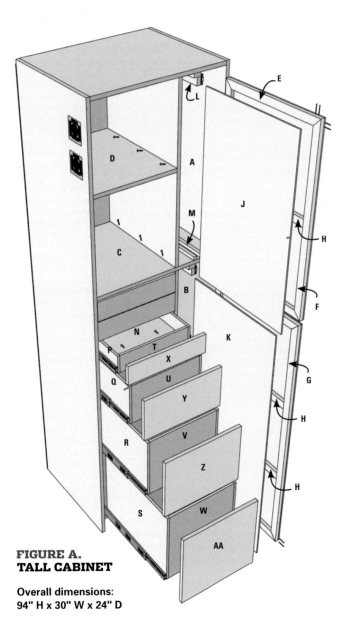

E

L

A

D

M

J

C

H

B

F

N

P

T

K

X

Q

U

G

Y

H

R

V

Z

H

S

W

AA

FIGURE A.
TALL CABINET

Overall dimensions:
94" H x 30" W x 24" D

Cutting List

KEY	QTY.	DIMENSIONS	PART
A	1	3/4"x 23" x 36"	Upper divider panel
B	1	3/4"x 23" x 51-3/4"	Lower divider panel
C	1	3/4"x 23" x 28-1/2"	Middle shelf
D	1	3/4"x 23" x 18"	Upper shelf
E	4	3/4" x 1-1/2" x 22"	Pegboard frame rails
F	2	3/4" x 1-1/2" x 36"	Upper pegboard frame stiles
G	2	3/4" x 1-1/2" x 50-3/4"	Lower pegboard frame stiles
H	3	3/4" x 1-1/2" x 19"	Panel crosspieces
J	2	22" x 36"	Upper pegboard panels
K	2	22" x 50-3/4"	Lower pegboard panels
L	4	3/4" x 3/4" x 1-1/2" x 22"	Slide support top and vertical
M	4	3/4" x 3/4" x 22"	Pullout guide cleats
N	6	3/4" x 16" x 20-1/2"	Drawer box bases
P	6	1/2" x 3-3/4" x 21-1/2"	Small drawer box sides
Q	2	1/2" x 8-1/2" x 21-1/2"	Medium drawer box sides
R	2	1/2" x 12-1/2" x 21-1/2"	Large drawer box sides
S	2	1/2" x 16" x 21-1/2"	X-large drawer box sides
T	6	1/2" x 3-3/4" x 16"	Small drawer box fronts and backs
U	2	1/2" x 8-1/2" x 16"	Medium drawer box front and back
V	2	1/2" x 12-1/2" x 16"	Large drawer box front and back
W	2	1/2" x 16" x 16"	X-large drawer box front and back
X	3	3/4" x 4-1/8" x 17-7/8"	Small drawer faces
Y	1	3/4" x 8-7/8" x 17-7/8"	Medium drawer face
Z	1	3/4" x 12-7/8" x 17-7/8"	Large drawer face
AA	1	3/4" x 6-3/8" x 17-7/8"	X-large drawer face

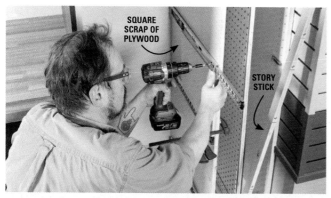

6 Lay out and install drawer slides. Rip a scrap of plywood to make a story stick, and mark the drawer spacing on it. Stand the stick in the cabinet and transfer those marks to the cabinet side and the lower divider. Install the first pair of slides on the bottom of the cabinet. Set the slides back the thickness of the drawer face plus 3/16 in.

7 Position and install drawer fronts. Using heavy-duty double-sided tape and shims, position the drawer faces (X–AA), keeping about a 1/8-in. gap around the perimeter. Attach each face from the inside of the drawer box using cabinet screws. The cabinet doors leave little space for drawer pulls. Drill 1-1/2-in. holes for finger pulls or make a hand-pull cutout.

8 Install the cord/hose ports. Drill two 4-in. holes through the side of the cabinet, then attach the ports to the outside of the cabinet with pan head screws.

9 Attach cabinet doors to tall cabinet. Join top and bottom door pairs using a piece of painted 1/4-in. hardboard cut to fit inside the hinges and with a 1-in. reveal around the other edges. With door pairs on a flat table and a 1/8-in. spacer between them, screw hardboard to the doors. Leave shims between the doors until the doors are installed.

Materials List

ITEM	QTY.
3/4" x 4' x 8' fir-core birch plywood	2
1/2" x 5' x 5' Baltic birch plywood	2
1x4 x 4' clear pine	1
3/4" x 16" x 4' S4S laminated spruce panel board	2
1/4" x 2' x 4' pegboard	4
1/4" x 4' x 8' hardboard	1
22" heavy-duty over-travel drawer slides	1 pair
22" soft-close drawer slides	8 pairs
3/4" x 2' piano hinge	2
Biometric cabinet lock	1
1/4" crown staples: 1" and 1/2"	
1-1/2" 18-gauge nails	
1-1/4" pocket screws	
1-1/2" trim screws	
1" cabinet screws	
3" corner braces	4
Construction adhesive	
Wood glue	
Heavy-duty double-sided tape	
Polyurethane finish	
Latex enamel	
50' cord reel	1
50' hose reel	1
4" hose ports	2
1-1/8" x 2' x 4' Kaizen foam	1
Heavy-duty 30 mm cup hinges	5

10 Make foam tool inserts. Use a box cutter and a straightedge to cut the foam drawer inserts. Place your tools on the foam where you want them, and trace them with a long-nose marker. Set the depth of a box cutter blade to match each tool and score the outlines. Kaizen foam is a stack of foam layers, so you can remove layers to the approximate depth of your cut.

FIGURE B.
BASE CABINET PULLOUT

Overall dimensions:34-1/2" H x 30" W
x 24" D

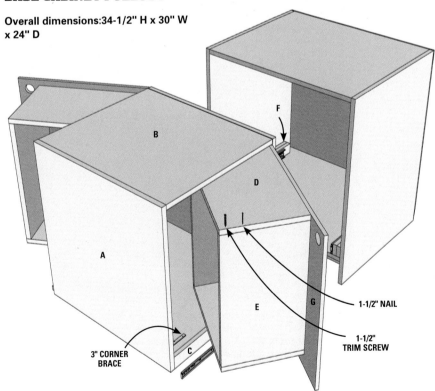

3" CORNER
BRACE

1-1/2" NAIL

1-1/2"
TRIM SCREW

Cutting List

KEY	QTY.	DIMENSIONS PART
A	2	3/4" x 24-1/2" x 25" Lower cabinet pullout front and back
B	2	3/4" x 24-1/2" x 20-1/2" Lower cabinet pullout top and bottom
C	2	3/4" x 2" x 20-1/2" Buildup
D	4	3/4" x 11" x 16-3/4" Inner storage box for lower pull out, top and bottom
E	4	3/4" x 11" x 19-1/4" Inner storage box for lower pull out, side
F	4	3/4" x 2" x 23" Slide supports for lower pullout
G	2	1/2" x 21-1/8" x 23" Backs for inner storage boxes

PRO TIP

Tape Gets
it Done

Use black electrical tape to black out the light plywood and create a shadow line in the gap between the two doors.

1 Attach drawer slides to large pullout. With the parts for the lower pullout (A–C) and storage boxes (D and E) assembled, use 1/2-in. spacers to attach the inner rail of the drawer slides to the base buildup (C) on the pullout box. Set the insert back about 3/16 in. from the front of the box. Attach the corner braces (E)—two on the top and two on the bottom—to square and stiffen the box.

2 Hang storage boxes on lower pullout. Cut the piano hinge to length. Install one side on the inner box, then attach the other to the lower pullout. A No. 4 self-centering bit gives quick and accurate screw placement for the hinges.

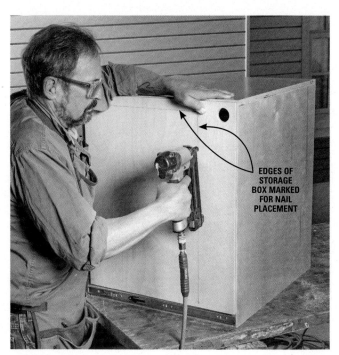

3 Install storage box backs. Mark the edges of the storage boxes on the backs (G) and fasten them using glue and brad nails. Using a 1-1/2-in. hole saw, cut a finger-pull hole in the upper front corner of each back.

4 Install lower pullout doors. With the drawer slides installed on their supports (F), slide the lower pullout into place. We recommend drawer slides rated for at least 250 lbs. Loaded with tools and fasteners, this pullout pushed the limits of the 150-lb. slides we used. Place the original doors using double-sided tape, maintaining a consistent gap against the adjoining cabinets. Attach them from inside the pullout with wood screws.

Garage Storage Tips

6 tips from our readers to tidy up the garage.

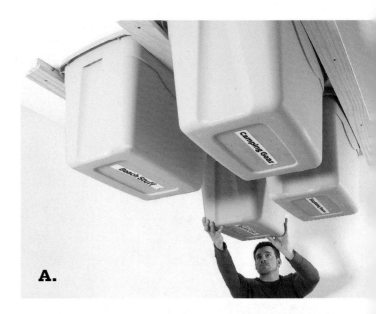

A.

A. GARAGE-CEILING BIN STORAGE

If you store stuff in big plastic storage bins and you need a place to put them, consider the garage ceiling. Screw 2x2s to the ceiling framing with 3-1/2-in. screws spaced every 2 ft. Use the bins as a guide for spacing the 2x2s. The lips on the bins should just brush against the 2x2s when you're sliding the bins into place. Then center and screw 1x4s to the 2x2s with 2-in. screws.

B. SHELF BAG

Toys, scooters and sports equipment can take up a lot of shelf space in the garage. Pick up a grill cover at a reuse center and repurpose it as a catchall bag for all that stuff. Attach the cover to your shelving unit with screws and washers.

C. ROTATING SMALL-PARTS ORGANIZER

Instead of mounting jar lids to a 2x4, attach them to a six-sided rotating beam. Draw a hexagon on the end of a 4x4 to use as a guide for setting the fence. Then set your table saw's blade to 60 degrees and make the rip cuts to form the sides. To allow the beam to rotate freely, drill dowel holes in the ends of the beam and run dowels through the posts into the beam ends.

D. SLIDE-OUT PARTS BINS

Make use of the narrow space between a shelving unit and a workbench with this slide-out rack. Mount 12-in. full-extension ball-bearing drawer slides to a plywood panel—one at the top and one at the bottom—with their mating parts attached to the side of the shelving unit. Then hang the parts bins on the plywood panel. The drawer slides have a 100-lb. load capacity.

E. TIGHT-SPACE GARAGE STORAGE

If your garage is too narrow for most shelving systems, here's a great way to store a lot of stuff in very little space. Hang several wire racks on the wall—the same kind as in the pantry. They hold a ton, and they don't get in the way.

F. PEGBOARD TOOL ORGANIZER

Collections of small screwdrivers can often roll around in a drawer, making it difficult to find the right one. To solve the problem, cut a scrap piece of pegboard and set it on standard pegboard shelf brackets. Now all of your small screwdrivers are neatly stored and easy to access.

GRILL COVER

B.

C.

D.

DRAWER SLIDE

SLIDING PANEL

E.

F.

Super Storage—Simplified

Simple and inexpensive, with huge storage capacity.

IT'S MOSTLY FRAMING LUMBER AND PEGBOARD

Check out **Figure A** to get the gist of the construction. After establishing the 2x2 grid work (see **Figure B**), frame the perimeter with 2x10s. Then cut the pegboard to fit and screw or glue it to the grid work. If you choose glue, you'll have to tack it in place until the glue sets. Then add the 2x8 partitions directly over the pegboard seams. Use a 4-ft. level to make sure those are plumb so your shelves will fit in any location within each bay.

Screw all the framing in place by end-screwing or toe-screwing as needed with 3-in. screws. In our example images, we show this project on a finished wall. But there's really no reason you can't install it over exposed studs or even over a concrete or a block wall.

If you're going to be installing it over masonry, be sure to anchor the 2x2s with 3-in. concrete screw anchors (Tapcon is one available brand). If the concrete where the shelves will be installed it is frequently damp, use treated 2x2s and they'll last forever.

WHAT IT TAKES	
TIME 1-3 days	**SKILL LEVEL** Intermediate
TOOLS & MATERIALS Circular saw, driver/drill, chalk line, level, stepladder (optional: nail gun)	

When at the store, check out the pegboard accessories. There are baskets, brackets, hooks, screwdriver holders, etc., all designed to hang just about anything you can think of. Wait until the project is done and think it through before buying any at this point.

Pegboard is dusty and messy to cut. Do it outside if possible or the entire garage and everything in it will be covered with dust. Wear a dust mask. Make the cuts with the good side down to eliminate tear-out on the show side.

WRITE UP A SHOPPING LIST

It's impossible to put together a materials list for this project because your wall will be different from ours. But it's easy to put one together. (See "Shopping Tips," below.) After you establish how many bays you want, look at **Figure A** and count the parts. That will give a pretty accurate custom materials list for the project.

Choose the lengths of the 2x10s in multiples of 4 ft. That way, they'll join directly over the pegboard splices, and the horizontal 2x10 splices will be supported by the vertical 2x8s **(Photo 4)**. That's why we used both 8- and 12-ft. 2x10s for the horizontal pieces. Joined together, they add up to our 20-ft. pegboard wall. Get one 8-ft. 2x8 for every two shelves **(Photo 7)**. Here's a heads-up: 2x8s and 2x10s will be 1/8 in. to 1/2 in. over the stated lengths. There will be a little built-in fudge factor, but you may have to do a little trimming from time to time. Place shelf standards in any bays where there will be adjustable shelves. Choose 6-ft. standards if they're available, and space them 1 ft. up from the bottom 2x10.

SIZE IT FOR YOUR GARAGE AND STORAGE NEEDS

Think of this project in terms of 4 x 8-ft. bays. They can be vertical like ours or horizontal if that better fits your needs. Do one bay or multiples; the construction is still the same.

NOW, ABOUT THE PEGBOARD

If you're willing to shop around, there are a lot of pegboard choices: thick, thin, metal, custom colors, etc. But home centers or lumberyards generally only offer 3/16-in.-thick plain brown and pegboard coated on one side with white melamine **(Photo 5)**. Either one will work fine for this project. Get the plain stuff to paint it a color or white if you're fine with that. Choose the thickest available with the larger (1/4-in.) holes.

PRO TIP

Shopping Tips

- Buy 10-ft.-long 2x10s for the end frames. The final lengths are a few inches longer than 8 ft.
- Pick horizontal frames in 4-ft. increments: 8 ft. for two bays, 12 ft. for three bays, etc.
- Get one 4 x 8-ft. sheet of pegboard for each bay.
- Buy four 8-ft. 2x2s for each bay.
- When it comes to hardware, buy a 1-lb. box of 3-in. screws and a 1-lb. box of 1-1/2-in. washer-head screws. You'll have more than you need, but they'll come in handy someday.

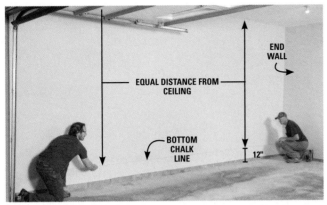

1 Establish the bottom first. Measure up from the floor 12 in., then measure down to get the distance from the ceiling. Transfer that measurement to the other end of the wall and snap the bottom chalk line for the base of the pegboard wall. Measure up from the bottom chalk line 93-1/8 in. and snap the top chalk line. Then snap horizontal lines spaced every 2 ft. from the top. Use a level to mark the stud centers and the other end of the wall.

2 Begin framing at the end wall. Cut the two 2x10s to 99-1/8 in. long (one for each end). Center one above and below the top and bottom chalk lines and screw it to the corner blocking. There should be blocking extending at least 1 in. away from the corner. Center an 8-ft. 2x2 between the 2x10 ends and screw it into place with 3-in. screws.

3 Build the grid work. Cut the horizontal 2x2s so they'll break in the middle of studs. Screw them to each stud with 3-in. screws using the chalk lines as a guide. Cut the last 2x2s 1-1/2 in. short of the end chalk line before fastening them to the studs. Then screw the last vertical 2x2 to the ends of each horizontal 2x2.

4 Build the 2x10 frame. Center and screw the last vertical 2x10 to the end 2x2. Cut the horizontal 2x10s so any splices will fall over the 2x8 dividers. (Get a helper to support the boards for this part.) Then begin attaching the horizontal 2x10s to the end 2x10s and to the horizontal 2x2s by using 3-in. screws.

5 Install the pegboard. Cut the pegboard to length if needed, then rest it on the bottom 2x10 and screw it to the 2x2s with 1-1/4-in. washer-head screws, four per 2x2. (You'll see the 2x2s through the pegboard holes.) If needed, cut the last pegboard panel to width.

6 Add the dividers. Cut the 2x8 dividers to length, and then center them over the pegboard seams. Plumb them with a 4-ft. level; screw them to the top and bottom 2x10s. Then toe-screw them to the horizontal 2x2s.

Overall dimensions: 20' 3-1/4" long x 9-1/4" deep x 8' 3-1/8" tall

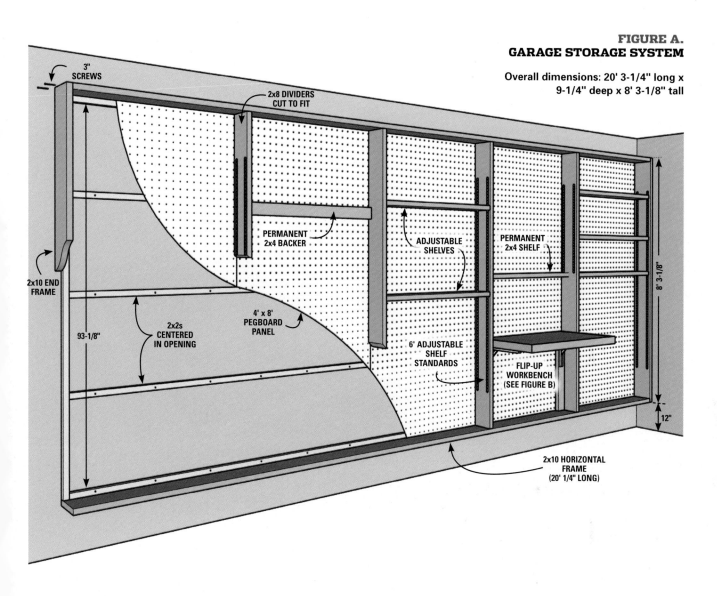

3"
SCREWS

2x8 DIVIDERS
CUT TO FIT

PERMANENT
2x4 BACKER

ADJUSTABLE
SHELVES

PERMANENT
2x4 SHELF

2x10 END
FRAME

93-1/8"

2x2s
CENTERED
IN OPENING

4' x 8'
PEGBOARD
PANEL

6' ADJUSTABLE
SHELF
STANDARDS

FLIP-UP
WORKBENCH
(SEE FIGURE B)

8' 3-1/8"

12"

2x10 HORIZONTAL
FRAME
(20' 1/4" LONG)

PAINT BEFORE ASSEMBLY

You'll spend as much time painting as you do building this system. We primed all the lumber with Zinsser Bulls Eye 1-2-3, not only to provide a good base for the paint, but also to keep knots from eventually bleeding through the color coat. After that, we rolled on two coats of latex wall paint, eggshell sheen.

A 3-in. roller frame with a 1/2-in.-nap sleeve works very well for all the painting. You can skip the paint tray and dip the sleeve right into the gallon paint can.

We used prefinished white pegboard, so there was no painting needed. If you want to custom-paint unfinished pegboard, rough up the surface with 100-grit sandpaper, then prime and paint it the same way. But use a 1/4-in.-nap roller to ensure thin coats. If you use a thick-nap roller, the peg holes will likely become plugged with paint. It took nearly a full gallon of paint to roll two coats over all of the framing members.

LAY OUT THE 2x2 MOUNTING GRID

Study **Figure A** to help you digest the following layout directions. Measure from the floor to make a mark at 12 in. **(Photo 1)**. Then measure down from the ceiling to the mark and transfer it to the other end of the pegboard wall. (Garage floors are rarely level, but you can usually trust the ceiling.) Snap the bottom line. Measure up from the bottom line 93-1/8 in. to snap the top line. The 2x2s will go below the bottom line and above the top line to give you 96-1/8 in. outside to outside when they're in place.

If your pegboard will butt against a wall, install the 2x10 end frame first and measure from that to establish the 20-ft. 1/4-in. vertical grid line at the other end. (Or make the line to suit the number of bays you wish to have: 4 ft. 1/4 in., 8 ft. 1/4 in., etc.) Then snap horizontal lines spaced about every 2 ft. for the 2x2s that support the pegboard. Lastly, use a 4-ft. level to mark the end of the wall and the center of each stud **(Photo 2)**.

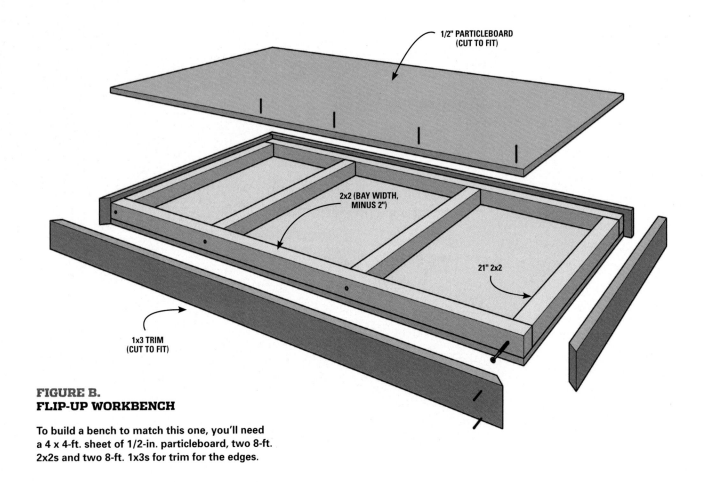

1/2" PARTICLEBOARD (CUT TO FIT)

2x2 (BAY WIDTH, MINUS 2")

21" 2x2

1x3 TRIM (CUT TO FIT)

FIGURE B.
FLIP-UP WORKBENCH

To build a bench to match this one, you'll need
a 4 x 4-ft. sheet of 1/2-in. particleboard, two 8-ft.
2x2s and two 8-ft. 1x3s for trim for the edges.

DEALING WITH OPENINGS

Our expanse of plywood didn't include any windows, doors
or electrical outlets or switches, but yours might. Surround
windows with 2x10s just like you did with the perimeter.
But beware of doors. Putting a 2x10 on the hinge side of
a door means it'll open only 90 degrees. Experiment with
the door swing to figure out which placement will work for
you. If you have electrical boxes, you're required by code
to install box extenders so the outlet or switch will be flush
with the pegboard surface.

STURDY, ADJUSTABLE SHELVING

You can buy dedicated pegboard shelving brackets, but we
wanted sturdy, adjustable 2x8 shelves, so we mounted 6-ft.
shelf standards on most of the 2x8s **(Photo 7)**. The 2x8s
can span the full bay width without sagging. Unless you
spend the time making all the bays exactly the same width,
the shelf length will vary from one bay to the next.

BUILT-IN, FLIP-UP WORKBENCH

Our bench is 40 in. high, and it can be folded down
into its own bay when you're not using it. The height
we've chosen is based on the pegboard wall base
being located 1 ft. above the floor and the how-to
steps shown in **Photos 8–11**. If you want a different
height, you'll have to do some design work. But make
sure to allow for a 1-1/2-in. gap between the bottom
of the bench and the 2x10 when it's folded down.
You'll need that gap for your fingers to safely open
and close the bench.

You will not find these special folding shelf brackets
in stores. Instead, conduct a search online for "KV
16 Folding Shelf Bracket" and you'll find plenty of
sources—and varying prices too. We paid about $65
with shipping for both. Make sure you get two. It's
easy to misorder and only get one. It happened to
us, folks!

Reconfigure As Your Needs Change

The items on your wall may come and go as your hobbies and storage requirements evolve. The beauty of this system is that you can rearrange shelves, add or substitute pegboard accessories, and even mount hanging systems that are designed for ordinary walls, so your wall will always suit your needs.

- Flip up the workbench when you need it; fold it down when you don't.
- Dozens of pegboard accessories are available to hang just about anything.
- Install 2x4 backers to hold storage brackets and hooks.
- Reposition shelves as your needs change.

7 Screw in the shelf standards. Mount standards on the dividers. Then cut the 2x8 shelves 1/4 in. shorter than the space between the standards and rest them on shelf standard brackets.

8 Assemble the workbench frame. Build a 2x2 framework 24 in. deep and 2 in. narrower than the bay opening you intend to install it in.

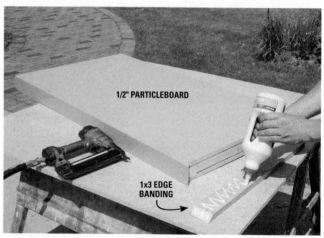

9 Sheathe the top and bottom. Cover both sides with 1/2-in. particleboard. Use it to square the ladder as you glue and nail it to the 2x2s. Then add 1x3 edge banding to the bench edges.

10 Add the folding shelf brackets. Cut 27-in.-long 2x4 hinge supports and screw them through the pegboard into the 2x2s with 3-in. screws. Then attach the folding shelf brackets with 1-1/2-in. washer-head screws.

11 Attach the top from underneath. Rest the bench on the top, centered between the 2x8 uprights and 1/4 in. away from the pegboard. Screw it to the brackets from underneath with 1-1/2-in. washer-head screws.

One-Day Garage Storage System

An incredibly easy solution for a cluttered garage.

This storage system is made mostly from wire shelving and plastic-coated particleboard (called "melamine"). Those two simple materials, along with some clever engineering, provide three big benefits:

Quick, simple construction. If you can make a few easy cuts (which don't have to be perfect), drive some screws and brush on a little paint, you can build this system in a weekend. If you're an experienced DIYer, you might be done in a day.

Fits any space. The system is made up of separate units, so you can build just one, cover an entire wall with several units or leave spaces between units.

Versatile storage. In addition to wire shelves, the system includes optional hanging spaces for clothes and outdoor gear, plus oversize upper shelves for bulky stuff. As your needs change, you can easily remove or reconfigure the shelves to fit what you need.

WHAT IT TAKES	
TIME 1 or 2 days	**SKILL LEVEL** Beginner
TOOLS & MATERIALS Circular saw or jigsaw, driver/drill, clamps, level, bolt cutter, paint brush (optional: stud finder)	

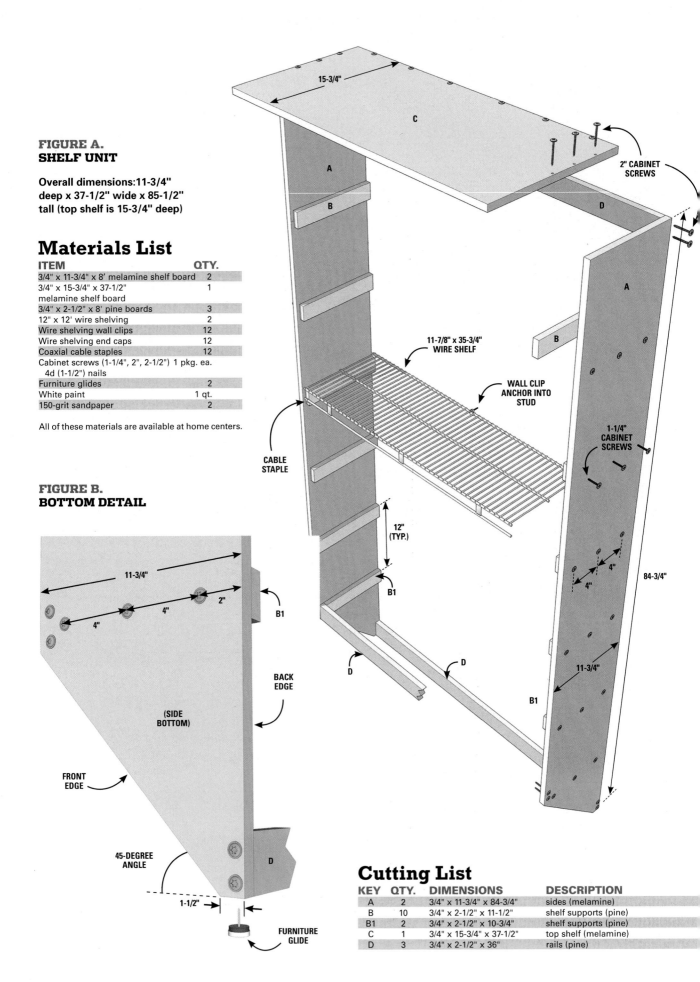

FIGURE A.
SHELF UNIT

Overall dimensions:11-3/4"
deep x 37-1/2" wide x 85-1/2"
tall (top shelf is 15-3/4" deep)

Materials List

ITEM	QTY.
3/4" x 11-3/4" x 8' melamine shelf board	2
3/4" x 15-3/4" x 37-1/2" melamine shelf board	1
3/4" x 2-1/2" x 8' pine boards	3
12" x 12' wire shelving	2
Wire shelving wall clips	12
Wire shelving end caps	12
Coaxial cable staples	12
Cabinet screws (1-1/4", 2", 2-1/2") 1 pkg. ea. 4d (1-1/2") nails	
Furniture glides	2
White paint	1 qt.
150-grit sandpaper	2

All of these materials are available at home centers.

FIGURE B.
BOTTOM DETAIL

11-3/4"

2"

4"

4"

B1

BACK EDGE

(SIDE BOTTOM)

FRONT EDGE

45-DEGREE ANGLE

1-1/2"

D

FURNITURE GLIDE

15-3/4"

C

A

B

D

2" CABINET SCREWS

A

B

11-7/8" x 35-3/4" WIRE SHELF

WALL CLIP ANCHOR INTO STUD

1-1/4" CABINET SCREWS

CABLE STAPLE

12" (TYP.)

B1

D

D

84-3/4"

4"

4"

11-3/4"

B1

Cutting List

KEY	QTY.	DIMENSIONS	DESCRIPTION
A	2	3/4" x 11-3/4" x 84-3/4"	sides (melamine)
B	10	3/4" x 2-1/2" x 11-1/2"	shelf supports (pine)
B1	2	3/4" x 2-1/2" x 10-3/4"	shelf supports (pine)
C	1	3/4" x 15-3/4" x 37-1/2"	top shelf (melamine)
D	3	3/4" x 2-1/2" x 36"	rails (pine)

1 Cut the sides. Cut one melamine board at a 45-degree angle and use it as a pattern to mark the others for cutting. Mark your cutting line on a strip of painter's tape—the tape reduces chipping as you cut.

2 Position the shelf supports. Mark where the edge of each shelf support is located and mark a centerline for the screw locations. Drill three 9/64-in. screw holes for each of the supports.

3 Fasten the shelf supports. Drive 1-1/4-in. screws through the sides and into the shelf supports. A clamp makes this step much easier.

4 Assemble the unit. Drill holes in the top, then drive cabinet screws to fasten the top to the sides.

BUILD THE UNITS

To get started, cut all the parts (see Cutting List, Page 68). The coating on melamine tends to chip when you cut it. For cleaner cuts, use a 60-tooth carbide circular saw blade and apply painter's tape over the cut **(Photo 1)**. Melamine is slippery stuff, so be sure to clamp it in place before cutting. Set the depth of your saw blade at 1 in. Chipping won't be a problem when you cut the solid wood parts (B and D). When you cut the supports for the lowest shelves (B1), note that they're shorter than the others. To avoid slow, fussy painting later, paint the wood parts before assembly. Our shelf spacing is 12 in., but any spacing you choose is fine. Lay pairs of sides

(A) next to each other when you mark shelf support locations. That way, you can be sure that the supports will match up after assembly. Drill screw holes **(Photo 2)** and then fasten the shelf supports **(Photo 3)**.

Pick out a flat spot on the floor and attach the top (C) to the sides **(Photo 4)**. Then tilt the assembly up a few inches and slide wood scraps beneath it so you can add the rails (D) with 2-in. screws **(Photo 5)**.

With the unit completely assembled, sand the exposed cut edges of the melamine using 150-grit sandpaper, then paint them **(Photo 6)**. Finally, hammer on some furniture glides **(Photo 7)** and the unit is ready for installation.

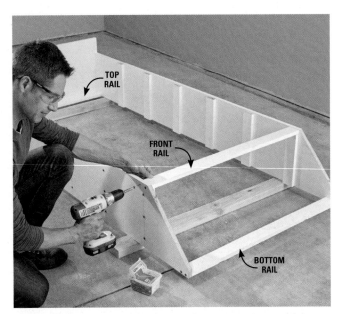

5 Install the rails. Drill screw holes in the sides and fasten the three rails. You'll need to raise the unit off the floor in order to screw the top and bottom rails.

6 Paint the cut edges. For looks and moisture protection, apply two coats of paint. If you slop paint onto the melamine surface, just wipe it off with a damp rag.

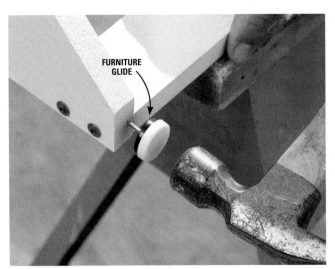

7 Add glides. Nail plastic furniture glides to the bottom of the sides to keep them from resting directly on damp surfaces, especially concrete.

INSTALL THE UNITS

If you have finished walls, locate the wall studs with a stud finder and mark them with masking tape. Get some help to lift the assembly up to the wall and hold it in place **(Photo 8)**. Our floor had a row of concrete blocks that protruded from the wall about 1-1/2 in., so we rested the glides on them. The blocks were level but the floor had a slight pitch toward the door, so this saved us the hassle of having to allow for the slope of the floor.

With the assembly located against the wall, you can shim underneath to level it (if necessary) and then plumb the sides with a level. Screw it to the wall studs with 2-1/2-in. screws **(Photo 9)**.

8 Install the first unit. Mark the stud locations with painter's tape and set the first unit in place. To ensure that the unit is level and square, check both the top and one side with a level.

If you're willing to spend $25 or so on a bolt cutter, cutting the wire shelves will be quick and easy **(Photo 10)**. Bolt cutters are sized by length; 24 in. is a good choice. When the shelves are cut, set them in place and "clip" them to the wall **(Photo 11)**. Also secure the shelf fronts with coaxial cable staples **(Photo 12)**, which are available in the electrical aisle at home centers. Remove the nails that come with the staples and use 4d nails instead. To store balls or other items that tend to roll off shelves, install a shelf or two upside down. The lip on the front of the shelf keeps stuff in place.

9 Add as many units as you like. With the first unit installed square and level, you can butt the next unit against it. Screw all of the units to studs at the top and bottom rungs.

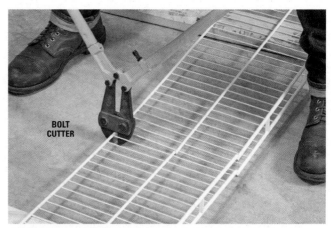

BOLT CUTTER

10 Cut the shelves. A bolt cutter is the best tool for cutting wire shelving to length. A hacksaw or a metal-cutting blade in a jigsaw will also do the job.

WALL CLIP

11 Anchor the shelves. Fasten each shelf to the wall with at least two clips. When you want to fasten the clip to a stud, simply cut off the drywall anchor part of the clip and drive a screw through the clip.

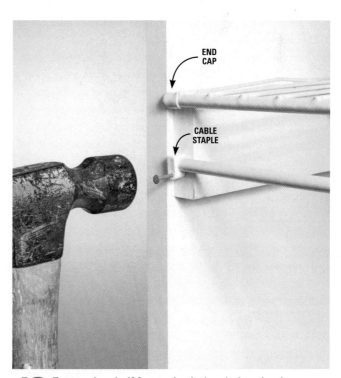

END CAP

CABLE STAPLE

12 Fasten the shelf fronts. Lock the shelves in place with coaxial cable staples. End caps give the shelves a finished look.

Super Sturdy Drawers

Super big, super tough, super easy.

This heavy-duty storage system is modeled after old metal filing cabinets, but these will hold more weight. We decided to build a bunch of them and add shelves and a continuous top. The first one (the prototype) took one full day to build and a couple hours to paint and finish, but we built the other three in just one more day. This isn't a project that requires a high-end furniture maker's craftsmanship: If you can build basic plywood boxes, you can build these drawer units.

GETTING STARTED

We'll focus on how to build one unit, but you can build as many as you like and arrange them whichever way works best. Refer to the cutting diagram (Page 75), and cut all the plywood components except the back (C), drawer bottoms (D) and hardwood drawer fronts (L, M, N). Cut these parts to size needed in case one or more components get a little out of whack. Many home centers will help you cut your plywood so it's easier to haul home, but don't wear out your welcome and expect them to make all the cuts for you.

CUT AND INSTALL THE DRAWER SUPPORTS

Lay the two sides (A) next to each other on your workbench. Position them so the surface with the most flaws faces up—this will be the inside and won't be visible once the drawers are installed. Also, determine which of the plywood edges have the fewest flaws and voids, and arrange the pieces so the best edges face toward the front. Measure up from the bottom on each side 14 in., 26 in. and 38 in., and make a pencil mark near the outside edge of each side. Use a straightedge, and draw a line between your marks and across the face of both sides at the same time. These will be the guidelines for the tops of the drawer supports (P).

Cut 18 in. off the 6-ft. pine 1x4, and set it aside to be used as the center brace (Q). Rip down what's left of the 1x4 into 1-in. strips to be used as the six drawer supports, and cut them to length (see Cutting List on Page 76).

Install the drawer supports with glue and 1-1/2-in. brads **(Photo 1)**. The drawer supports should be 1/2 in. short on the front side to accommodate the thickness of the hardwood drawer fronts. Flip the sides over and install three 1-1/2-in. screws in each support. Countersink all the screws a bit on the outside of the entire carcass so the holes can be filled with wood filler before painting.

WHAT IT TAKES

TIME
2 days

SKILL LEVEL
Intermediate

TOOLS & MATERIALS
Table saw (or circular saw), router, clamps, wood glue
(optional: 18-gauge brad nailer)

18-GAUGE BRAD NAILER WITH 1-1/2" BRADS

DRAWER SUPPORT

DRAWER SUPPORT GUIDELINE

1 Mount the drawer supports. Attach the drawer supports to the side panels before assembling the cabinet. Glue each support and tack it down with brads. Flip the panel over and drive 1-1/2-in. screws into the supports.

ASSEMBLE THE CARCASS

Apply wood glue and tack on the top or bottom (B) to the sides with three or four brads. Even the straightest plywood available at the home center or lumberyard will probably cup and curl a bit after it's cut up. So whenever you join two pieces of plywood, start on one end and straighten out the plywood as you go.

Secure each joint with three 1-1/2-in. screws before moving on to the next one. Whenever drilling close to the edge of plywood, avoid puckers and splits by predrilling 1/8-in. holes for the screws. And stay at least 1-1/2-in. from the end of the plywood that's being drilled into **(Photo 2)**. If a screw is installed too close to the end, it will just split the plywood instead of burying into it.

Spread glue on the back edge of the carcass and fasten the back with 1-1/2-in. brads along one whole side first. Then use the back as a guide to square up the rest of the carcass **(Photo 3)**. Finish attaching the back with screws every 16 in. or so.

The center brace keeps the plywood sides from bowing in or out. Measure the distance between the drawer runners at the back of the carcass. Cut the center brace that same length. Install the brace between the two middle runners 4 in. back from the front. Make sure the brace is flush or just a little lower than the drawer supports or the drawer will

STAY 1-1/2" FROM END

1-1/2" TRIM HEAD SCREWS

2 Assemble the carcass. Fasten the sides to the top and bottom with glue and brads, and then add screws. To avoid splitting the plywood, drill pilot holes for the screws and stay 1-1/2 in. from the ends.

3 Add the back. Use the back to square up the cabinet. Fasten the whole length of one side, and then align the other sides with the back as you go.

FIGURE A.
STORAGE UNIT

Overall dimensions:
16" wide x 51-1/2" tall
x 24" deep

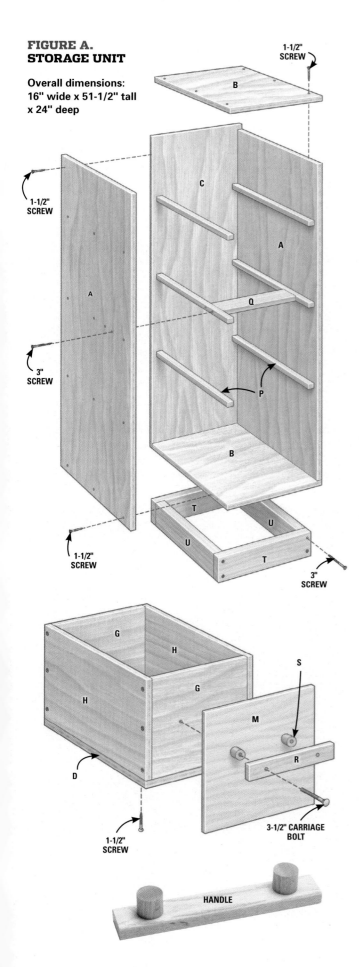

1-1/2" SCREW

1-1/2" SCREW

3" SCREW

B

C

A

A

Q

P

B

T

U

U

T

1-1/2" SCREW

3" SCREW

G

H

G

H

S

M

R

D

1-1/2" SCREW

3-1/2" CARRIAGE BOLT

HANDLE

Materials List

ITEM	QTY.
4' x 8' x 3/4" BC sanded plywood	2
2' x 4' x 1/2" hardwood plywood	1
1x6 x 6' pine	1
2x4 x 8' pressure-treated lumber	1
1x2 x 4' oak	1
1-1/4" x 16" oak dowel	1
1-1/2" screws (small box)	1
3" trim head screws (small box)	1
1-1/2" 18-gauge brads (small box)	1
1/4" x 3-1/2" carriage bolts	8
1/4" nut and washer	8
Wood filler, patch or putty	1
Paint, quart	1
Polyurethane, quart	1

teeter back and forth on it. Hold it in place with a clamp and secure it with two 3-in. screws through each side **(Photo 4)**. Install a brace at more than one drawer-support location if your plywood is particularly unruly.

ASSEMBLE THE DRAWERS

Lay out each drawer so all the best edges face up. Then, just as you did with the carcass, assemble the drawers with glue, brads and screws. Cut the drawer bottoms after the sides (F, H, K) and fronts/backs (E, G, J) are assembled. That way you can cut the bottoms exactly to size. A perfectly square bottom will ensure your drawers are also square. Make sure the bottom is flush or a little short on the front side of the drawer; otherwise the hardwood drawer fronts won't sit flat on the front of the drawer **(Photo 5)**.

FASTEN THE DRAWER FRONTS

The home center closest to us carried three options of hardwood plywood: oak, birch and one labeled just "hardwood." We went with the generic hardwood, but if you do the same, make sure to get enough to finish the project because the grain and color will vary from one batch to the next—and you don't want your project to be mismatched.

The drawers may not sit perfectly flat until they are filled with stuff, so before securing the hardwood drawer fronts, add some weight to the drawer you're working on and the one above it. Center each drawer in the opening before you secure the drawer front.

Start at the bottom, and cut the hardwood drawer fronts to size one at a time. Cut them so there's a 1/8-in. gap between the bottom and the sides and the bottom of the drawer above it. Rest the drawer front on a couple of shims to achieve the gap at the bottom and eyeball the gaps on the side. Glue it and secure it with four brads, one in each corner **(Photo 6)**. There's no need for screws; the handle bolts will sandwich everything together. If you're building several of these storage units and purchased a piece of hardwood plywood larger than 2 x 4 ft., you'll have the option to line up the grain on the drawer fronts the same way it came off the sheet. It's a small detail that can add a lot to the looks of the project.

BUILD AND ATTACH THE HANDLES

Rout the edges of the handle with a 1/4-in. round-over bit before cutting the handles (R) to length. Next, cut the dowels for the handle extensions (S) to length.

Build one simple jig to align the dowels on the handles, and to position the handles on the drawer fronts. Cut a 3/4-in. piece of plywood the same width as the drawer fronts and rip it down to 4-3/8 in. Fasten a scrap of 3/4-in. material to the end of the jig. Measure in from each side and mark a line at 2-1/8 in., 3-1/8 in. and 4-3/8 in.

This jig is designed to center the top handle on the top drawer front and keep the others the same distance down from the top on all the other drawers. If you want all the handles centered, build two more jigs or mark center lines on the other drawers.

Set the jig on the workbench and line up the handle with the two outside lines. Line up the dowels on the inside and middle lines on the jig and glue the dowels to the center of handles. No need for clamping—just keep pressure on them for 10 to 20 seconds. Then set them aside for an hour or so to let the glue dry. The glue is just to keep the dowels in place until the handle bolts are installed.

Clamp the jig onto the top of the drawer front, and line up the handle with the guidelines. Drill a starter hole through each handle and the drawer front with a 1/8-in. drill bit

4 Install the center brace. The brace prevents the sides from bowing in or out. Clamp the brace in place, and then fasten it with 3-in. trim head screws.

Cutting List

KEY	QTY.	DIMENSIONS	DESCRIPTION
3/4" BC sanded plywood			
A	2	46-1/2" x 23-1/4"	sides
B	2	16" x 23-1/4"	top/bottom
C	1	48" x 16"	back*
D	4	22-3/4" x 14-1/4"	drawer bottoms*
E	2	12-3/4" x 12"	bottom drawer front/back
F	2	22-3/4" x 12"	bottom drawer sides
G	4	12-3/4" x 10"	middle drawer front/back
H	4	22-3/4" x 10"	middle drawer sides
J	2	12-3/4" x 7-1/4"	top drawer front/back
K	2	22-3/4" x 7-1/4"	top drawer sides
1/2" hardwood plywood			
L	1	14-1/4" x 13-7/8"	bottom drawer front*
M	2	14-1/4" x 11-7/8"	middle drawer fronts*
N	1	14-1/4" x 8-3/8"	top drawer front*
Cut from 6' pine 1x4			
P	6	22-1/2" x 1" x 3/4"	drawer supports
Q	1	12-1/2" x 3-1/2" x 3/4"	center brace
Cut from 4' oak 1x2			
R	4	10" x 1-1/2" x 3/4"	handles
Cut from 1' oak 1-1/4" dowel			
S	8	1" x 1-1/4"	handle extensions
Cut from 8' pressure-treated 2x4			
T	2	16" x 1-1/2" x 3-1/2"	base front/back
U	2	17" x 1-1/2" x 3-1/2"	base sides

*Cut to fit

5 Build the drawers. Assemble the drawers as you built the cabinets: Glue, nail and screw the sides, front and back. Then square up the box as you fasten the bottom.

FIGURE B.
CUTTING DIAGRAM

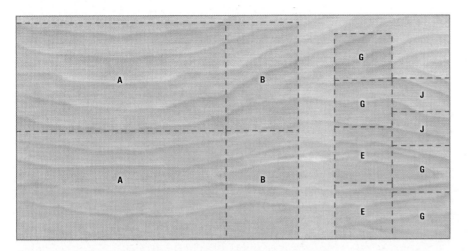

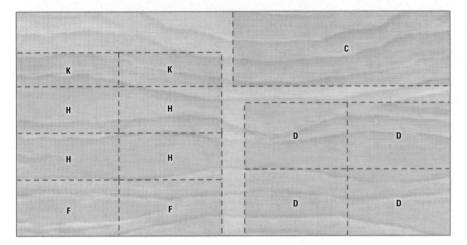

on the insides, backs or sides that were going to be sandwiched together. Cover the hardwood drawer fronts and edges with two coats of polyurethane, or another similar coating. Avoid discoloration around the brad hole on the drawer fronts by filling them with matching putty between coats of poly. We stained the oak handles with a medium-tinted stain to make them "pop" a little more before finishing them with two coats of poly.

Install the handles with the carriage bolts, washers and nuts. Seat the carriage bolts with a hammer so they don't spin while you turn the nut, and turn them tight.

INSTALL MULTIPLE UNITS

If you're building several units, build the base and then set each unit in place individually (**Photo 8**). Create a toe space by building the base 4 in. narrower than the units. Our garage floor slants down toward the overhead door, so we had to rip down the base to make the whole thing level. You may just need a few shims to make the units level. Level each storage unit as you go and screw them to the base and to one another with 1-1/2-in. screws. Angle the screws a bit so they don't poke through when you screw the units together.

Rip down a couple of cleats and screw them to the sides for the middle shelf to sit on. Leave them a couple of inches short of the front so you don't see them. Attach the lower shelf to the base before installing the middle shelf (**Photo 9**).

Once all the units are in place, attach the top(s) so that the seams fall in the middle of one unit. Screw the whole thing to the wall studs last using one screw per unit. The front side of the base may end up needing a few shims to make it sit flush against the wall.

Touch up the exposed screw holes and scuff marks with paint. Now all that's left is to file away all that clutter.

before drilling the final holes with a 1/4-in. bit (**Photo 7**). The 1/8-in. bit probably won't be long enough to clear all the material, but it still helps make a cleaner hole when you drill through the second time.

Mark the bottom of each handle extension and the area near the hole on each drawer with the same number so that you can install that same handle on the same drawer after you apply the finish.

BUILD AND SECURE THE BASE

If you're building only one unit, cut the base parts (T) and assemble them with glue and two 3-in. screws that are compatible with pressure-treated lumber. Secure the base to the bottom of the carcass with glue and 1-1/2-in. screws: three on the sides and two each on the front and back.

FINISH THE COMPONENTS

Patch all the screw holes, brad holes and voids on the carcass with wood filler or wood patch. We painted only the outside and front of the cabinet. We didn't bother painting the wood

6 Position the drawer fronts. Slip the drawer boxes into the cabinet. Center the drawer fronts and shim under them to achieve 1/8-in. gaps. Secure the fronts to the drawer boxes with glue and one brad in each corner.

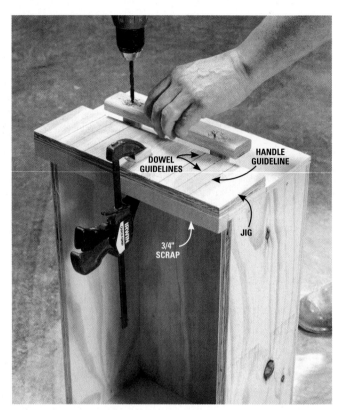

7 Add the handles. Build a simple jig and clamp it onto the drawer front. Hold the handle in place and drill holes for the carriage bolts.

8 Set the carcass on the base. When installing multiple units, build, paint and lay down the base first, and then attach each unit to the base.

9 Hang shelving between units. Install the bottom shelf on the base. Install cleats to support other shelves.

Ultimate Garage Cabinets

Inexpensive, enormous and surprisingly easy to build.

If you're looking for easy, attractive, economical cabinets, you've found them. Keep in mind that this cabinet system can easily adapt to any situation: You can build one cabinet or a dozen, adjust the height or width to suit the space, or combine closed cabinets and open shelves in different ways. This system can also be configured for a laundry room, closet or basement.

TOOLS, MATERIALS & MONEY

You could build this system with just a few hand tools, a drill and a circular saw, but a table saw would save lots of time. The skills needed are as basic as the tools. If you can make long straight cuts and screw parts together, you can build this system.

This whole system is made from just two materials: plastic-coated particleboard, usually called "melamine," and construction-grade pine 1x4s. (Melamine is the type of plastic used as the coating.) You could use 3/4-in. plywood

or particleboard, but we chose melamine because it didn't require a finish.

The materials for this floor-to-ceiling system cost less than we would have paid for those wimpy "utility" cabinets that you'd find at a home center. Our garage walls were 10 ft. tall. If your ceiling is about 8 ft. tall, you can eliminate the deep upper cabinets. That will lower the cost per linear foot.

If you opt for completely open shelving and you skip the cabinet doors, that lowers the cost even further. You'll find your cost will drop to about $20 per linear foot.

WHAT IT TAKES	
TIME 1-3 weekends	**SKILL LEVEL** Intermediate
TOOLS & MATERIALS Circular saw (or table saw), driver/drill, stepladder, 4-ft. level (optional: steam iron, edge-banding trimmer)	

PLAN THE SYSTEM TO SUIT YOUR STUFF

Roughly block out the cabinet locations on the wall, using masking tape. Remember to space the garage cabinets to leave room for shelves in between. Experiment with different cabinet widths and spacing until you find a layout that works well. Follow these guidelines:

- Each cabinet must have at least one stud behind it so you can fasten the cabinet securely to the wall.
- Limit door widths to 24 in. or less. To cover a wider opening, install double doors. We limited most of our doors to 12-in. widths so we could open them even when the car was parked in the garage.
- Shelves longer than 2 ft. often sag. If you make yours longer, stiffen the melamine by screwing 1x4 cleats to the undersides.
- Size the cabinets to make the most of a full sheet of melamine. By making our cabinets 16 in. deep, for example, we were able to cut three cabinet sides from each sheet with no wasted material (see **Figure A** for other dimensions). Don't forget that a saw blade eats up about 1/8 in. of material with each cut. Some sheets of melamine are oversized by about 1 in. to account for this.

BUYING MELAMINE

Most home centers carry melamine in 4 x 8-ft. sheets, usually only in white. For colors other than white, try a lumberyard that serves cabinetmakers. These suppliers often charge more and might sell only to professionals, so call before you visit.

Home centers carry plastic iron-on edge banding. Some also carry peel-and-stick edge banding, which lets you skip the ironing. Either way, white will be the only choice at most home centers.

WORKING WITH MELAMINE

With your cabinet dimensions in hand, begin cutting the melamine into parts. Cut the material into equal widths for the sides and the fixed and adjustable shelves, but don't cut the parts to length until they're edge banded.

Here are some pointers:

- Get help. Melamine is too heavy to handle solo. If you have a large, stable table saw, you and a helper can cut full sheets. But it's usually better to slice a sheet into manageable sections with a circular saw first. Then make finish cuts on the table saw.
- Wear gloves when handling large pieces. The edges of melamine are sharp enough to slice your hands.
- Avoid scratching the melamine surface. If your workbench has a rough surface, cover it with cardboard or old carpet. Pad sawhorses the same way. Run a few strips of masking tape across the shoe of your circular saw so it doesn't mar the melamine.

Cutting List

KEY	QTY.	DIMENSIONS	DESCRIPTION
A	#	16" x 96"	side
B	#	16" x 23-5/8"	fixed shelf
C	#	3-1/2" x 23-5/8"	pine (cleat)
D	#	12" x 95-1/4"	door
E	#	16" x 23-5/8"	adjustable shelf

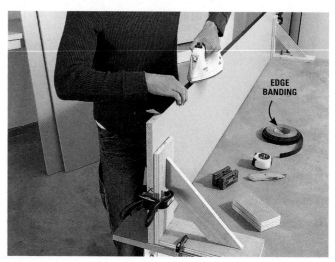

1 Iron on the edge banding. Cut the melamine to width and iron on edge banding. Position the banding so that it overhangs the ends and sides. Let the banding cool before you begin trimming.

2 Trim the ends. Hold a wood block firmly over the end and carefully slice off the excess banding. Use a sharp new blade in your utility knife.

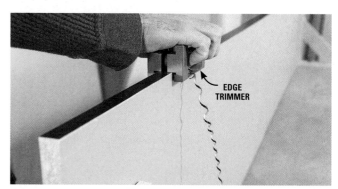

3 Trim the edges. Slice off the excess banding with an edge trimmer. Test the trimmer on a banded scrap first; you may have to adjust the blades for a perfect cut.

FIGURE A.
UPRIGHT CABINET CONSTRUCTION

Overall dimensions: 96" tall x 25-1/8" wide x 16-3/4" deep.
Your dimensions may differ.

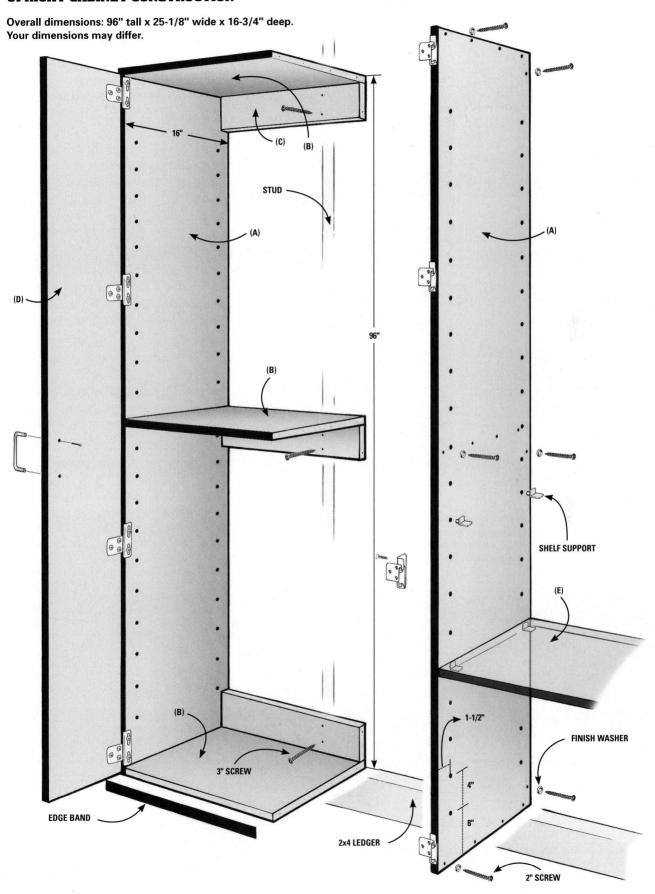

16"

(C)   (B)

STUD

(A)

(D)

96"

(B)

(A)

SHELF SUPPORT

(E)

(B)

3" SCREW

1-1/2"

FINISH WASHER

EDGE BAND

2x4 LEDGER

4"

8"

2" SCREW

4 Drill shelf support holes. Drill 1/4-in. shelf-support holes through cabinet sides using a scrap of pegboard as a guide. For end panels that won't support shelves on one side, place a stop collar on the drill bit.

5 Crosscut the parts. Cut parts to length using a crosscut guide. A stop block screwed to the guide lets you mass-produce identical lengths fast. Support the melamine on both sides of the cut with 2x4 scraps.

6 Assemble the cabinets. Predrill and screw 1x4s to melamine to form the fixed shelves. Screw all of the fixed shelves to one cabinet side, then add the other side to complete the cabinet.

- Be careful with edges. They're easy to chip. When standing parts on edge, set them down gently. Don't drop sheets or drag them across the floor.
- Plan for chip-out. Saw blades often leave slightly chipped edges in the melamine coating. A new carbide blade will chip less than a dull one, but you can't completely prevent chips. Chipping is worse on the side where the saw teeth exit the material. When you are running melamine across a table saw, the underside of the sheet is particularly prone to chipping. With a circular saw or a jigsaw, chipping is worse on the face-up side. Plan cuts so that all the chipped edges are on the same side of the part. Then you can hide them during assembly by facing them toward the inside of cabinets.

IRON ON THE EDGE BAND

Set your iron to the "cotton" setting and iron the banding on in two or three passes (**Photo 1**). On the first pass, run the iron quickly over the banding just to tack it into place. Center the banding so it overhangs on both sides. Make a second, slower pass to fully melt the glue and firmly adhere the banding. Then check the edges for loose spots and make another pass if needed.

Trim the ends of the banding with a utility knife (**Photo 2**) before trimming the edges (**Photo 3**). If you damage the banding while trimming, just reheat it, pull it off and start

FIGURE B.
CROSSCUT GUIDE

This guide takes a few minutes to make but saves time when you're cutting the fixed shelves (**Photo 5**) and even more time later when cutting adjustable shelves (**Photo 14**). Our system required 30 shelves. To make a crosscut guide, screw a guide strip to the base and run the saw against the guide strip to trim the excess off the base. Add a squaring strip positioned perpendicular to the guide strip. Position the stop block to set the length of the parts.

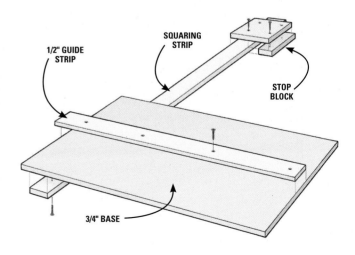

over. For more information, visit familyhandyman.com and search for "edge banding."

DRILL SHELF SUPPORT HOLES

The adjustable shelves rest on shelf supports that fit into holes drilled into the cabinet sides (**Photo 4**). Drill all the way through the sides that will support shelves inside and outside the cabinet. Drill holes 3/8 in. deep in cabinet sides that form the outer ends of your shelf system. Tape wrapped around a drill bit makes a good depth marker when you're drilling just a few holes, but a stop collar is better for this job.

Check your shelf supports before drilling. Some require 1/4-in. holes; others require 5 mm holes. Use a brad-point drill bit for a clean, chip-free hole. To limit blowout where the bit exits the melamine, set a "backer" underneath. You can make a drilling guide from just about any material, but a strip of pegboard is a perfect ready-made guide. Label the bottom of the guide and the bottoms of the cabinet sides so all the holes will align.

BUILD FIXED SHELVES AND ASSEMBLE THE CABINETS

The fixed shelves that fit between the cabinet sides (A) are made from melamine panels (B) and pine 1x4s (C). Paint the 1x4s to match the melamine. Cabinets less than 4 ft. tall need only top and bottom fixed shelves. Taller cabinets also need a middle fixed shelf (**Figure A**). To make the fixed shelves, just cut melamine and 1x4s to identical lengths and then screw them together.

Assembling the cabinets is a simple matter of fastening the sides to the fixed shelves (**Photo 6**). Predrill and drive a screw near the front of each fixed shelf first, making sure the banded edges of the fixed shelf and side are flush. Then drill and drive another screw near the back of the cabinet to hold the fixed shelf in position before you add the other screws. Handle the completed cabinet boxes with care—they're not very strong until they're fastened to the wall.

HANG THE DOORS

Make the doors after the cabinet boxes are assembled. To hang the doors, first screw hinges to the cabinets (**Photo 7**). The type of hinge we chose is called a "wrap" hinge because it wraps around the corner at the front edge of the cabinet. If you don't find them at a home center, search online for "1/4 overlay wrap hinge." This design has a couple of big advantages: It mounts more securely to the cabinet and it lets you position the doors perfectly (**Photo 8**) before you fasten them (**Photo 9**).

We used four hinges for each of our 12-in.-wide double doors. If you opt for a single wide door, use at least five hinges. The hinges themselves are strong enough to hold much more weight, but they're fastened with just two screws

7 Install the hinges. Screw hinges to the cabinets. Position the top and bottom hinges 1/4 in. from each corner and space the others equally apart.

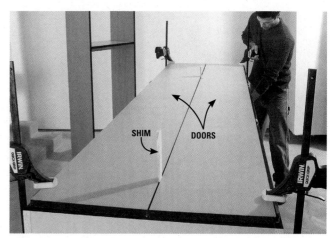

8 Position the doors. Position the doors over the hinges using shims to maintain a 1/8-in. gap. Use clamps or weights to hold the doors in place.

9 Fasten the doors from below. Predrill with a self-centering bit and drive one screw through each hinge from inside the cabinet. Add the other screws with the doors open. A self-centering drill bit (above) makes positioning screw holes easy.

Making Screws Work in Melamine

Screws are the only fastening method used in this entire project. They make fast, strong joints. But screwing into melamine presents a few complications:

- **Strip-out**: As with any other particleboard product, melamine strips easily if you overdrive screws. Go easy on the drill trigger as you drive screws home. Use coarse-thread screws only. Fine-thread screws will strip every time. Longer screws also minimize stripping. If this project had been built from plywood, 1-5/8-in. screws would have worked fine. But we used 2-in. screws to assemble the boxes.

- **Splits**: Particleboard splits easily. Never drive a screw into particleboard without drilling a pilot hole. We drilled 7/64-in. holes and used No. 8 screws. Even with a pilot hole, screws will split particleboard if you place them close to ends. Keep them at least an inch from the ends of parts.

- **Countersinking**: Tapered screw heads will sometimes sink into melamine, but often they'll strip out before the head is flush with the melamine surface. Next to an edge, they'll crush out the particleboard. Always drill countersink holes to create a recess for screw heads. You can drill countersink and pilot holes in one stroke with a countersink bit.

- **Appearance**: Even with a clean countersink hole, screw heads are a blemish in melamine's perfect surface. For a neater look, use finish washers (photo below) with screws that will be visible. Finish washers would eliminate the need for countersink holes.

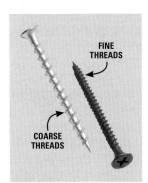

FINE THREADS

COARSE THREADS

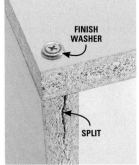

FINISH WASHER

SPLIT

CRUSH-OUT

PILOT/COUNTERSINK BIT

LEDGER

10 Install a ledger. Fasten a 2x4 ledger to the wall framing with 3-in. screws. Choose a straight 2x4 and make sure the ledger is level.

1/2" OR MORE CLEARANCE FROM WALL

LEDGER

11 Hang the cabinets. Set the cabinet into place and then screw it to the ledger. Then level the cabinet and fasten it to the wall with pairs of 3-in. screws driven through the upper and middle cleats into studs.

FIGURE C.
UPPER CABINET CONSTRUCTION

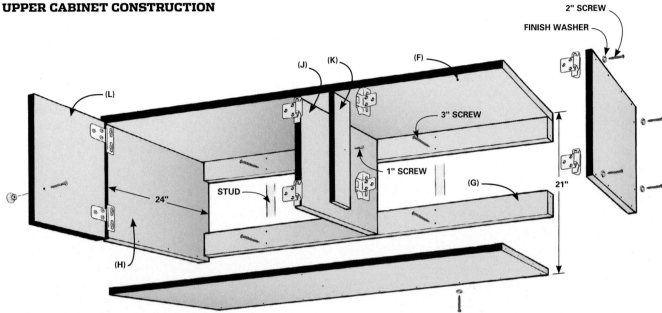

Overall dimensions: 21" tall x 72" wide x 24" deep.
Your dimensions may differ.

Cutting List

KEY	SIZE & DESCRIPTION
F	24" x 70-1/2" (top/bottom panel)
G	3-1/2" x 70-1/2" pine (cleat)
H	21" x 24" (side panel)
J	19-1/2" x 23-1/4" (divider)
K	4" x 23-1/4" (hinge spacer)
L	17-7/16" x 20-1/4" (door)

each. The particleboard core of melamine doesn't hold screws very well. So when in doubt, add more hinges.

With the hinges in place, measure between them to determine the door width (with double doors, allow a 1/8-in. gap between them). To determine the length, measure the cabinet opening and add 3/4 in. Cut the doors and set them in place to check the fit before banding the edges. When the doors are complete and screwed to the hinges, label each door and cabinet. Then unscrew the doors to make cabinet installation easier.

MOUNT THE CABINETS

Don't install the cabinets directly on the garage floor. Water puddles from dripping cars will quickly destroy particleboard. We mounted these cabinets about 6 in. off the floor—just enough space to allow for easy floor sweeping. This height also let us level the ledger and fasten it to the wall framing **(Photo 10)** rather than to the concrete foundation. We drove screws into the studs and sill plate.

You'll need a helper to install the cabinets **(Photo 11)**. Install the two end cabinets first, then position the others between them, leaving equal spaces for the shelves that fit between the cabinets. Watch out for obstructions that prevent cabinet doors from opening. End cabinets that fit into corners, for example, should stand about 1/2 in. from the adjacent wall.

UPPER CABINETS

The upper cabinets provide deep, enclosed storage space and tie the upright cabinets together so they can't twist away from the wall. Instead of installing upper cabinets, you could simply run a long shelf across the tops of the upright cabinets.

The upper cabinets are simply horizontal versions of the upright cabinets; you use the same techniques and materials (see **Figure C**). Here are some building tips:

- Minimize measuring and math errors: Build the upper cabinets after the upright cabinets are in place.
- To allow easy installation, leave a 1/2-in. gap between the ceiling and the upper cabinets. You could leave the resulting gap open, but we chose to cover it. Here's how: We ripped 1x4s into 1-in.-wide strips, painted the strips to match the edge band and screwed the strips to the tops of the cabinets. After the uppers were installed, we cut trim strips from 1x4, painted them and used them to cover the gap.
- You can build upper cabinet sections up to 8 ft. long. For strength and ease of installation, size the sections so that they meet over the upright cabinets, not over open shelves.
- Remember to add hinge spacers (K) to dividers (J) so you can install hinges back to back.

SHELVES AND HARDWARE COME LAST

Cut the shelves at the very end of the project (**Photo 14**). That way, you can take exact measurements inside and between shelves and use up any scraps. The number of shelves is up to you; we made four for inside each cabinet and six for each between-cabinet space. Install cabinet knobs or pulls after the doors are in place to make drilling a hole in the wrong location just about impossible.

12 Assemble the upper cabinets. Build the upper cabinets with the same techniques and materials used for the uprights. Install a blank panel where cabinets will meet at a corner.

13 Install the upper cabinets. Place the upper cabinets on top of the lower cabinets and screw the uppers together with 1-1/4-in. screws. Then screw them to the wall studs and to the lower cabinets.

14 Add shelves between cabinets. Measure the spaces inside and between cabinets. Subtract 1/4 in. and cut shelves using the crosscut jig.

Quick & Easy Shed

Building a home for all your garden gear is as easy as building a fence. You can make these shed walls from posts, rails and boards—just like a fence. We'll show you fast, foolproof roof-building tricks, too!

If you need more space to store and organize your lawn and garden gear, consider this simple, elegant 5 x 12-ft. shed. It's large enough for wheelbarrows, lawn mowers and even a moderate-size garden tractor. And there's still plenty of room left over for garden hoses, tools and supplies, pots and other stuff. We also included a built-in bench for potting plants.

The shed will look good for years because it's built from durable cedar siding, pressure-treated wood and a 30-year steel roof. The front is attractive, but the back is all business—it's wide open for easy access and storage. But if leaving it open just won't work in your yard, you can install doors, too.

Another nice feature of this shed design is that you can very easily enlarge the plan. Build it up to 12 ft. deep and make it as long as you like. Even in larger sizes, the shed uses exactly the same techniques and materials, so there's

no adjustment needed there. Just be sure to keep the post spacing under 6 ft., adding more posts as needed.

The following pages will show you how to assemble this shed, which requires no more skill than building a fence. We simplified the tough spots—laying out the posts, assembling the roof and marking the angles—so that you can successfully build it even if this is your first shed. This project costs about the same as a store-bought kit, but ours is quite a bit better

WHAT IT TAKES

TIME	SKILL LEVEL
3 weekends	Beginner

TOOLS & MATERIALS
Circular saw, driver/drill, tin snips, 4-ft. level

and prettier. And best of all, you can complete the project in three easy weekends.

SITING YOUR SHED

If you build the shed and leave the back open, it's best to position the open back against a backdrop of foliage, a fence or a garage wall. That'll keep the finished side most visible and the clutter out of sight. Still, if security is an issue, you may not want to store any valuable items there.

It's best to position your shed on a level site. The greater the slope, the more work you'll have leveling the floor. Our site sloped about 6 in. from one end to the other. The floor in this shed is simple concrete pavers laid over a 6-in. layer of level sand. It's inexpensive, drains well and can be cleaned with a few squirts from the garden hose. Other options are pouring a concrete slab or even framing in a deck-like floor. Whatever floor you choose, make sure it's higher than the surrounding yard to keep runoff water out of the building.

You probably won't need a building permit for this shed because in most communities it will fall under the minimum size that requires a permit. But it's a good idea to check with

Material List

QTY.	ITEM & USE
6	4x4 x 10' (treated) for posts
1	2x4 x 10' (treated) for bottom rail (end walls)
1	2x4 x 12' (treated) for bottom rail (front wall)
2	2x4 x 10' for end wall framing
3	2x4 x 12' for front wall and window framing
5	2x8 x 12' for beams
6	2x4 x 10' for rafters
1	2x6 x 16' for ridge beam
6	2x4 x 16' for purlins
10	1x12 x 10' (cedar) for end wall siding
8	1x6 x 10' (cedar) for end wall siding
8	1x12 x 8' (cedar) for front wall siding
10	1x6 x 8' (cedar) for front wall siding
2	1x6 x 8' (cedar) for window jambs (all trim for two windows)
2	1x6 x 6' (cedar) for window jambs
4	1x4 x 8' (cedar) for window trim
8	60-lb. bags of concrete mix for footings

Metal roofing

10	56-in.-long sheets of steel roofing (roof panels)
2	10-ft. residential ridge cap
3	1-lb. boxes of roofing screws

Hardware

34	1-1/2 x 2-in. angle brackets (framing-to-post connections)
18	Hurricane ties (beam-to-post and rafter-to-beam connections)
2	Boxes of 1-1/4-in. joist hanger screws
2	1-lb. boxes of 16d nails
2	24-in. x 43-1/2-in. barn sash windows with handles
2	Pairs of storm window hanger brackets
2	Pairs of storm window adjusters

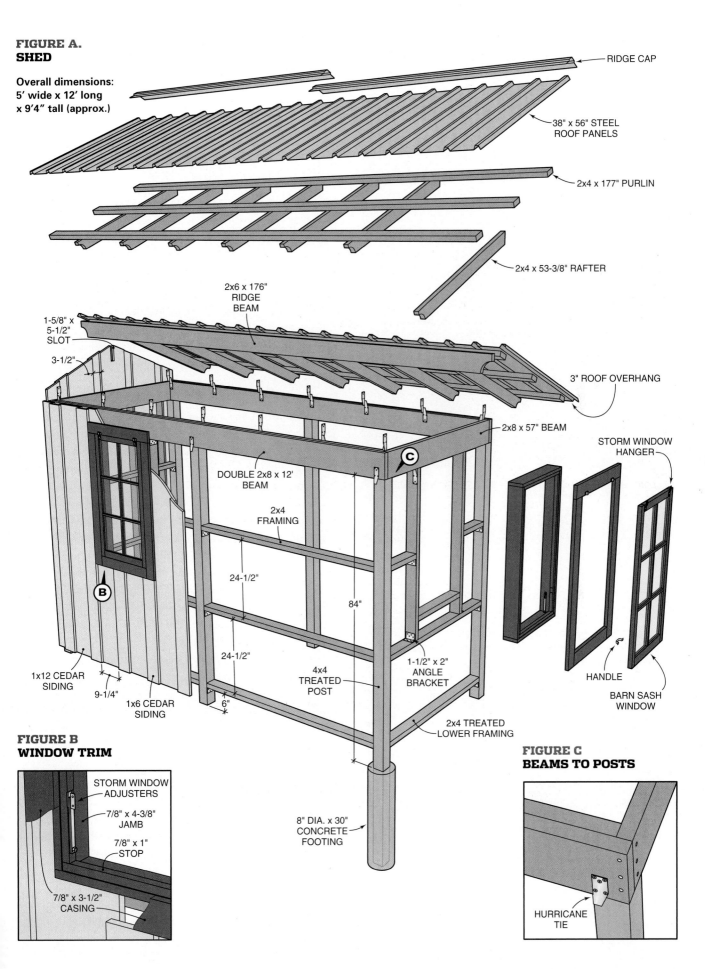

FIGURE A.
SHED

**Overall dimensions:
5' wide x 12' long
x 9'4" tall (approx.)**

RIDGE CAP

38" x 56" STEEL
ROOF PANELS

2x4 x 177" PURLIN

2x4 x 53-3/8" RAFTER

2x6 x 176"
RIDGE
BEAM

1-5/8" x
5-1/2"
SLOT

3-1/2"

3" ROOF OVERHANG

2x8 x 57" BEAM

STORM WINDOW
HANGER

DOUBLE 2x8 x 12'
BEAM

2x4
FRAMING

24-1/2"

84"

C

B

24-1/2"

1x12 CEDAR
SIDING

9-1/4"

1x6 CEDAR
SIDING

6"

4x4
TREATED
POST

1-1/2" x 2"
ANGLE
BRACKET

HANDLE

BARN SASH
WINDOW

2x4 TREATED
LOWER FRAMING

8" DIA. x 30"
CONCRETE
FOOTING

FIGURE B
WINDOW TRIM

STORM WINDOW
ADJUSTERS

7/8" x 4-3/8"
JAMB

7/8" x 1"
STOP

7/8" x 3-1/2"
CASING

FIGURE C
BEAMS TO POSTS

HURRICANE
TIE

ANGLE BRACE

STAKE POSTHOLES

LAYOUT TEMPLATE

1 Build a 2x4 template to the shed dimensions, square it and mark the post locations with stakes. Set the template aside and dig 3-ft.-deep postholes.

TOE-SCREW

2 Drop the posts into the holes, position them using the template, plumb them and screw them into place. Fill the holes with concrete.

Adding Doors

If you want to enclose your shed, you have a few options. You could build a wall covering half the back, framing and siding it just as you did the front. Then cover the other half with a pair of swinging doors or install one sliding door. For easier access, skip the wall and cover the whole back with two sliding "bypass" doors. Some home centers carry sliding door hardware designed for farm buildings. To shop online, go to hardwarestore.com and search for "barn door hardware." If your shed has board-on-board cedar siding like ours, you can make doors that match the siding using rough-sawn plywood framed with rough-sawn boards.

the building permit department at city hall to be sure before you get started on the project.

Remember to keep your shed to the proper setback distance from your neighbor's property line. Even if you don't need a permit, it's important to check with your local building department to learn the setback rules and shed building requirements. In any case, call 811 before you dig to have underground utilities marked.

ONE-STOP SHOPPING FOR MATERIALS

You can buy everything you need at a home center and take it home in one (rather large) pickup load (see the Materials List, Page 88). All of the framing is standard construction lumber; just make sure to get treated posts and treated 2x4s for the bottom horizontal rail **(Photo 5)**.

If the home center stocks metal roofing, it'll probably only have green, brown or white, but you can special order other colors and have the panels cut to length for a small extra charge. If you're comfortable cutting panels to length and are happy with stock colors, just buy 8-ft. lengths. Our roofing was special order and took a couple of weeks to arrive, so plan accordingly. Be sure to order residential ridge caps to match **(Photo 13)**. Otherwise, you'll get the large ridge caps used on farm buildings. Also order the special roofing screws that are colored to match your roof.

Our siding is vertical "board-on-board" cedar; 1x12s overlaid with 1x6s. This is by far the most expensive feature of our shed. Substitute any type of siding you wish, either to save money or to match the siding on your home. The construction details are the same if you're using plywood siding. But if you use horizontal lap siding, substitute a 4x4 for the 2x4 around the bottom. Then add vertical studs every 16 in. between that and the top beam instead of the horizontal 2x4 framing we show.

You have complete creative freedom with the windows: You can use any window you wish, wherever you wish. We chose an inexpensive "barn sash" type window **(Photo 10)**. Add storm window hanger brackets and storm window adjusters and you'll have low-cost windows that open like awnings to let the breeze flow through.

POSITION THE POSTS WITH A TEMPLATE

Screw a 2x4 template together as a guide for locating the posts **(Photo 1)**. Make the inside dimensions of the frame exactly 5 x 12 ft. Square the template by racking until the diagonal measurements are equal and then add an angled brace to hold it square. Measure and mark the posthole positions on the template. Drive stakes at the post marks, remove the template and dig 8-in.-diameter holes with a posthole digger.

Screw the posts to the template to hold them plumb while you mix and pour the concrete. To make sure the tops of the posts are also perfectly aligned, unscrew the template and move it up about 5 ft. before the concrete hardens. Carefully level the template as you screw it to the posts; you'll use it later to gauge the post cutoff heights. Then plumb and brace the whole assembly **(Photo 3)**. Leave the braces in place overnight and get back to work the next morning after the concrete has set up.

SET THE BEAMS AND FRAME THE WALLS

Choose the post that's closest to the highest point on the ground and mark it 6 ft. 8 in. above your estimated finished floor height. You'll have to guess somewhat at this. The idea is to keep from bonking your head when you enter the shed. Cut off the post at the mark by cutting from two opposite sides with a circular saw. Then measure from the top of the template to the newly cut top. Match that distance to mark and cut the other posts to the same height. (This is why that template had better be level!) Preassemble the doubled 2x8 beams, toenail them on top of the posts and add the end 2x8s **(Photo 4)**. Set 2x8 beams on the posts, toenail them in place and then anchor them with hurricane ties **(Photo 4)**.

Now add the rest of the wall framing, using **Figure A** as a guide. It's easiest to toenail the 2x4s into place, then anchor them with angle clips **(Photo 5)**.

Size window openings to fit your windows. If you're using barn sash windows, measure the width and height of the window sash and add 1-7/8 in. to each dimension to arrive at the rough opening size.

FRAME A SUPER-SIMPLE ROOF

Hand-framing a roof is usually challenging, but we've made the job foolproof with a simple trick: You use the siding to center and support the ridge board while you scribe, cut and install the rafters.

Start the roof by cutting a 5-1/2-in.-deep by 1-5/8-in.-wide slot at the ends of two 10-ft.-long 1x12s. Then cut the boards to length so the bottoms will be at least 2 in. above grade and the top will project past the beam 16 in. **(Photo 6)**. Center, plumb and nail those boards to each end wall.

Cut a 2x6 ridge board to length and cut coves (we used a 1-qt. can for a pattern) at the ends with a jigsaw. Drop the ridge board into the slots, making the overhang equal at both ends **(Photo 6)**. Eyeball the ridge board from one end. If there's a bow, straighten and brace it from the beams with a 2x4 **(Photo 8)**.

Scribe the first rafter angle by screwing a short cleat on the top. Then rest the board on the ridge and scribe the angle with a scrap 2x4 **(Photo 7)**. Cut the angle and test the fit. Then cut it to length and add the decorative end cut. Use this

3 Slide the template up 5 ft. and level it, screwing it to the posts. Recheck the posts for plumb and brace the assembly. Let the concrete harden overnight.

STAGGER ENDS
HURRICANE TIE
DOUBLED FRONT BEAM

4 Cut the post tops to length. Then cut and assemble the 2x8 beams. Anchor them with hurricane ties.

WINDOW OPENING
ANGLE BRACKETS
TREATED BOTTOM RAIL

5 Cut the rails to fit and fasten them between the posts with angle brackets. Frame the window openings to suit your windows.

6 Cut a slot, then center and nail a 1x12 siding board to each end wall. Then drop the ridge board into the slots and center it.

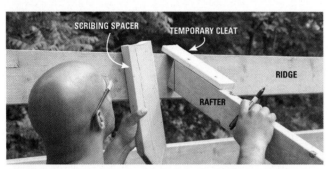

7 Scribe the ridge angle cut on one of the rafters and cut it to length. Use it as a pattern to mark the other rafters.

8 Lay out the rafter positions on the ridge and beams. Then toenail the rafters to the ridge and anchor the other ends to the beam with hurricane ties.

9 Space and nail the siding to the end walls (Figure A). Trim it even with the rafters. Then add the rest of the 1x12 siding.

rafter as a pattern to mark the rest and then cut and install them (Photo 8).

FINISH THE SIDING

To save time, finish the ridge board, the rafter and all of the siding on all four sides before installation (we even stained the interior framing to brighten the inside of the shed). To inhibit rot, coat the freshly cut bottom ends of the siding boards before nailing the boards into place.

Begin siding by nailing up the 1x12 boards on the ends. Raise them 2 in. above the ground and run them long at the top (Photo 9). Fasten them in the center of each board with a single nail at each framing member (the overlapping 1x6s will hold the edges). Use a 2x4 block to space the boards 3-1/2 in. apart. That way the 1x6s will overlap 1 in. on both sides. Determine the length of each siding board on the front of the shed by measuring from the ground to the top of the beam and subtracting 2 in.

Install the window frame and exterior trim before you install the 1x6s. Rip the 1x6 jamb boards to 4-1/4 in. wide so they'll be flush with the outside of the 1x12s and the wall framing on the inside of the shed. (Use the leftover strips for the window stops; see Photo 10.) That way you can add the window trim around the openings and surround them with 1x6 siding for a nice, clean look (Photo 10).

Draw marks 1 in. from the edge of the 1x12s to help align the 1x6s. You can cheat the 1x6s left or right a bit if it helps them clear window openings or arrive at corners at a better point. Small variations won't be noticeable. Just make sure you have at least a 3/8-in. overlap and that you plumb each one with a level. Nail each side of the 1x6s through the 1x12 below it and into the framing. Use a reciprocating saw to cut off the long siding boards at the end walls flush with the end rafters (Photo 9). Or snap a chalk line on the outside and use a circular saw. Use the leftover pieces to fill in above or below the windows.

HANG THE WINDOWS

Screw the hanger brackets to the windows. Then center the window in the opening to position and screw the bracket clips to the window trim. Shim the window sash so it's 1/4 in. back from the window trim and centered in the frame. Nail the 1x1 window stops to the jambs, holding them snug against the window sash (Photo 10). Add the storm window adjusters, following the instructions on the packaging.

SCREW DOWN THE METAL ROOFING

Cut the 2x4 purlins to length and nail them to each rafter with two 16d nails (Photo 11). If they're twisted and won't lie flat, screw them down. Otherwise the metal roofing will deform or kink when you screw it down. Nail together a 2x4 "L", push it against the bottom purlin and screw it into place

10 Mount the storm window brackets to the window and trim and then hang the window. Nail the 1x1 window stop tight against the window.

STORM WINDOW HANGER

WINDOW STOP

11 Cut the purlins to length, then center and nail them to each rafter with two 16d nails.

PURLIN

3" FROM END

12 Screw a 2x4 "L" to the rafter tails tight against the bottom purlin. Then rest the roof panels against it and screw the panels to the purlins.

PURLIN

TEMPORARY 2X4 "L"

13 Cut both ridge caps to length, then center and clamp them into place. Screw them to every third rib.

RESIDENTIAL RIDGE CAP

from the underside so you can remove it later **(Photo 12)**. This will hold the metal roof panels in place while you screw them to the purlins. If you need to cut roof panels, before installation, cut them from the underside with a jigsaw and metal-cutting blade.

Starting at one end, lay the first panel in place, hanging one edge 3 in. over the purlin ends. Center the screws in the flat areas between the ribs and over the purlins. The screws are self-tapping; push down firmly as you run the screw gun and they'll drill their way through the metal and into the wood. Tighten them up until the special neoprene washer mushrooms against the metal. Measure carefully and keep

all the screws exactly in line. It'll look bad if lines of screw heads wander all over the place. And if you drive a screw in the wrong place and miss the purlin, there's no good way to repair a screw hole.

Cut both pieces of ridge cap to length with a tin snips so they overlap 6 in. near the middle. Center and clamp the ridges while you screw them to the ribs of the underlying panels **(Photo 13)**. It's best to predrill these holes with an 1/8-in. bit.

Then you're done! Enjoy having a brand-new, built-by-hand shed in your yard to keep things organized and to last for years to come.

Garden Storage Closet

Ideal for smaller backyards, this shed sits against the back or side of the house for maximum convenience and storage space.

If you don't have room in your yard for a large, freestanding shed, you can still create plenty of space for garden tools with a shed attached to the back or side of the house. If you're an experienced builder, you can build this shed in a couple of weekends. Save money by using treated lumber, pine, and asphalt shingles instead of cedar as shown here.

FRAME THE WALLS AND ROOF

Nail together the side walls, then square them with the plywood side panels. Overhang the panels 3/8 in. at the front—this will hide the gap at the corner when you hang the doors.

Join the two sides with the top and bottom plates and rim joists. The sides, top and bottom are all mirror images of each other except for the top front rim joist, which is set down 1/2 in. from the top so it stops the doors (**Photo 1**). Use screws to fasten the framework together except in the front where fasteners will be visible—use 2-1/2-in. casing nails there. Screw the 4x4 footings to the bottom plates, then nail on the plywood base. Cut and screw together the

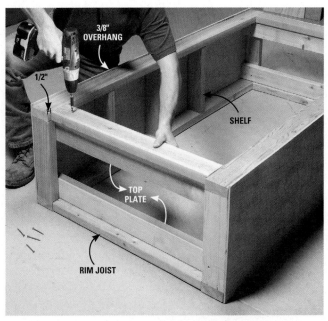

1 Frame and sheathe the walls, then join them with plates and joists. Use the best pieces of lumber in the front where they'll show.

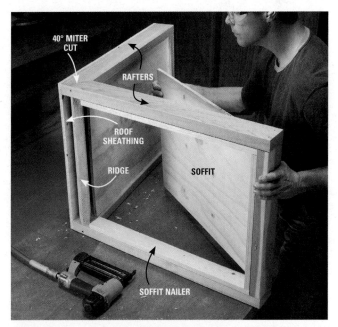

2 Build the roof on your workbench. Start with an L-shaped 2x4 frame, then add the nailers, soffit, sheathing and trim. Shingle with cedar or asphalt shingles.

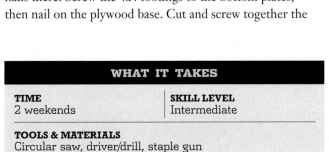

WHAT IT TAKES	
TIME 2 weekends	**SKILL LEVEL** Intermediate

TOOLS & MATERIALS
Circular saw, driver/drill, staple gun

FIGURE A.
GARDEN CLOSET CONSTRUCTION DETAILS

Overall dimensions:
86" H x 38-3/8" W x 24" D

The shed is made from three components—the roof, the walls and the doors, with edges covered by trim boards.

F NOT SHOWN

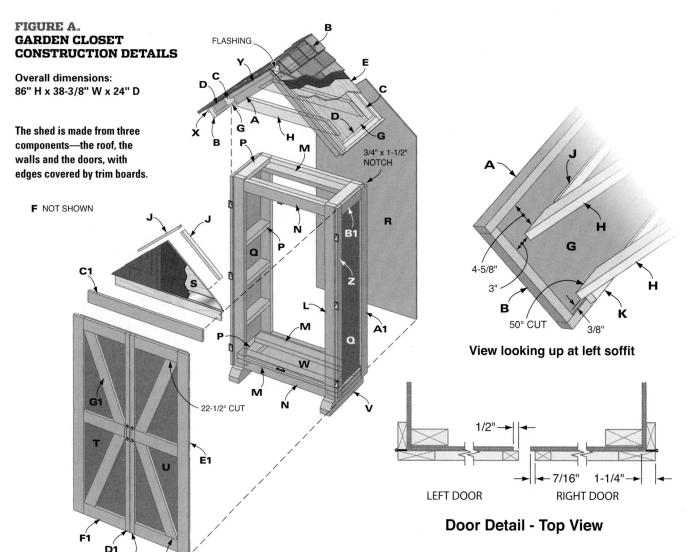

FLASHING

3/4" x 1-1/2" NOTCH

22-1/2° CUT

22-1/2° CUT

View looking up at left soffit

4-5/8"
3"
50° CUT
3/8"

Door Detail - Top View

1/2"
7/16"   1-1/4"
LEFT DOOR   RIGHT DOOR

Cutting List

KEY	QTY.	DIMENSIONS	DESCRIPTION
A	4	1-1/2" x 3-1/2" x 32"	rafters
B	3	1-1/2" x 3-1/2" x 20"	fascia and ridge
C	4	3/4" x 2-1/2" x 27"	nailers (pine)
D	2	3/4" x 2-1/2" x 18-1/2"	nailers (pine)
E	1	1/2" x 23" x 31-7/8"	right roof sheathing
F	1	1/2" x 23" x 32-1/4"	left roof sheathing
G	2	1/2" x 20" x 28"	soffit
H	2	1-1/2" x 3-1/2" x 38-3/8"	collar ties
J	2	3/4" x 1-1/2" x 18"	front nailers (pine)
K	2	3/4" x 1-1/2" x 23"	rear nailers (pine)
L	2	1-1/2" x 3-1/2" x 64"	studs
M	4	1-1/2" x 3-1/2" x 36"	top and bottom plates
N	4	1-1/2" x 3-1/2" x 29"	rim joists
P	10	1-1/2" x 3-1/2" x 13-1/2"	shelves
Q	2	3/8" x 16-7/8" x 64"	side panels
R	1	3/8" x 36-5/8" x 79-1/4"	back panel
S	1	3/8" x 36" x 19-1/2"	front panel
T	1	17-5/16" x 60-1/8"	left door
U	1	18-5/16" x 60-1/8"	right door
V	2	3-1/2" x 3-1/2" x 19-1/2"	footings
W	1	13-3/8" x 35-7/8"	plywood base
X	2	3/4" x 1-1/2" x 23"	roof trim
Y	2	3/4" x 1-1/2" x 33-1/8"	roof trim
Z	2	3/4" x 2-1/2" x 64"	side battens
A1	2	3/4" x 3-1/2" x 64"	rear side battens
B1	4	3/4" x 3-1/2" x 11-1/8"	horizontal side battens
C1	1	3/4" x 3-1/2" x 38-3/8"	front trim
D1	2	3/4" x 1-1/2" x 60-1/8"	door edge
E1	2	3/4" x 3-1/2" x 60-1/8"	door edge
F1	6	3/4" x 3-1/2" x 14-1/8"	horizontal door trim
G1	4	3/4" x 3-1/2" x 28-3/8"	(long edge to long edge) diagonal door trim

Materials List

ITEM	QTY.
3/8" x 4' x 8' rough-sawn exterior plywood	3
1/2" x 4' x 8' BC grade plywood	1
1x2 x 8' pine	1
1x2 x 8' cedar	3
1x3 x 8' pine	2
1x3 x 8' cedar	2
1x4 x 8' cedar	7
Cedar shakes	1 bundle
2x4 x 8' cedar	11
4x4 x 4' pressure treated	1
2-1/2" exterior screws	2 lbs.
1-5/8" exterior screws	1 lb.
2-1/2" galv. finish nails	1 lb.
1-1/2" galv. finish nails	1 lb.
1" narrow crown staples (for cedar shingles)	1 lb.
30-lb. felt	1 roll
10" x 10' roll aluminum flashing	1
2-1/2" x 2-1/2" rust-resistant hinges	3 prs.
Magnetic catches	1 pr.
Handles	1 pr.

Note: Shown are rough-sawn cedar boards—which usually (but not always!) measure 7/8 in. thick—for the trim. If you substitute pine, which measures 3/4 in., subtract 1/8 in. from each door width.

3 Set the completed roof on the shed base. Screw on the front and back panels to join the roof and the base.

ROOFING FELT

1" MINIMUM OVERLAP

FLASHING

4 Cover the front panel with roofing felt and shingles. Place metal flashing over the trim so water won't seep behind it.

How to Mortise a Hinge

Mark the hinge locations on the doorjamb, then on the door, less 1/8 in. for clearance at the top of the door. Separate the hinge leaves, then align the edge of the leaf with the edge of the door or jamb. Predrill and fasten the leaf, then cut along all three edges with a razor knife to about the same depth as the hinge leaf **(Photo 1)**.

Remove the hinge and make a series of angled cuts to establish the depth of the mortise **(Photo 2)**. Turn the chisel over and clean out the chips using light hammer taps.

Holding the chisel with the beveled front edge against the wood, chip out the 1/4-in. sections. Check the fit of the hinge leaf and chisel out additional wood until the leaf sits flush.

If the hinges don't fit back together perfectly when you hang the door, tap the leaves up or down (gently) with a hammer.

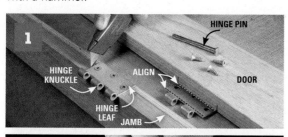

1

HINGE PIN

HINGE KNUCKLE

ALIGN

DOOR

HINGE LEAF

JAMB

2

DEPTH OF HINGE LEAF

two pairs of rafters, then nail on the fascia and ridge boards. Nail on the roof sheathing and the soffit, butting the corners together **(Photo 2)**. Screw on the collar ties at the points shown in **Figure A**, then screw on the front and rear nailers. Nail on the roof trim, staple on a layer of roofing felt, then shingle the roof. If you use cedar shingles, fasten them with narrow crown staples or siding nails. Leave 1/8-in. to 1/4-in. gaps between cedar shingles for expansion, and nail a strip of aluminum flashing across the ridge under the cap shingles.

Tip the shed upright, then set the roof on, aligning the front collar tie with the front rim joist and centering it side to side **(Photo 3)**. Nail the cedar trim to the sides, aligning the 1x3s on the sides with the overhanging edge of plywood along the front edge. Glue and screw on the back and front siding panels to join the roof and base together. Use the back panel to square the structure and make it rigid.

Nail on the front trim piece, aligning it with the horizontal side battens (Z). Attach flashing and felt to the front panel, then cover it with cedar shakes **(Photo 4)**.

HANG THE DOORS

Construct the doors (see **Figure A**, Door Detail, Page 96), cut the hinge mortises (see left) and hang the doors. Leave a 1/8-in. gap between the doors and trim along the top. Paint or stain if desired, then set the shed against the house on several inches of gravel. Add or take away gravel under the footings until the shed is tight against the siding and the gap above the doors is even. Screw the shed to the studs in the wall to keep it from tipping. Drill two 1/2-in. holes for the screws through the plywood near the rim joists, then loosely fasten the shed to the wall with 2-1/2-in. screws and large fender washers so the shed can move when the ground freezes and thaws.

Pine Garden Hutch

With a handsome roof and a unique shape, this hutch holds all of your stuff in style.

Wouldn't it be nice to have all your gardening tools and supplies in one handy location? This copper-roofed pine hutch holds long-handled tools such as shovels, rakes and hoes on one side, and smaller tools and supplies on shelves on the other side.

START BY BUILDING THE FACE FRAME

Build the face frame **(Photo 3)** first and use it as a guide for assembling the doors and cutting the curve on the back panel.

A full sheet of 3/4-in. MDF (medium-density fiberboard) or particleboard set on sawhorses makes a good workbench for this project. Set up for marking the arcs (for the curved

pieces) by drawing a center line parallel to the long edge of the sheet. Center a 4-ft. length of 1x12 on the line. Line up the top edge with the edge of the workbench and clamp it. Screw the point of the homemade compass in the center line 21-5/8 in. below the bottom edge of the 1x12 **(Photo 1)**.

<table>
<tr><th colspan="2">WHAT IT TAKES</th></tr>
<tr><td>**TIME**
2 weekends</td><td>**SKILL LEVEL**
Advanced</td></tr>
<tr><td colspan="2">**TOOLS & MATERIALS**
Circular saw, jigsaw, driver/drill, pocket hole jig, sander, framing square, tin snips, crimper</td></tr>
</table>

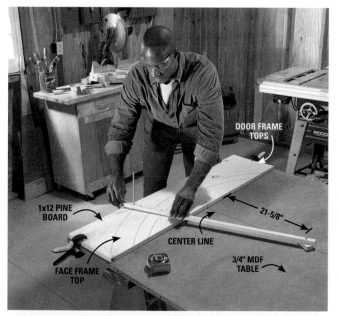

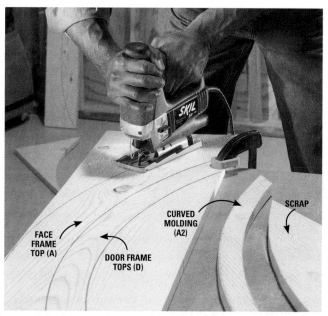

1 Build a large compass by drilling holes in a 36-in.-long stick using Figure B as a guide. Draw arcs for the face frame top (A1) and door frame tops (D) on a 4-ft. 1x12. On a second 4-ft. 1x12, draw arcs for the curved molding (A2) under the front roof (Figure B, p. 101).

2 Saw out the curved pieces with a jigsaw. Use the pattern on p. 101 to draw the curve on the face frame bottom (C1) and saw it out.

Draw three arcs for the face frame top and door top pieces (**Figure B**, p. 101). Then replace the 1x12 with another 48-in. 1x12 and relocate the screw point (see Figure B). Draw two arcs to outline the 1-1/2-in.-wide curved roof trim molding. Cut out the curves **(Photo 2)**.

Even with careful jigsaw work, sand the curves for a smooth arch. Use 80-grit sandpaper on a sanding block to even out the curve and remove saw marks. Then sand again with 100- and 120-grit paper. For the best-looking finish, sand all the boards before assembly. Use a random orbital sander or hand-sand along the grain of the wood.

After cutting and sanding the curved pieces, rip the remaining face frame and door trim pieces to width and cut them to length according to **Figure A** and the Cutting List, both on Page 101. Use the pattern on Page 101 to cut the curve on the 39-in.-long 1x6 bottom frame piece (C1). Cut the same curve on the 44-in.-long x 5-in.-wide piece (C2). Use this for the bottom cleat **(Photo 5)**. Assemble the face frames and door frames and the back frame with pocket screws. **Photos 3 and 6** show how to mark for the angle cuts where the curved pieces join the straight ones.

Use a miter box to cut angles on the ends of the curved pieces, and steady them by supporting them with one of the scrap concave corners cut from the 1x12. Place the straight edge of the concave scrap against the fence and nestle the curves. Then sight along the blade and adjust the angle to cut along the line. Use this same technique for cutting the angles on the ends of the curved door frame tops (D) as shown in **Photo 6**.

After assembling the face frame, flip it over and screw on the cleats (B2 and C2; **Photo 5**). The cleats overlap the joints to add strength and serve as a nailing surface for the floorboards and side panels.

TAKE TIME BUILDING THE DOORS

Use the completed face frame as a guide to check the fit of the doors as they're built. The goal is to end up with a 1/8-in. space between the doors and the face frame and between the two doors. Sand or plane them as needed to create an even gap. Build and fit the door frames first. Then use them as a guide to cut out the tongue-and-groove boards that make up the door panels **(Photo 7)**. Rip the groove off the first board in each door panel and then rip the last board to fit. Glue and nail the boards to the frames and then sand the edges flush. A belt sander works great for this task.

BUILD THE SIDE AND BACK PANELS

The panels for the sides and back are constructed just like the door panels. Rip the tongues and grooves from the outermost boards after figuring out how wide they should be **(Photo 8)**. The exact ripping widths will probably vary between projects, based on the boards that are used. The easiest approach is to temporarily assemble the tongue-and-groove boards, using clamps if needed to draw them tight together. Then mark the panel widths on them, making sure to measure over the panel to remove an equal amount from the outside boards. Rip the outside boards to width. Then assemble the panels. Run a small bead of water-resistant wood glue along the tongue of

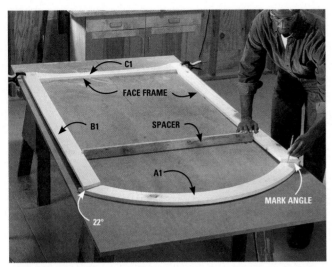

3 Cut the side pieces (B1) to length with 22-degree angles on the tops. Snug the face frame sides to the bottom (C1) and to a 39-in.-long spacer and clamp them to the table. Scribe lines on the curved top (A1) and cut off the ends.

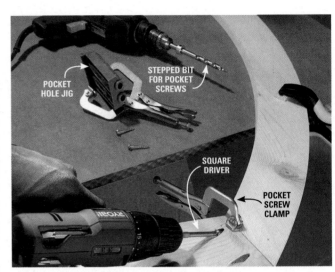

4 Drill pocket holes on the back side of the face frame pieces with a pocket hole jig. Glue the joints and connect them with pocket screws.

each board before sliding it into the groove. Clean up any squeezed-out glue right away with a damp cloth. When the glue hardens, the panels will be rigid and strengthen the cabinet. Use construction adhesive to glue the panels to the frames and/or cleats.

Here are a few special considerations for building the panels. First, use a framing square to make sure the panels are perfectly square before the glue dries. Cut the curve on the back panel after it's constructed **(Photo 9)**. The beveled top cleat (K) on the side panels (H) is a little tricky. Take a good look at **Photos 10 and 13** and **Figure A** to see its location and orientation.

ASSEMBLE THE CABINET, THEN MOUNT THE DOORS

Glue and nail the completed panels and face frame together **(Photo 10)**. Then add the floorboards and center panel **(Photo 12)**. Center the curved molding (A2) and nail it to the top of the face frame. Finally, glue and nail the roof boards along the curve **(Photo 13)**. Start with 1x4s aligned with the ends of the curved molding. Then complete the roof with 1x3s, working from both sides to the center. To make sure everything is square, temporarily tack the 1x4 in place. Then set four of the 1x3s on the roof with their ends perfectly aligned and measure the front overhang to make sure it's consistent. If the overhang is getting larger or smaller, move the back end of the 1x4 down or up, respectively, to correct the problem.

When the cabinet is complete, tip it on its back to install the doors **(Photo 14)**. Use any strong, gate-type hinge. Make sure to leave an even space around the perimeter of the doors and between them. Use a belt sander to trim tight spots.

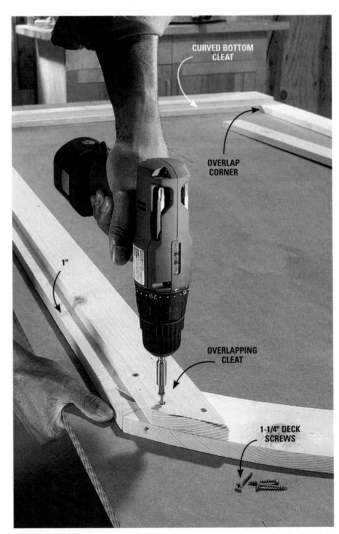

5 Cut backing cleats (B2 and C2) that overlap the face frame joints (Figure A, parts A1, B1 and C1). Predrill and screw them to the back of the face frame.

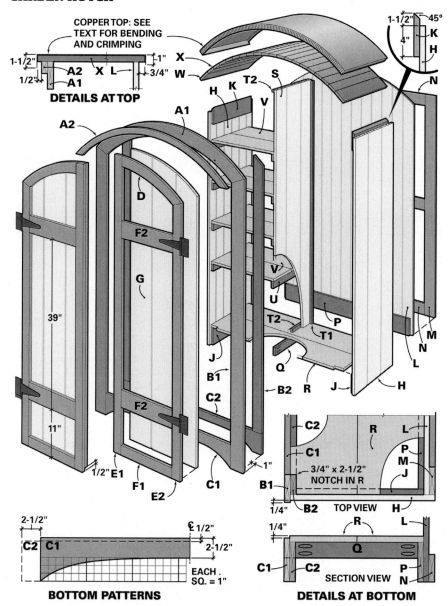

FIGURE A.
GARDEN HUTCH

COPPER TOP: SEE TEXT FOR BENDING AND CRIMPING

DETAILS AT TOP

BOTTOM PATTERNS

EACH SQ. = 1"

TOP VIEW

NOTCH IN R
3/4" x 2-1/2"

SECTION VIEW

DETAILS AT BOTTOM

Cutting List

KEY	QTY.	DIMENSIONS DESCRIPTION
Face frame		
A1, D	1	48" x 3/4" x 11-1/4" (curved frame and door tops)
A2	1	48" x 3/4" x 11-1/4" (curved molding; cut curve and ends)
B1	2	68" x 3/4" x 3-1/2" (sides)*
B2	2	66" x 3/4" x 2-1/2" (side cleats)*
C1	1	39" x 3/4" x 5-1/2" (bottom; cut curve to pattern)
C2	1	44" x 3/4" x 5" (bottom cleat; cut curve to pattern)
Doors		
D	2	Curved tops (cut from "door top" above)
E1	2	68-5/8" x 3/4" x 2-1/4" (door sides)*
E2	2	61" x 3/4" x 2-1/4" (door sides)*
F1	2	14-13/16" x 3/4" x 2-1/4" (door bottom rail); see Figure B
F2	4	14-13/16" x 3/4" x 4" (intermediate rails)
G	6	72" t&g 1x8 (door panels); cut to fit
Sides		
H	6	68-1/4" t&g 1x8 (19-1/2" x 68-1/4" side panels)
J	2	5" x 3/4" x 17-1/4" (bottom cleats)
K	2	5-1/2" x 3/4" x 17-1/4" (top cleats; bevel top to 45 degrees)
Back		
L	7	78" t&g 1x8 (44" x 78" back panel; cut top curve)
M	2	3-1/2" x 3/4" x 68" (frame sides)
N	3	3-1/2" x 3/4" x 37" (frame crosspiece)
P	1	5" x 3/4" x 42-1/2" (bottom cleat)
Interior Parts		
Q	1	2" x 3/4" x 16-1/2" (floor crosspiece)
R	2	9" x 3/4" x 44" (floorboards)
S	3	72" t&g 1x8 (17-1/4" x 72" center panel)
T1	1	3/4" x 3/4" x 72" (center panel cleats)
T2	2	3/4" x 3/4" x 17-1/4" (center panel cleats)
U	8	1-1/2" x 3/4" x 17-1/4" (shelf cleats)
V	8	8-5/8" x 3/4" x 21-5/8" (shelf boards)
W	3	3-1/2" x 3/4" x 21-1/2" (roof boards)
X	18	2-1/2" x 3/4" x 21-1/2" (roof boards)

*Cut top angles at 22 degrees

Materials List

ITEM	QTY.
1x2 x 8' pine	3
1x3 x 8' pine	9
1x4 x 6' pine	4
1x4 x 8' pine	3
1x6 x 6' pine	4
1x10 x 8' pine	3
1x12 x 8' pine	1
1x8 x 6' t&g pine	15
1x8 x 8' t&g pine	7
8" gate hinges	4
Latch	1
Tubes of construction adhesive	2
Magnetic catches	4
Water-resistant wood glue	
1-1/4" finish nails	
Copper or brass weather strip nails	
Pocket screws and jig	
2' x 5' 16-oz. copper sheet (available from roofing or sheet metal suppliers)	

FIGURE B.
ARC PATTERNS

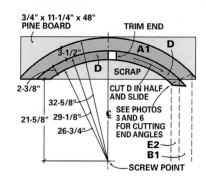

3/4" x 11-1/4" x 48" PINE BOARD

TRIM END

A1

D

3-1/2"

D

SCRAP

CUT D IN HALF AND SLIDE

SEE PHOTOS 3 AND 6 FOR CUTTING END ANGLES

2-3/8"

32-5/8"

21-5/8" 29-1/8"

26-3/4"

E2

B1

SCREW POINT

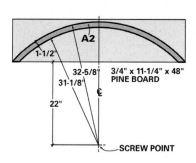

A2

1-1/2"

32-5/8"

31-1/8"

22"

3/4" x 11-1/4" x 48" PINE BOARD

SCREW POINT

CRIMPING TOOL SIMPLIFIES CURVE OF THE METAL ROOF

Start with a 24-in. x 60-in. piece of 16-oz. copper sheeting. Screw down a 2x4 frame on the bench top to provide clearance for bending down the edges. Start by snipping the corners of the copper with tin snips (**Photo 15**). Then hand-bend the edges of the sheet down over the 2x4s. The last step is to crimp the edges with the five-blade downspout crimper to curve the sheet (**Photo 16**). Keep the crimps parallel by aligning one of the crimping blades in the previously made crimp before squeezing it. Crimp about 12 in. on the front. Then crimp 24 in. on the back to even up the curve. Continue alternating until the end. Adjust the arch for an exact fit once the copper is back on top of the cabinet. Hold off on nailing the copper in place (**Photo 17**) until after a finish has been applied to the hutch.

Since the hutch is pine and will rot quickly if left unprotected outdoors, apply a durable finish. This hutch has an oil stain and three coats of spar varnish. Be sure to seal the bottom edges thoroughly. If putting the hutch in a wet location, install metal or plastic feet on all four corners to elevate it slightly. Setting the hutch on an uneven surface can cause the doors to bind or fit poorly. Shim under the cabinet to level it, if needed.

6 Assemble the door frame with pocket screws as shown. Then cut the curved top (D) in half and cut angles on the ends to fit. Attach them with pocket screws as well. Place the assembled door frames in the face frame to check the fit. Plane and sand as needed to allow a 1/8-in. space around and between the door frames.

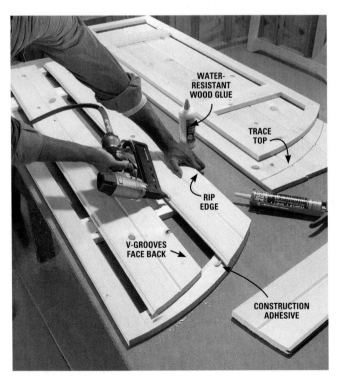

7 Temporarily assemble the door panels and center the frames over them. Mark the bottom, sides and top. Rip the sides and cut the top curve. Cut the bottoms 1/4 in. shorter than marked. Then glue and nail the boards together with wood glue and fasten them to the frame with construction adhesive.

8 Assemble the back frame (M and N) with pocket screws. Glue and nail tongue-and-groove boards to it to form the cabinet back. Rip the first and last boards to fit.

9 Center the face frame over the back panel and line up the bottoms. Mark the top curve, and then saw it out with a jigsaw.

10 Assemble the side panels (Figure A). Then glue and nail the side panels to the back panel and face frame.

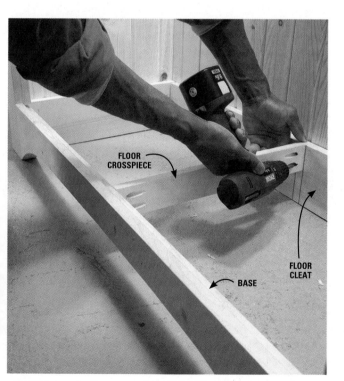

11 Screw in the crosspiece (Q) with pocket screws to support the floorboards. Notch the first floorboard (R) to fit around the face frame then glue it and nail it down. Cut the back floorboard to fit and nail it in.

12 Glue and nail together the center divider and attach it to the bottom and back with cleats (T1 and T2) and screws. Attach the top to the ceiling boards after they're installed (Photo 13).

13 Nail the curved molding (A2) to the face frame. Then glue and nail the ceiling boards to the top of the cabinet. Start by overhanging the 1x4s as shown and work from both sides to the center with the 1x3 boards. Cut the last piece to fit.

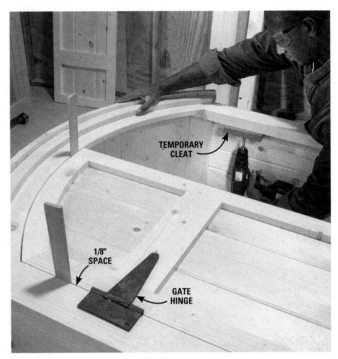

14 Screw temporary cleats to the back of the face frame to support the doors. Set the doors in place and trim them if necessary to allow 1/8-in. clearance all around. Predrill for hinge screws and then screw on the door hinges and hardware.

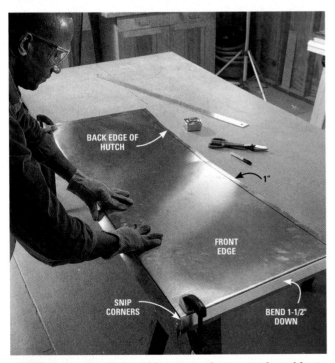

15 Center the 24-in. wide copper sheet over the cabinet top with a 1-1/2-in. overhang in front. Mark along the back, front and ends with a permanent marker. Add 1-1/2 in. to the ends and cut the copper sheet to length with tin snips. Snip the corners as shown. Bend the front, back and ends down over the 2x4 frame.

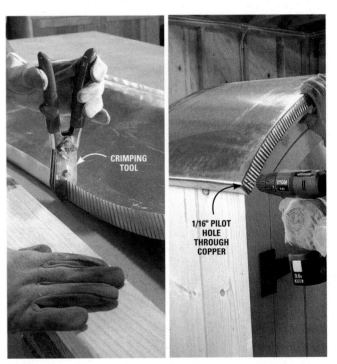

16 Crimp the front and back edges to form the curved top using a special sheet metal crimping tool. Alternate between the front and the back until you reach the end.

17 Drill 1/16-in. pilot holes (through the copper only) about every 12 in. along the edges. Drive small copper or brass weather strip nails through the copper into the wood slats to hold the copper roofing in place.

Ultimate Garden Shed

Two sheds in one, this rustic cedar gem will keep everyone happy.

This cedar garden shed is the perfect storage solution for every gardener and family member who enjoys working and playing in the backyard. At 8 ft. x 9-1/2 ft., the storage area has loads of room for all your lawn and garden equipment. And you can access it easily through the 46-in.-wide sliding door in the back. With the addition of workbenches and shelves, the smaller 5-1/2-ft. x 8-ft. room makes a perfect potting shed. The concrete paver floor, natural cedar siding and steel roofing add up to a low-maintenance shed that will last for generations.

Building this shed isn't complicated, nor does it require more than basic carpentry experience. Still, it's a big job, and if you've built a deck or done other major remodeling, you'll find this project the next step up in skill level. It'll take you and a helper three or four weekends to build plus another few days to seal the siding and put on the finishing touches. If this shed is beyond your budget, save several hundred dollars by

simplifying the exterior trim details and using less expensive flooring material.

In addition to basic hand tools, you'll need a circular saw, drill, table saw and power miter saw. You'll also need 6-ft. and 10-ft. stepladders to work on the roof and tall gable ends. To speed up the work and simplify your job, rent scaffolding with a set of casters. For more building details and a complete materials list, go to familyhandyman.com/project/2014shed

WHAT IT TAKES	
TIME 3-4 weekends	**SKILL LEVEL** Advanced
TOOLS & MATERIALS Driver/drill, circular saw, table saw, miter saw, ladder	

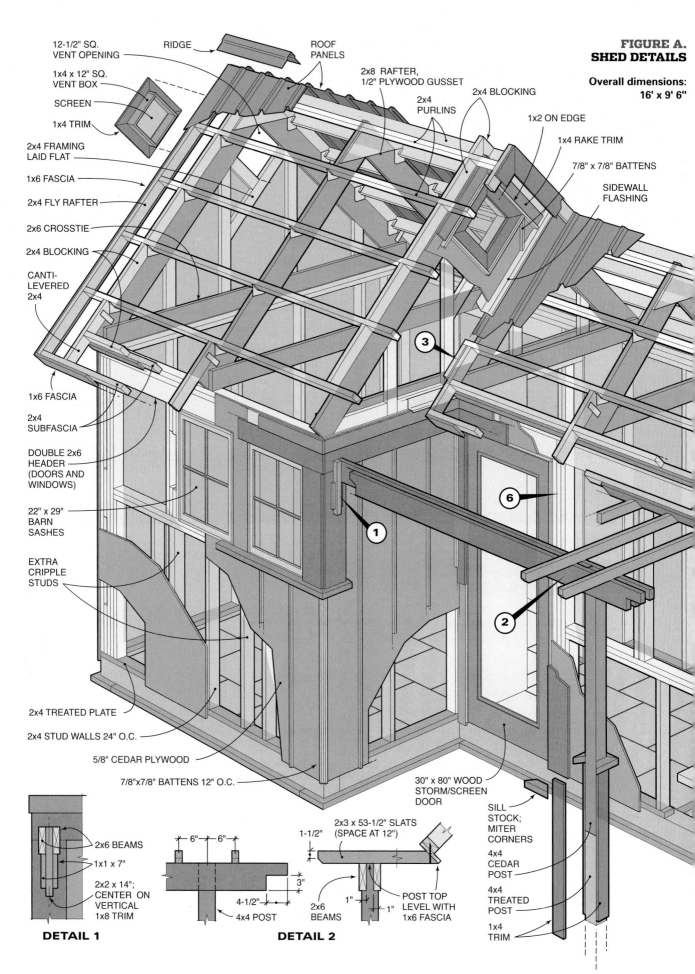

FIGURE A.
SHED DETAILS

Overall dimensions:
16' x 9' 6"

12-1/2" SQ. VENT OPENING

RIDGE

ROOF PANELS

2x8 RAFTER, 1/2" PLYWOOD GUSSET

2x4 BLOCKING

1x4 x 12" SQ. VENT BOX

2x4 PURLINS

1x2 ON EDGE

SCREEN

1x4 RAKE TRIM

1x4 TRIM

7/8" x 7/8" BATTENS

2x4 FRAMING LAID FLAT

SIDEWALL FLASHING

1x6 FASCIA

2x4 FLY RAFTER

2x6 CROSSTIE

2x4 BLOCKING

CANTI-LEVERED 2x4

1x6 FASCIA

2x4 SUBFASCIA

DOUBLE 2x6 HEADER (DOORS AND WINDOWS)

22" x 29" BARN SASHES

EXTRA CRIPPLE STUDS

2x4 TREATED PLATE

2x4 STUD WALLS 24" O.C.

5/8" CEDAR PLYWOOD

7/8"x7/8" BATTENS 12" O.C.

30" x 80" WOOD STORM/SCREEN DOOR

SILL STOCK; MITER CORNERS

4x4 CEDAR POST

4x4 TREATED POST

1x4 TRIM

DETAIL 1

2x6 BEAMS

1x1 x 7"

2x2 x 14"; CENTER ON VERTICAL 1x8 TRIM

DETAIL 2

6" 6"

3"

4-1/2"

4x4 POST

2x6 BEAMS

1-1/2"

2x3 x 53-1/2" SLATS (SPACE AT 12")

1"

1"

POST TOP LEVEL WITH 1x6 FASCIA

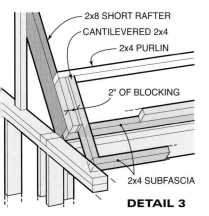

2x8 SHORT RAFTER
CANTILEVERED 2x4
2x4 PURLIN
2" OF BLOCKING
2x4 SUBFASCIA

DETAIL 3

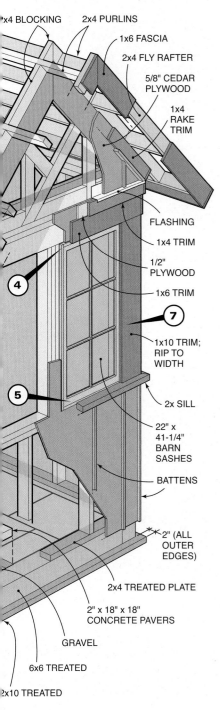

x4 BLOCKING
2x4 PURLINS
1x6 FASCIA
2x4 FLY RAFTER
5/8" CEDAR PLYWOOD
1x4 RAKE TRIM
FLASHING
1x4 TRIM
1/2" PLYWOOD
1x6 TRIM
4
7
1x10 TRIM; RIP TO WIDTH
5
2x SILL
22" x 41-1/4" BARN SASHES
BATTENS
2" (ALL OUTER EDGES)
2x4 TREATED PLATE
2" x 18" x 18" CONCRETE PAVERS
GRAVEL
6x6 TREATED
2x10 TREATED

CHECK WITH THE CITY—YOU MAY NEED A PERMIT

Most cities require a building permit for large sheds. Consult with the building department to find out. This shed is 120 sq. ft. Also check for restrictions on where the shed can be placed on the lot. If you're planning to build near the edge of the lot, you may have to hire a surveyor to locate the lot lines. Start this planning process at least a month in advance in case there's a snag. A few days before you intend to start digging, call 811 to have buried utility lines located and marked.

YOU MAY HAVE TO SPECIAL-ORDER THE ROOFING

Most of the materials for this shed are readily available at home centers and lumberyards. You may have to order the barn sash windows and the grooveless cedar plywood, however. If your lumber supplier doesn't sell the metal roofing material, check local roofing or farm supply retailers. A few colors are stocked, but you'll have to special-order the roofing materials to get a custom color or have the panels cut to the exact length needed.

START BY OUTLINING THE SHED WITH STAKES AND STRING

The first step in the construction process is to accurately stake out the perimeter (**Photo 1**). We're using 2x10s as our foundation with 6x6s resting on them. The 2x10s will stick out beyond the 6x6s about 2 in., so set your stakes 2 in. beyond the shed dimensions to mark their outer edges. Use a line level to level the strings. Then double-check the distance between stakes and make sure the diagonal measurements of each rectangular section are equal before you start digging.

Remove all the sod or other organic material inside the perimeter of the strings. Then dig the trench and set the 2x10 footing plates on a bed of gravel. Roughly level the 2x10s by measuring down from the string. Then fine-tune with a 4-ft. or longer level. Take your time here. An out-of-level foundation will cause you problems later.

Complete the wood foundation by adding the 6x6s (**Photo 1 and Figure B** online). The edge of the 6x6s should be about 2 in. inside the string line and the top should be level with the string. Square the 6x6s (**Photo 1**) and level them with shims. Pack gravel around the perimeter to hold it all in place. You'll need about 3-1/4 yards of 3/8-in. to 1/2-in. crushed gravel.

LOOSE-LAID PAVERS ARE EASY TO INSTALL AND ALLOW WATER TO DRAIN

You can choose any size or style paver for the floor. Notch the 2x4 screed board to match the thickness of the pavers you choose (**Photo 2**). We used 18-in. square cement pavers. We used a circular saw and diamond blade to cut the 2-in. thick pavers to fit, but if I had it to do over, I'd rent a larger, masonry-cutting saw instead. We offset the joints for a more interesting look and to avoid having to keep the pavers precisely aligned.

BUILD THE ROOF TRUSSES BEFORE YOU BUILD THE WALLS

First cut the rafters and crossties according to the dimensions in **Figure C** online. Arrange the truss parts on the shed floor as shown in **Photo 4**. The angles at the top should fit tightly together. Tack positioning blocks at the top and mark the bottoms on the 6x6 as a guide for building the remaining trusses. Repeat this process at the narrow end to build the three small trusses.

Connect the pairs of rafters at the top with a plywood gusset and ten 6d nails. Connect the bottoms with a 2x6 nailed to each rafter with three 10d nails. On the end trusses, cut and nail additional 2x4 framing as shown to provide nailing for the plywood siding and square openings for the screened vents (**Photo 4**). Mark location of purlins along the top of each truss (**Figure C** online). Cut purlins to length and mark the truss locations on them as well (**Figure E** online).

PRO TIP

Great Floor—But a Little Extra Work

Knowing that the smaller section would be used as a potting area, I thought it would be nice to have a floor that allowed drainage. I came up with the plan to set pavers between a foundation of treated 6x6s. But leveling the 6x6s and cutting the thick pavers to fit in was more work than I expected. Poured concrete would have been a lot simpler. Also, if your shed site is sloping, a platform on posts would be a better choice for the shed floor.

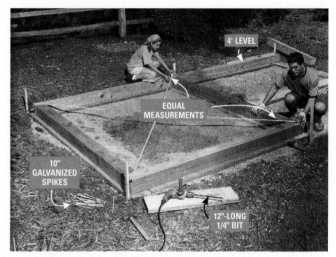

1 Build the foundation. Cut treated 6x6s to form perimeter of shed. Check with a level and slip treated shims under them at low spots. Drill pilot holes and nail corners together with galvanized timber spikes. Adjust 6x6s until diagonal measurements are equal. Toe-screw 6x6s to 2x10s to hold them in place.

2 Prepare for pavers. Add 3-in. layers of gravel and pack each layer with a hand tamper to within 2 in. of the top. Drag a notched 2x4 over the gravel to create a flat, level base for the concrete pavers.

FRAME THE WALLS ON THE FLOOR AND STAND THEM UP

Cut the plates to length (**Figure D** online) and tack them to the 6x6 exactly where they'll go to check the fit. Leave them tacked while you lay out the stud and opening locations on the plates (**Photo 5**).

Then cut the studs and other wall framing parts to length according to the dimensions shown in **Figure D**. Build the headers by sandwiching a layer of 1/2-in. plywood between 2x6s and nailing them together with pairs of 10d sinkers spaced every 8 in. Choose a pair of straight 2x4s for each corner and nail them together with short lengths of scrap 2x4s as spacers. Once all the parts are cut and the headers and corners are built, you're ready to assemble the walls.

Build the long back wall first. We're using a framing nailer (**Photo 6**) to speed things up. This is a dangerous tool. We recommend avoiding this tool and hand-nail this entire project unless you have experience using a framing nailer. Stand and brace the back wall (**Photo 7**), then the front walls, and the end walls. Tie them together with doubled top plates and finally plumb and brace the corners (**Photo 8**).

STAND THE TRUSSES AND CONNECT THE PURLINS

Once the walls are plumbed and braced and the trusses are built, it's time to frame the roof. It'll take shape quickly, but you'll need some help lifting and positioning the trusses. Also line up a few tall ladders or scaffolding. The key to this roof is to make sure truss positions are marked on the top plates, purlin positions on the rafters, and rafter positions on the purlins. Then all will go together smoothly. Start by nailing a long 2x4 brace to the end walls. It should extend up to the rafter (**Photo 9**). Once these are in place, you can install the two end trusses and connect them with a purlin (**Photo 9**).

3 Make rafter patterns. Mark and cut a pair of long and a pair of short rafters from the dimensions in Figure C. Check the fit (Photo 4); use them as a pattern for the rest.

PRO TIPS

Change Window Sizes Easily

The walls with windows have continuous support beams, called headers, over the windows. This means that if you would like to use windows that are a different width, all you have to do is adjust the position and size of the window spacers. If you want to use windows that are a different height, simply adjust the length of the cripples under the windows.

Ditch the Line Level

We used a line level attached to a string to level the foundation. But now that affordable self-leveling laser levels are available, we would use one of these for this project instead.

4 Build the trusses. Align rafters with outside edges of 6x6s as shown to build three large trusses. Do the same on the narrow end to build three small trusses. Use temporary wood blocks to center tops of rafters on the end wall while you nail them together with triangular plywood gussets. Add flat 2x4s 24 in. on center to create one small and two large gable end trusses. Build one large and two small trusses without the studs.

5 Lay out the plates. Cut treated 2x4 bottom plates and 2x4 top plates and tack them into place around the perimeter. Mark window and door rough openings and the edge of each stud according to the dimensions in Figure D.

6 Assemble the walls on the floor. Nail full-length studs between top and bottom plates. Assemble 2x6 headers; nail them into place. Add trimmers under ends of headers. Cut cripples and rough sills to complete window openings. Build short posts that separate windows and toenail them into place.

7 Stand the walls. Stand and brace the front and the back walls first, making sure tops tilt out slightly to allow room for walls that fit in between. Align outside edges of walls with 6x6s and nail down through the bottom plates. Build the end and center walls and stand them up. Remove the temporary braces and nail the corners together, making sure the top plates are aligned with each other.

8 Plumb and brace the corners. Tape a level to a long straight board with equal spacers at each end. Push or pull the wall until it's plumb and hold it in this position while a helper nails on a temporary diagonal brace. Repeat this process for each wall. Plumb both end walls first. Then sight down the long back wall to make sure it's straight before nailing the diagonal brace across the center wall.

Then install the intermediate truss. Toenail everything with 8d nails and add metal hurricane ties where there's space to do so **(Photo 10)**.

Complete the roof framing by building the cantilevered overhangs. Connect them to the trusses with metal tie plates **(Photo 10 inset)**. Then complete the overhangs by cutting and nailing up the 2x4 rough fascias. Finally, cut and install the blocking to complete the roof framing.

INSTALL THE METAL ROOFING

Since this design doesn't include a metal fascia that would typically cover the edge of the metal roofing at the gable ends, you'll have to cut the first rib from the starting sheet to leave a flat spot **(Photo 11)**. We tried tin snips and abrasive metal-cutting blades but settled on a standard 24-tooth carbide blade mounted in a circular saw as the best method for making the long, straight cuts in the metal sheets. Be careful, though. The blade throws metal chips quite a distance. Keep bystanders away and make sure to wear safety glasses, hearing protection and leather gloves. Smooth the cut edges with a mill bastard file to remove sharp burrs.

Photos 12 and 13 show how to install the sheets. Screw down each sheet before moving to the next. Use special hex head roofing screws that have a built-in rubber washer to seal the hole. Set the last sheet into place, overlapping at the seams as usual, and mark it 1 in. past the fascia for cutting. On the back side of the roof, you'll have to notch one panel where the roof transition occurs. If your last panel is a few inches short of the end as ours was, rather than cutting a 2-in. strip, cut a piece 13 in. wide and run it underneath the previous panel so the seam won't show from below.

It's difficult to reach the top of the roof to install the ridge cap after all the roofing is on. One solution is to complete one side of the roof, then cut the ridge and screw it down over the completed side. Slide the panels on the opposite side of the roof under the ridge and screw down the ridge as you fasten each panel.

FINISH THE EXTERIOR WITH CEDAR PLYWOOD PANELS AND CEDAR BATTENS

Since all of the cedar plywood panels for the walls are the same height, you can start by marking and cutting them all to 91 in. long. A drywall square works great for marking the 4x8 sheets. Mark and cut from the back side of the sheets. The studs are spaced so you'll be able to start each wall with a full-width sheet and cut the last sheet to fit.

Drive 6d galvanized nails every 6 in. around the perimeter of the panels and at 8-in. intervals along the studs **(Photo 14)**.

9 Set the trusses. Erect the two end trusses and brace them with 2x4s nailed to the walls. Line up the outside edges with the walls and toenail them into place. Align the one long purlin and toenail it into place. Tip up the remaining trusses and toenail them to the purlin. Toenail the ends of the trusses to the top plates.

10 Add the purlins. Nail on the remaining purlins using hurricane ties (inset photo) where possible. Complete roof framing as shown by adding the cantilevered 2x4s that support the overhang and nailing on the 2x4s that form the rough fascia. Add 2x4 blocking between the purlins on the end walls to keep out birds.

CLAMP

UPSIDE-DOWN ROOF PANEL

STRAIGHT BOARD

CLAMP

BACKER BOARD

11 Cut the roof panels. Cut metal panels with a 24-tooth carbide blade in a circular saw. Clamp the panel between a straight board to guide the saw and a 2x4 that backs up the cut. Cut the first rib from the starting piece to create a flat edge (see Photo 12).

CUT EDGE

FULL ROOF PANEL

OVERLAP SEAM

1x6 CEDAR FASCIA

12 Install the metal roofing. Nail 1x6 cedar fascia boards to the 2x4 subfascia boards. Overhang the metal panel 1 in. on the end and 2 in. on the bottom and attach it to the purlins with special self-sealing hex head screws. Overlap the second panel onto the first and screw it into place (Photo 13). Measure and cut the last panel to overhang the cedar trim by 1 in. Finally, cap the top with the metal ridge cap (Figure A).

LINE UP WITH PURLINS

HEX DRIVER

SCREW ONE SIDE

SCREW BOTH SIDES

OVERLAPPED SEAM

13 Fasten the roof panels. Drive special self-sealing hex head screws into the purlins to secure the panels. Place screws along one side of each rib and on both sides of ribs where panels overlap. Snug up screws to compress the rubber washer but don't overdrive.

PRO TIPS

Save Money On Siding

We used 5/8-in. rough-sawn plywood with no grooves for the siding. At most lumberyards this is a special-order item and it's quite expensive. You could save several hundred dollars by substituting the more commonly available grooved siding and then eliminating the battens.

Recycled Windows Are a Great Option

You could use old windows instead of barn sash. Get in touch with someone who does window replacements—there are probably all kinds of cool, divided-lite sash for available for free. Of course, you'll have to plan ahead and build the openings to fit.

Consider Shingles

Metal roofs look great and last almost forever. But asphalt shingles have improved in both looks and longevity. So shingles are a great option for this or any shed.

BUILD YOUR OWN WINDOWS

Adding the windows, doors and trim can be time consuming. But it's these details that make the shed look sharp. Patience pays off here. Construct the window frames by screwing together 1x4 cedar boards to form a box that's about 1/4 in. wider and taller than the window sash. You'll have to pull out the table saw to cut out the 1/2-in. x 7/8-in. stops, as well as the sills (15-degree angles), battens and window trim. Mount the larger barn sash in the frames with a pair of 3-in. screen door hinges at the top. We chose to mount the smaller sashes between stops and leave them permanently closed. Then mount storm window hold-open hardware 10 in. up on each side to hold the windows open or closed. Finally, shim and install the windows **(Photo 15)**.

Add the trim and battens. Position the battens so every other one falls over a stud (24 in. on center). That way, you can use 8d galvanized finish nails. Fasten intermediate battens with 4d nails and construction adhesive. A layout stick **(Photo 17)** speeds up the layout. After you've completed the siding, trim and drip cap on the lower walls and seal the gap between the small front roof and the gable end wall with sidewall flashing.

THE OPTIONAL CEDAR ARBOR IS A GREAT PLACE TO HANG PLANTS OR GROW VINES

You can be as creative as you want with this part of the project. **Figure A** shows how we built our arbor. The key is to temporarily brace the post and level across from the bottom of the fascia to mark the height and cut the notches. Then it's a simple matter to plumb the post, attach the beams and finally top them with the 1-1/2-in. x 2-1/2-in. cedar lattice pieces. We screwed the lattice through the fascia and into the 2x4 subfascia with 4-in. galvanized deck screws run in at a 45-degree angle.

ADD SIMPLE SHELVES AND BENCHES

We fitted the smaller side of the shed with two full-length workbenches and 1x6 wall shelves. The workbenches are simply 2x4 frames screwed to the studs and supported by angled 2x4 braces. We covered the tops with three 1x6 boards for a width of 16-1/2 in. For the shelves, we notched 1x6 boards to fit around each stud and supported them by nailing 2x4 spacers to the studs under each shelf.

BUILD THE SLIDING DOOR

Referring to **Figure G** online and **Photo 18**, build the sliding door from a sheet of 5/8-in. cedar plywood. Then mount the heavy-duty sliding door track to the wall of the shed and hang the door. To keep the bottom of the door from bumping into the battens, cut 1-1/2 in. from the bottom of each batten that's under the track and nail on a horizontal 1x2 for

the door to ride against. Keep the bottom of the door from swinging out by mounting a metal 2x4 bar holder to the foundation 6x6 just to the left of the door **(Figure G)**. Install a gate latch to hold the door shut.

PROTECT THE CEDAR WITH EXTERIOR FINISH

We finished the outside of this shed with an exterior-grade penetrating oil finish. Recoating every few years with a cedar-tinted stain should maintain the natural beauty of the cedar.

PRO TIPS

Upgrade the Finish
We used penetrating oil finish on the siding and exterior trim. But you could use a product like Sikkens Cetol SRD. It's more like a varnish than like a penetrating oil, so the wood will look more "finished" and less natural. But the advantage is a longer lasting finish that provides better protection against water damage.

MARK STUDS

5/8" CEDAR PLYWOOD

6D GALVANIZED SIDING NAILS

14 Nail on the siding. Cut 5/8-in. cedar plywood panels to fit; nail them to the studs with galvanized siding nails. Lap the bottom of the panels 1 in. over the 6x6. Complete the lower panels and window and door installation and trim before installing the panels on the gable end trusses.

15 Build and install the windows. Build 1x4 cedar frames for the barn sash, allowing for a 1/8-in. gap around the sash. Hinge the sash at the top and nail 1/2-in. x 7/8-in. stops around the inside. Level the frames in the openings and adjust with shims until the gap between the sash and the frame is even and the space between pairs of windows is equal on the top and bottom. Nail through the frame and shims from inside to secure the windows. Cut off the shims.

16 Attach a beveled sill. Rip 2-in.-wide cedar sills with 15-degree bevels on each side with a table saw. Cut 45-degree miters where the sills wrap around the walls. Nail the sill pieces below the windows with 16d galvanized casing nails.

17 Add trim and battens. Cut the cedar boards to fit around windows and doors and nail them into place. Continue the top 1x6 cedar board across the end of the shed. Shim out the 1x4 board over this with 1/2-in. plywood strips and add a metal drip cap overtop before cutting and installing the gable end plywood. Mark the batten locations every 12 in. and nail them up with galvanized siding nails.

18 Build the sliding door. Glue and screw 1x3s flat and then 1x3s on edge to the perimeter of a 48-in. x 80-1/2-in. sheet of 5/8-in.-thick cedar plywood to create a sliding door. Screw pocket door wheel brackets to the top, 4 in. from the ends and entered in the top 1x3.

CHAPTER THREE

LAUNDRY ROOM, CLOSETS & CLOTHES

Easy Textile Storage

No need to let piles of clothes and accessories gather dust on your clean floors. With these tips, you'll be able to quickly and easily store them.

A. COMPACT STORAGE FOR COMFORTERS

Billowy comforters, pillows and blankets take up lots and lots of storage space in your closet. To save room, toss those puffy items into a heavy-duty (2 mm or thicker is best) plastic bag. Then use your shop vacuum to remove as much air as possible before tying off the bag.

To keep the items fresh in storage, toss in a fabric softener sheet before you use the vacuum.

B. QUICK-INSTALL CLOTHES ROD

If you need a clothes rod in the laundry room and you have exposed joists, check out this simple, solid and fast way to get it. Attach some 3/4-in. J-hooks (these are used for hanging pipe) to the joists and snap a 7/8-in. dowel rod in the curve.

C. ACCESSORY CLIP-UP

Create the perfect hangers for soft items like hats and gloves using a length of metal or plastic chain and binder clips. Squeeze the metal handles to free them from the clips, slip them through the chain links, then reattach the clips. You'll have a neat hangout for all your winter gear.

D. SUPER STUFF SACKS

Ever try, unsuccessfully, to fit 10 lbs. of blankets and clothes into a 5-lb. bag? Now you can do it with ease. Space-saving storage bags use a vacuum to ensure that you're only storing stuff, not air.

If you put lots of winter clothes and bedding in storage every spring, then spend the summer trying to stop the bulky winter stuff from tumbling out of closets and drawers, you'll like these vacuum-pack bags. Just fill the bag with clothes or bedding, seal the top, and pull the air out using a vacuum. Seal the vacuum port and you're good to go. The bags can be reused, so come fall you can store your summer stuff.

No matter how you put items into the bag, the vacuum suction will compress them. However, the more neatly you fill the bag, the flatter it will end up. Various sizes are available, so you can match the size to the items you're storing. Several brands of these bags are on the market.

A.

HEAVY-DUTY GARBAGE BAG

3/4" J-HOOK

7/8" DOWEL ROD

B.

SQUEEZE HANDLE

C.

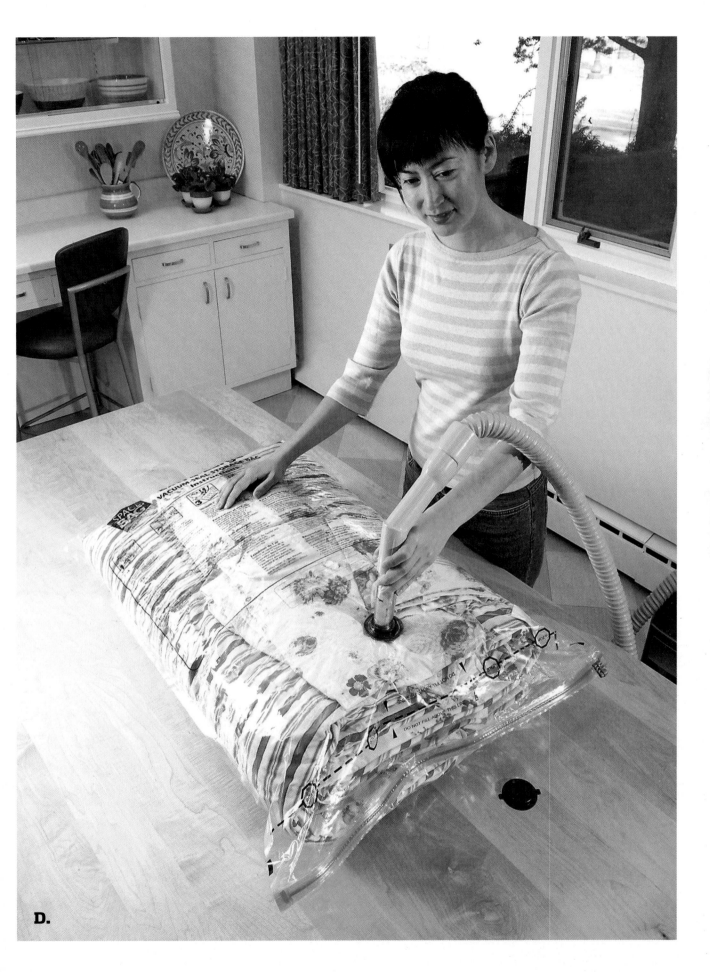

D.

E. BELTS AND OTHER HANG-UPS

Where do you store your belts? (A) on the floor, (B) over a chair, (C) stuffed in a drawer or (D) all of the above? Well, you can now choose (E)—on an inexpensive and easy-to-make belt holder. All you need is a wooden hanger and some cup hooks. If some of your belts have unusually thick buckles, just widen the cup hook slightly with a needle-nose pliers. This is a great way to hang small handbags too.

F. HANGER SLIDING FREEDOM

A common complaint about wire shelving is that it restricts the movement of hangers because they're stuck between the shelves. Fix that irksome problem by adding a hanger rod. Most manufacturers make some version of one. A hanger rod allows you to slide clothes from one end of the closet to the other, even past an inside corner. This upgrade will add a bit to the cost of the materials on a standard shelf design. Make sure the type of shelving you buy will work with the hanging-rod hardware you plan to use.

G. REVIVE AN AROMATIC CEDAR CLOSET

Everyone likes the woodsy smell of a new aromatic cedar closet. But the fragrance diminishes once the cedar oils evaporate and dust clogs the wood pores. You can revive much of the aroma by sanding and cleaning the paneling.

Start by emptying the closet, laying down floor protection and draping the area with plastic sheeting to control the sanding dust.

Sand the emptied closet using an orbital sander fitted with 100-grit sanding paper. For the best results, move the sander in overlapping side-to-side strokes. Achieve an even finish by moving the sander slowly back and forth under medium pressure and changing the sanding paper when it's clogged with dust. To avoid "chatter marks" on inside corners and door trim, grip the sander firmly and move it up and down without touching the adjacent walls and trim.

Clean the paneling by vacuuming and then wiping it with tack cloths. Avoid using a damp cloth or sponge to remove the cedar dust. Wet-cleaning may raise the wood grain and leave a rough surface and water stains.

H. SUPER STURDY CLOSET SHELVES

Here's a fast, strong and easy way to install closet shelves. Paint a 1x4 to match your shelf. Then draw a level line and locate the studs. Nail the 1x4 to the studs with 8d finish nails. Run the strip across the back and ends of the closet. Then put blocks in the locations where you want brackets. Now you have solid wood to attach the brackets and the closet-pole sockets to. And the back of the shelf is fully supported to prevent sagging.

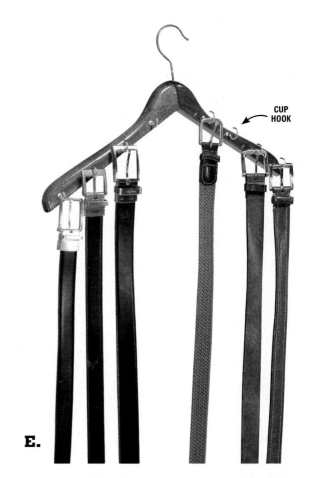

CUP HOOK

E.

CORNER HANGING BAR

BAR HANGER SUPPORT

F.

ORBITAL SANDER WITH 100-GRIT SANDPAPER

G.

HOOK STRIP

H.

Tie, Scarf And Belt Organizer

You don't need tons of materials or time to build this organizer—but the results are well worth the couple of hours you'll spend on it.

Clean up a messy closet by hanging your ties, belts and scarves on this three-in-one closet organizer. All you need is a 2 x 2-ft. piece of 1/2-in. plywood, a wooden hanger, a hook (the one shown came from the hanger) and a few hours.

This organizer is 12 in. wide and 16 in. tall, but yours can be taller or narrower. To get a nice curve at the top, use the wooden hanger as a guide. Center it, trace the edge and cut it out with a jigsaw. Make a pattern of holes, slots and notches on a piece of paper and transfer it to your board. Use a 2-in. hole saw to cut the holes, making sure the board is clamped down tightly to keep the veneer from chipping **(Photo 1)**. Use a jigsaw to cut out the side notches. To cut the slots, punch out the ends with a 5/8-in. Forstner drill bit (or a sharp spade bit) to prevent chipping, and then use a jigsaw to finish cutting out the center of each slot **(Photo 2)**.

Sand the hanger and apply several coats of sealer or poly to smooth the edges so your scarves and ties don't snag (this is the most time-consuming step). Using a 1/4-in. round-over bit with a router makes the sanding go faster. Drill a small hole into the top of the hanger for your hook, squeeze in a bit of epoxy glue to hold it and then screw it in.

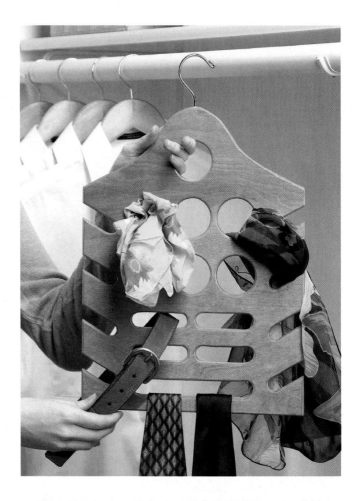

WHAT IT TAKES	
TIME 1-2 hours	**SKILL LEVEL** Beginner

TOOLS & MATERIALS
Jigsaw, driver/drill, 5/8" Forstner bit or spade bit, router, 2-hole saw

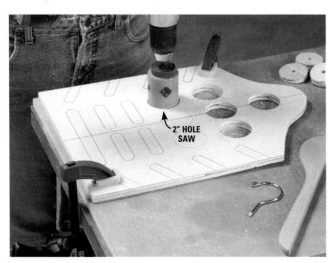

1 Drill scarf holes with a 2-in. hole saw. Clamp the plywood tightly against a piece of scrap wood to prevent chipping as the hole saw exits the plywood.

2" HOLE SAW

2 Use a 5/8-in. Forstner drill bit or a sharp spade bit to punch out the ends of the slots, and then finish cutting them out with a jigsaw.

Small-Closet Organizer

Decluttering will be easy with this simple-to-build organizer.

Most standard bedroom closets suffer from a serious lack of organization—stuff on the floor; a long, overloaded closet rod; and a precariously stacked, sagging shelf. The simple shelving system shown here cleans up some of that clutter. It provides a home for shoes; several cubbies for loose clothing, folded shirts, sweaters or small items; and a deeper (16 in.) top shelf to house the stuff that keeps falling off the narrow shelf. Besides the storage space it provides, the center tower supports the shelf above it as well as the hanging clothes, since it uses two shorter rods rather than a long one.

Here you'll learn how to cut and assemble this shelving system from a single sheet of plywood (for a 6-ft. long closet), including how to mount drawer slides for the shoe trays. Birch plywood is used because it's relatively inexpensive yet takes a nice finish. The edges are faced with 1x2 maple for strength and a more attractive appearance.

The key tool for this project is a circular saw with a cutting guide, which works for cutting the plywood into nice straight pieces **(Photo 1)**. An air-powered brad nailer or finish nailer makes the assembly go quite a bit faster, and a miter saw will help you produce clean cuts. But neither of them is absolutely necessary.

CUT THE BIRCH PLYWOOD TO SIZE

First, rip the plywood into three 15-3/4-in. x 8-ft. pieces **(Photo 1)**, then cut the sides and shelves from these with a shorter cutting guide. For an average-size closet—6 ft. wide with a 5-1/2-ft.-high top shelf—cut all the sides and shelves from one piece of 3/4-in. plywood. Making the shelving wider means settling for fewer shelves/trays or buying

WHAT IT TAKES	
TIME 2 days	**SKILL LEVEL** Intermediate

TOOLS & MATERIALS
Circular saw with cutting guide, driver/drill, profile gauge (optional: brad nailer, miter saw)

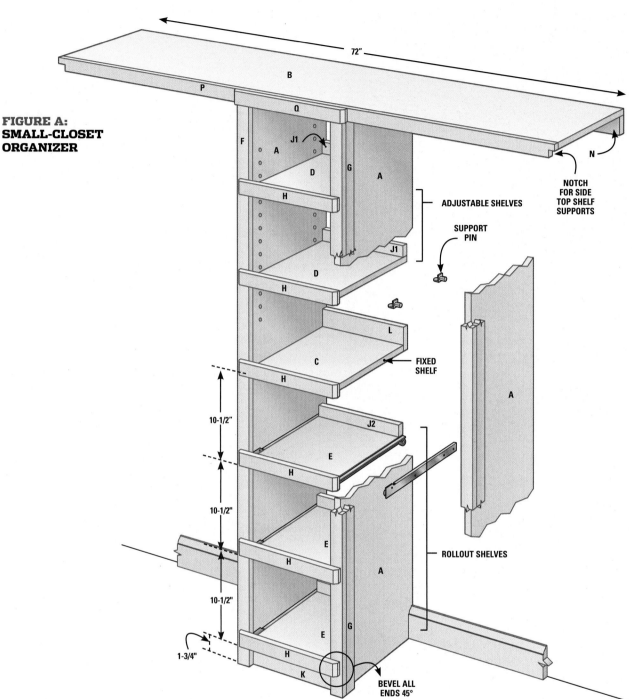

FIGURE A:
SMALL-CLOSET ORGANIZER

72"

B

P

Q

N

NOTCH FOR SIDE TOP SHELF SUPPORTS

F

A

J1

D

G

A

H

ADJUSTABLE SHELVES

SUPPORT PIN

D

H

J1

C

L

FIXED SHELF

H

A

J2

E

H

E

ROLLOUT SHELVES

10-1/2"

H

E

10-1/2"

H

E

G

10-1/2"

H

A

K

1-3/4"

BEVEL ALL ENDS 45°

Cutting List

KEY	QTY.	DIMENSIONS	DESCRIPTION
A	2	15-3/4" x 65-1/4"	plywood (sides)
B	1	15-3/4" x 72"	plywood (top shelf)
C	1	15-3/4" x 12"	plywood (fixed shelf)
D	2	15-3/4" x 11-7/8"	plywood (adjustable shelves)
E	3	15-3/4" x 11"	plywood (rollout shelves)
F	2	3/4" x 1-1/2" x 64-1/2"	maple (vertical front trim)
G	2	3/4" x 1-1/2" x 65-1/4"	maple (vertical side trim)
H	6	3/4" x 1-1/2" x 14-1/2"	maple (shelf fronts)
J1	2	3/4" x 1-1/2" x 11-7/8"	maple (shelf backs)
J2	3	3/4" x 1-1/2" x 11"	maple (rollout shelf backs)
K	1	3/4" x 1-1/2" x 12"	maple (base)
L	5	3/4" x 3-1/2" x 12"	pine (bracing)
M	2	3/4" x 3-1/2" x 24"	maple (side top shelf supports not shown)
N	2	3/4" x 3-1/2" x 29-1/4"	maple (rear top shelf supports)
P	1	3/4" x 1-1/2" x 72"	maple (top shelf edge)
Q	1	3/4" x 1-1/2" x 15-3/4"	maple (top trim)

Materials List

ITEM	QTY.
4' x 8' x 3/4" birch plywood	1
3/4" x 1-1/2" x 8' maple	6
3/4" x 3-1/2" x 8' No. 2 pine	1
3/4" x 3-1/2" x 12' maple	1
14" bottom-mount drawer slides	3
2' x 4' x 1/4" pegboard	1
1/4" shelf support pins	8
1-1/4" and 1-1/2" brads for a brad nailer	

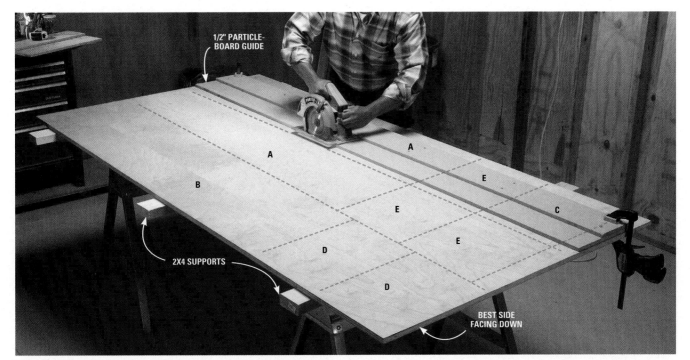

1 Cut the sheet of plywood into three equal widths using a saw guide. Then crosscut the sections into the pieces shown in Figure A, Page 124, using a shorter guide.

additional plywood. Be sure to support the plywood so the pieces won't fall after completing a cut, and use a guide to keep the cuts perfectly straight. Use a plywood blade in a circular saw to minimize splintering. Cut slowly on the crosscuts, and make sure the good side of the plywood is down—the plywood blade makes a big difference, but the thin veneer will splinter if you rush the cut.

Mark and cut the baseboard profile on the plywood sides, using a profile gauge **(Photo 2)** or a trim scrap to transfer the shape, or remove the baseboard rather than cutting the plywood and reinstalling it later. Either method works fine.

ATTACH THE MAPLE EDGES

Glue and nail the side 1x2s (G) to the best-looking side of the plywood (so it faces out), holding them flush with the front edge **(Photo 3)**. Be sure to use 1-1/4-in. brads here so the nails don't go completely through the side. Use 1-1/2-in. brads everywhere else.

Then attach the front 1x2s (F). These 1x2s should be flush with the bottom of the sides, but 3/4 in. short of the top. The 1x2s will overlap the edge slightly because 3/4-in. plywood is just slightly less than a full 3/4 in. thick. Keep the overlap to the inside.

Lay out the locations for the drawer slides and the fixed center shelf before assembling the cabinet—the 12-in. width is a tight fit for a drill. Use the dimensions in **Photo 4** and **Figure A** for spacing. Vary any of these measurements to better fit shoes or other items. Then take the drawer slides apart and mount them on the tower sides **(Photo 4)**.

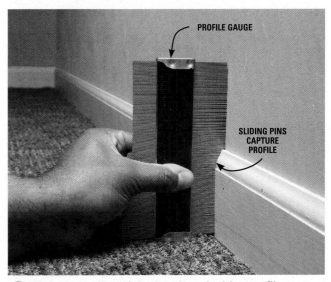

2 Make an outline of the baseboard with a profile gauge and, using a jigsaw, cut out the pattern on the lower back side of the two shelving sides. (See Figure A and Photo 4.)

Remember that one side of each pair is a mirror image of the other.

To position the shelf support pins for the two adjustable shelves, align the bottom of the 1/4-in. pegboard with the fixed shelf location, then drill mirror-image holes on the two sides **(Photo 5)**. Mark the holes to be used on the pegboard—it's all too easy to lose track when flipping the pegboard over to the second side. Use a brad point drill bit to prevent splintering, and place a bit stop or a piece of tape for a 5/8-in. hole depth (1/4-in. pegboard plus 3/8 in. deep in the plywood). Most support pins require a 1/4-in.-diameter hole, but measure to make sure.

CUT THE BEVELS AND ASSEMBLE THE SHELVES

Cut the bevels in all the 1x2 shelf fronts, then glue and nail them to the plywood shelves, keeping the bottoms flush (**Photo 6**). Nail 1x2 backs (J1 and J2) onto the adjustable and rollout shelves. Next, nail together the bracing (L) and the base piece (K), which join the cabinet. And add the slides to the rollout shelves (**Photo 7**).

Assembling the shelving tower is straightforward (**Photo 8**). Position the L-shaped bracing at the top and braces at the bottom, add glue to the joints, then clamp and nail. Because of the lip where the 1x2 front trim (F) overlaps the plywood, it requires chiseling out a 1/32-in.-deep x 3/4-in.-wide notch so the fixed shelf will fit tightly (**Photo 9**).

SET THE CABINET IN THE CLOSET

Remove the old closet shelving and position the new cabinet. If there's carpeting, it's best to cut it out under the cabinet for easier carpet replacement in the future (**Photo 10**). For the cleanest look, pull the carpet back from the closet wall, cut out the padding and tack strip that fall under the cabinet, and then nail new tack strips around the cabinet position. Then reposition the cabinet, push the carpet back against it and cut the carpet. Or, simply cut out the carpet and tack strip under the cabinet and tack the loose carpet edges to the floor (but it won't look as nice).

Plumb and level the cabinet, then screw it to the wall. Use hollow wall anchors if the studs are hard to find. The cabinet will be firmly anchored by the upper shelf anyway.

SCRIBE THE TOP SHELF FOR A TIGHT FIT

Closet shelves are tough to fit because the corners of the walls are rarely square. To cut the shelf accurately, scribe a leftover 16-in.-wide piece of particleboard or plywood in both corners (**Photo 11**) and use it for a template for cutting the ends of the shelf. Then the shelf will drop right into place and rest on 1x4 supports nailed to the side walls and back wall. Make sure the front of the shelf is flush with the front of the tower and nail it to the top. If the back wall is wavy, scribe the back of the shelf to the wall and trim it to make the front flush. Then cut and notch the front 1x2 and nail it to the shelf (**Photo 12**).

Lightly sand all the wood and apply a clear finish. When it's dry, mix several shades of putty to get an exact match to your wood and fill the nail holes. Add another coat of finish and let it dry. Screw on the clothes rod brackets, aligning them with the bottom of the 1x4. Then pile on the clothes.

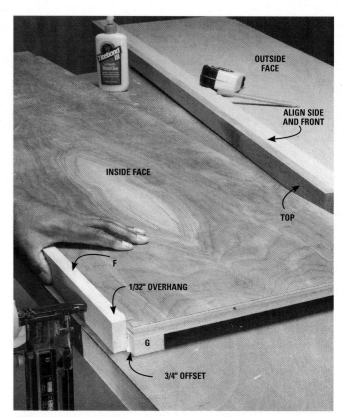

3 Cut the 1x2s to length. Then glue and nail them to the plywood sides (Figure A) with 1-1/4-in. brads. Note the slight (1/32-in.) overhang along the inside.

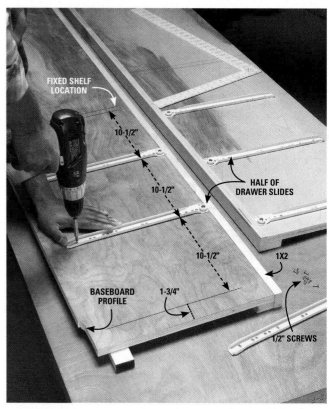

4 Mark the center and rollout shelf locations using a framing square. Then mount half of each of the two-piece drawer slides even with the 1x2 on each side.

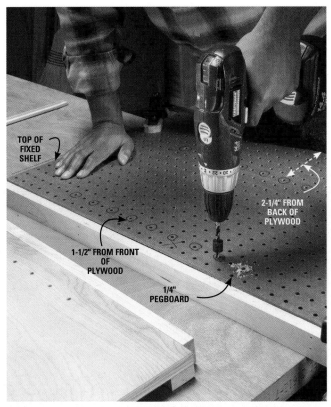

TOP OF FIXED SHELF

2-1/4" FROM BACK OF PLYWOOD

1-1/2" FROM FRONT OF PLYWOOD

1/4" PEGBOARD

5 Drill 1/4-in matching holes 3/8 in. deep for the adjustable shelf pins using a pegboard template. Flip the pegboard when switching sides.

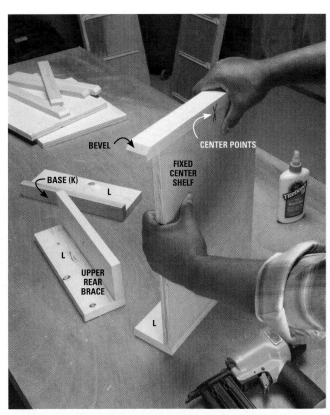

BEVEL

CENTER POINTS

FIXED CENTER SHELF

BASE (K) L

L

UPPER REAR BRACE

L

6 Assemble the shelves and shelving braces using glue and 1-1/2-in. brads. Align the centers of each piece for accurate positioning.

FRONT 1X2

7 Attach the other halves of the slides to the rollout shelves with 1/2-in. screws. Butt them against the front 1x2.

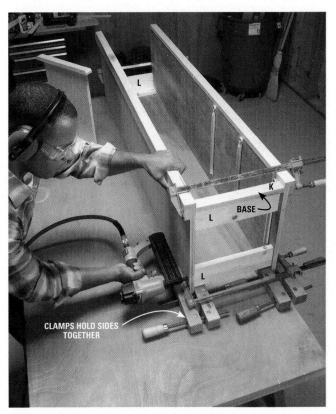

L

K

BASE

L

L

CLAMPS HOLD SIDES TOGETHER

8 Set the sides on edge, glue and clamp the braces (L) in place and nail the assembly together with 1-1/2-in. brads. Make sure the braces are square to the sides.

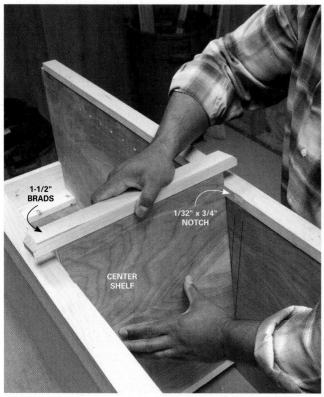

9 Chisel shallow slots in the 1x2 overhang, then slide the center shelf into place. Nail at the front, back and sides.

1-1/2" BRADS

1/32" x 3/4" NOTCH

CENTER SHELF

10 Center the cabinet in the closet against the back wall, mark its position and cut the carpet out around it. Tack the loose edges of carpet to the floor.

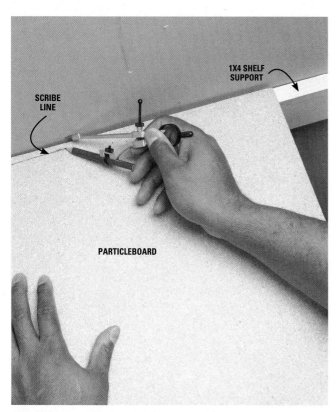

11 Shove a 16 x 24-in. sheet of particleboard into the shelf corners and scribe a line. Cut along the scribe line and use the particleboard as a pattern. Nail the shelf to the supports and cabinet top.

1X4 SHELF SUPPORT

SCRIBE LINE

PARTICLEBOARD

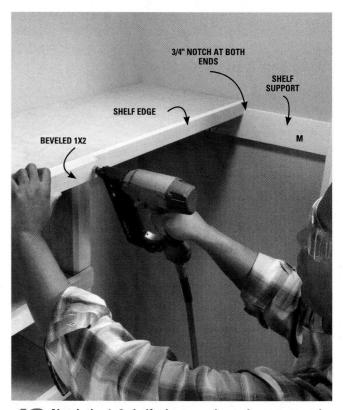

12 Notch the 1x2 shelf edge over the end supports and nail it into place. Then trim the top of the cabinet with a beveled 1x2.

3/4" NOTCH AT BOTH ENDS

SHELF SUPPORT

SHELF EDGE

BEVELED 1X2

M

Versatile Clothes Cabinets

Add extra clothes storage space to any room with these attractive cabinets.

It seems like no matter how much closet space you have, there's never quite enough. But building attractive clothes cabinets like these allows you to expand storage into your bedroom or a spare room and gain the extra space you need. You can build one storage tower or connect several together. Each tower consists of a drawer base, a wall cabinet with doors, and two side panels with holes for adjustable shelves. We'll show you how to build the cabinets and assemble the towers. And we'll also include details for adding a clothes hamper drawer, a pullout pants-hanging rack and shoe storage between the two towers.

Even though the style here is simple, building these cabinets requires close attention to detail and accurate cuts. If you can cut plywood precisely and have the patience to carefully assemble

the parts, you shouldn't have any trouble with the process of building this project.

We used 3/4-in. maple plywood for everything but the drawers and the backs of the cabinets. For these we used good-quality shop-grade plywood. You could substitute less expensive plywood for the cabinet boxes to save a little money.

WHAT IT TAKES	
TIME 2-3 weekends	**SKILL LEVEL** Advanced

TOOLS & MATERIALS
Table saw, miter saw, driver/drill, brad nailer, steam iron, edge-banding trimmer, 35 mm (or 1-3/8") Forstner bit

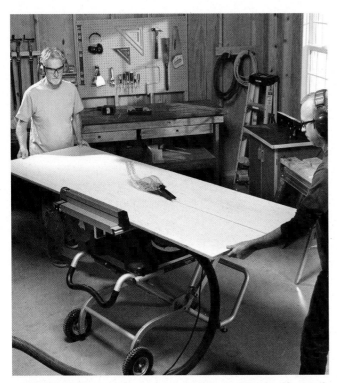

1 Rip the plywood. Round up a helper and rip the plywood sheets into strips according to Figure E. Choose the best-looking plywood for the tall end panels because these are the most visible.

2 Crosscut the plywood. A crosscutting sled is the best tool for accurately cutting the plywood strips to length. Take the time to build a sled if you don't already have one. Clamp a stop to the crosscutting sled to cut the same-size parts accurately.

CUT AND PREPARE THE PLYWOOD

The most important step in the building process is cutting the parts accurately. Use the Cutting List and **Figure E** (Page 137) as a guide. Our plywood was a full 3/4 in. thick, and the sizes shown are for 3/4-in. plywood. If yours is slightly thinner, cut the shelves, doors and drawer parts after you've assembled the cabinet boxes so you can adjust the fit.

A stationary table saw with an accurate fence and outfeed tables would be ideal for this job. But you can get great results with a portable saw, too. You'll need a top-quality blade designed to crosscut plywood. We splurged on a 90-tooth 10-in. blade and were amazed at the glass-smooth, splinter-free cuts we got.

After all the parts are cut, separate out the uprights and shelves that receive solid wood nosing. Then cover the raw plywood edges of the remaining 3/4-in. plywood parts with edge-banding veneer. For the cabinet boxes, you only need to cover the front edges. On the doors and drawer fronts, you'll want to cover all four edges.

BUILD THE CABINET BOXES

The cabinets are simple plywood boxes with drawers or doors added. The key to accuracy is to make sure that the edges of the plywood remain perfectly aligned as you assemble the boxes and that the cabinet box is square. **Photos 6-8** show you how.

3 Cover the raw plywood edges. Finish the edges of the cabinet parts and the shoe shelves with edge banding. We're using self-adhesive edge banding, but iron-on edge banding works well, too. Center the edge banding and press or iron it on as per manufacturer's instructions.

4 Trim the ends. Place the banded edge down on the work surface and use a sharp utility knife to trim the ends so they are flush.

5 Trim the edges. Use a veneer edge trimmer to slice off the excess edge banding along the sides. A double-edge trimmer like this one trims both edges at once. Single-edge trimmers cost about half as much and work well. They just take a little longer. Use sanding paper to remove any overhanging edge banding to create a perfectly flush edge.

CENTERLINE

6 Install the slides first. It's easier to attach slides to the cabinet sides before the cabinet is assembled. Draw lines to indicate the center of the slides. Then center the screw holes on the line and attach the slide with the included screws.

7 Nail, then screw the parts. To prevent the plywood from sliding around when you're drilling pilot holes, tack the parts first with a brad nailer. Then drill countersink pilot holes and connect the parts with screws.

8 Attach the back. If you're careful to cut the back perfectly square, you can use it to square the cabinet. Apply a bead of glue and set the back onto the cabinet. Make sure one edge of the back is flush with one side of the cabinet box and fasten it with 1-in. nails. Adjust the cabinet box until the other sides align, then partially drive a nail to hold it. Check the cabinet for square, then finish nailing on the back.

9 Groove the drawer parts. Set your table saw fence at 1/2 in. and raise the blade 1/4 in. above the table. Cut a groove in the drawer sides and fronts. Move the fence away from the blade about 1/16 in. and make a second pass to widen the groove. Check the fit of the drawer bottom plywood. It should be snug but not too tight. You may need a third pass. After cutting the grooves, rip the backs to width.

10 Build the drawer boxes. Glue and nail the sides to the front and back. Use glue sparingly to avoid squeeze-out mess. Use 1-1/4-in. nails and aim carefully to prevent them from shooting out the sides. Make sure the grooves line up—it's easy to get a part upside down.

11 Slide in the bottom. Check the fit of the drawer bottom and trim the width a little if needed. Don't force the plywood or it may push the drawer sides apart.

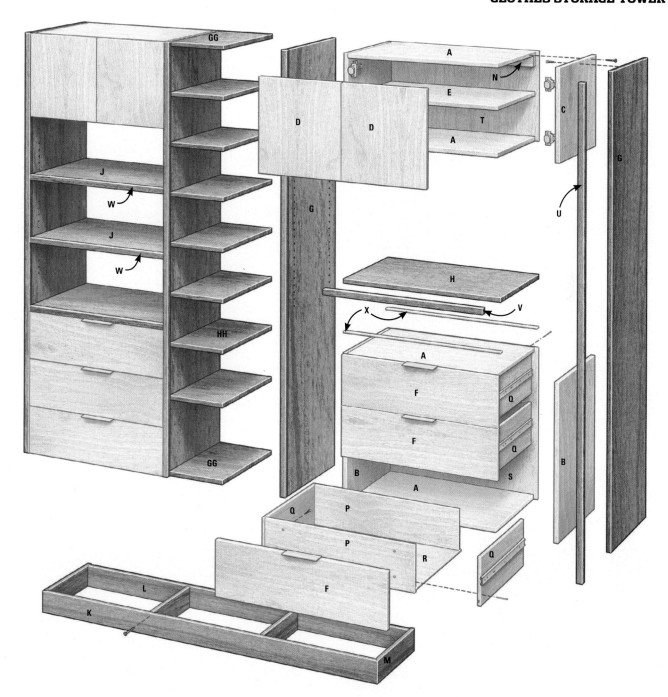

BUILD THE DRAWERS

The most critical part of the drawer-building process is to make sure the finished drawer is between 1 in. and 1-1/16 in. narrower than the inside dimensions of the cabinet to allow for the drawer slides. To determine the exact dimensions of the front and back of the drawers (parts P), measure between the cabinet sides and then subtract twice the thickness of the drawer plywood. Then subtract another 1-1/16 in. **Photos 9-14** show how to build and install the drawers.

HANG THE DOORS WITH EURO HINGES

This type of cabinet construction is perfect for Euro-style hinges. You simply mount a plate to the cabinet and drill a 35-mm (1-3/8-in.) recess in the door to accept the hinge. The Blum 120-degree clip hinges we're using are adjustable up and down, in and out, and side to side, making final door fitting a breeze. **Photos 15-21** show how to install the hinges and hang the doors.

12 Nail the drawer bottom. Measure drawer diagonally to ensure it is square. Then drive 1-in. nails through the drawer bottom into the drawer back to hold it in place.

13 Attach the drawer slide. Draw a line 3-3/4 in. from the top edge of the drawer. Center the drawer slide on the line, keeping the front edge lined up with the front of the drawer. Attach it with two screws. Add the remaining screws later to secure the drawer slide in place after making any adjustment.

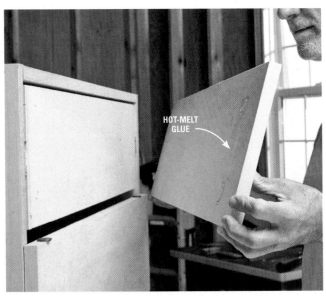

HOT-MELT GLUE

14 Install the drawer fronts. Mount each drawer front with hot glue; pull it out and secure it with four screws driven from inside the drawer. Set the bottom door flush with the bottom of the cabinet. Then use two stacks of two pennies as spacers between the drawer fronts. The top drawer should be 1/8 in. below the top of the cabinet.

15 Mark the hinge locations. Mark the hinge position on the doors, 3 in. from the top and bottom. Then align the door with the cabinet and transfer the marks to the cabinet side.

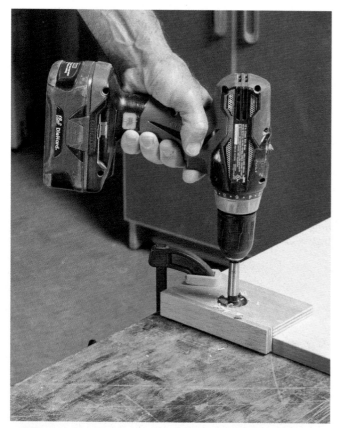

16 Start the hinge holes. We built this plywood jig as a guide for starting the hinge holes. You can also buy a jig, or mark the center of the hinge and use a center punch to create a starting hole. For these Blum hinges, the center of the hole is 7/8 in. from the edge of the door. Start drilling the hole with the 35-mm (or 1-3/8-in.) Forstner-style bit.

17 Complete the hinge hole. Remove the guide so you can judge how deep to drill. With most bits you can drill until the top of the bit is flush with the surface. The recess should be 1/2 in. deep. Drill a hole in a scrap first to check the depth before drilling a door.

FIGURE B.
PIN LOCATIONS

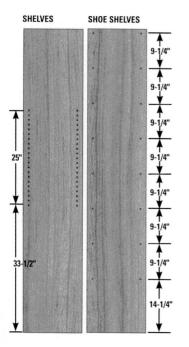

SHELVES SHOE SHELVES

9-1/4"
9-1/4"
9-1/4"
25"
9-1/4"
9-1/4"
9-1/4"
9-1/4"
33-1/2"
9-1/4"
14-1/4"

FIGURE C.
SUPERSIZE DRAWER OR
PANTS RACK

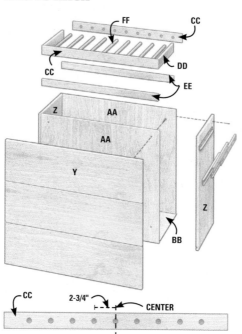

FF
CC
DD
CC
EE
Z
AA
AA
Y
Z
BB

CC
2-3/4"
CENTER

FIGURE D.
DRAWER SLIDE CENTERS

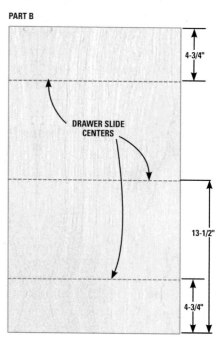

PART B

4-3/4"

DRAWER SLIDE
CENTERS

13-1/2"

4-3/4"

18 Mount the hinge. Press the hinge into the recess and align it with a square. Use a self-centering bit to drill pilot holes for the hinge screws. Then attach the hinge with the screws provided.

19 Mark for the hinge plates. Draw lines 1-7/16 in. from the front of the cabinet to locate the center of the hinge plates. If you're using a different hinge, check the instructions to find the correct distance.

20 Attach the hinge plates. Center the hinge plates on the marks and line up the center of the screw holes with the second mark. Drill the pilot holes with a self-centering bit and attach the plates with the screws.

BUILD THE SIDE PANELS

The side panels have 1-in.-wide solid wood edging on one side and shelf-pin holes on one face. If you'll be adding shoe shelves between two towers as shown in the photo on Page 129, then drill holes for these shelf pins, too. Be careful to attach the nosing to the correct edge of each panel. Since the shelf-pin holes are not an equal distance from top and bottom, the two sides are not interchangeable but are mirror images.

INSTALL THE CABINETS IN YOUR ROOM

After all the cabinets and side panels are built, you'll want to stain and varnish or paint them before installing them in your room. Remove all the drawers, doors and hardware to make finishing easier. Carefully sand all the parts. We used a random orbital sander and 120-grit sanding paper. Then we stained the side panel and shelves and brushed two coats of polyurethane on all the parts. After the finish dries, reinstall the hardware and carry the cabinets, side panels and base into your room. Mark the studs in the location where you'll install the cabinets. **Photos 24 – 27** show the installation steps.

Cutting List

KEY	QTY.	DIMENSIONS	DESCRIPTION
3/4" maple plywood			
A	4	15-7/8" x 30-1/2"	Cabinet tops and bottoms
B	2	15-7/8" x 27"	Lower cabinet sides
C	2	15-7/8" x 16"	Upper cabinet sides
D	2	15-3/4" x 15-7/8"	Upper cabinet doors
E	1	15-7/8" x 30-3/8"	Upper cabinet shelf
F	3	8-7/8" x 31-3/4"	Lower cabinet drawer fronts
G	2	16-1/8" x 79-3/4"	Side panels
H	1	16-1/8" x 32"	Lower cabinet top
J	2	15-1/4" x 31-7/8"	Shelves
K	1	4" x 30-1/2"	Base front (extend as needed for two towers)
L	1	4" x 29"	Base back
M	2	4" x 13-1/2"	Base sides
N	1	2" x 30-1/2"	Upper cabinet hanging strip
1/2" shop-grade plywood			
P	6*	7-1/2" x 28-1/2"	Drawer fronts and backs (cut backs to fit)
Q	6	7-1/2" x 15-3/4"	Drawer sides
1/4" shop-grade plywood			
R	3	15-1/2" x 29"	Drawer bottoms
S	1	27" x 32"	Lower cabinet back
T	1	16" x 32"	Upper cabinet back
3/4" solid maple			
U	2	1" x 79-3/4"	Side panel edging
V	1	1" x 32"	Lower cabinet top edging
W	2	1" x 31-7/8"	Shelf edging
X	2	1/4" x 32"	Spacers
OPTIONAL LARGE DRAWER			
3/4" maple plywood			
Y	1	26-7/8" x 31-3/4"	Grooved drawer front
1/2" shop-grade plywood			
Z	2	15-3/4" x 25"	Drawer sides
AA	2	28-1/2" x 25" *	Drawer front and back (cut back to fit)
1/4" shop-grade plywood			
BB	1	15-1/2" x 29"	Drawer bottom
OPTIONAL LARGE DRAWER			
3/4" maple plywood			
CC	2	2" x 28-3/8"	Front and back
DD	2	2" x 13-1/8"	Sides
EE	2	1-1/2" x 28-1/2"	Cleats
5/8" dowels			
FF	9	13-7/8"	Dowels
OPTIONAL SHOE SHELVES			
GG	2	16" x 12"	Top and bottom shelves
HH	7	16" x 11-7/8"	Middle shelves

*Adjust size to compensate for plywood thickness

3/4" PLYWOOD

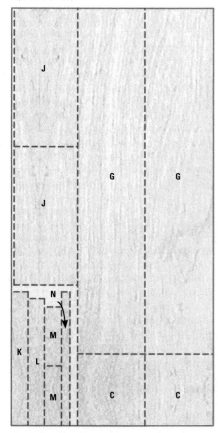

1/4" PLYWOOD

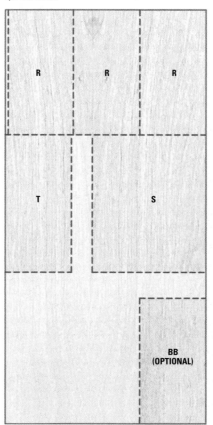

Materials List

ITEM	QTY.
4' x 8' x 3/4" maple plywood	3*
4' x 8' x 1/2" shop-grade plywood	1
4' x 8' x 1/4" shop-grade plywood	1
3/4" x 5-1/2" x 8' maple board	1
13/16" maple veneer edge banding	75 ln. ft.
16" full-extension drawer slides	3 pairs
Blum 120-degree clip-top hinges	4
Blum frameless 0mm screw-on mounting plates	4
1/4" shelf pins	12
Screws, nails, wood glue, drawer and door pulls, finishing supplies	
Optional 6" file drawer slide for supersize drawer	1
Optional hamper for supersize drawer	2

* Leftover materials can be used to make a drawer front for the supersize laundry drawer and the shoe shelves.
The Blum hardware and the file drawer slide are available at woodworking stores and online.

1/2" PLYWOOD

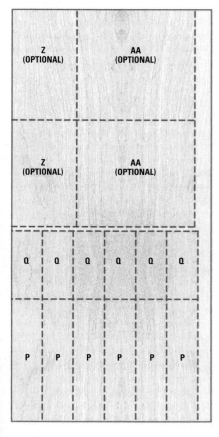

3/4" PLYWOOD

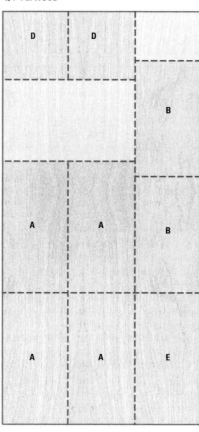

3/4" PLYWOOD

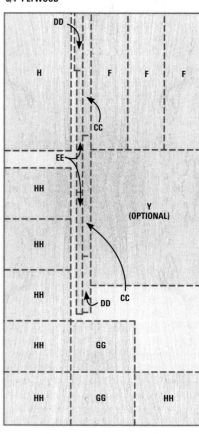

21 Hang the door. Clip the hinges to the plates to hang the doors. Don't bother to adjust the hinges until after the cabinet is mounted to the wall.

22 Drill the pin holes. We're using a store-bought jig, but you can also use a length of 1/4-in. pegboard as a template for drilling the holes. Mount a stop on your 1/4-in. drill bit to drill the holes 3/8 in. deep.

23 Glue and nail the nosing. Spread a bead of glue along the plywood edge. Align the wood edging flush to the inside edge of the panel and attach it with 1-1/4-in. nails.

Supersize Drawer

Replacing three drawers with one huge drawer allows you to hang pants or store two clothes hampers. The big drawer is just a deeper version of the small drawers. But to keep it from sagging, we mounted the drawer on file-cabinet drawer slides instead. To simulate three drawers, we grooved a single sheet of plywood by running it through the table saw with the blade raised 1/4 in., and used this for the drawer front. To convert the drawer to use for pants storage, just build the dowel rack and rest it on cleats.

Supersize Laundry Drawer

Figure C shows the parts for the deep drawer. Center the cabinet part of the file-drawer slide 4-3/4 in. from the top of the cabinet, and the drawer part 1 in. down from the top of the drawer. Finish by mounting the grooved drawer front.

Pullout Pants Rack

Use Figure C as a guide to build this rack from 2-in. strips of plywood and 5/8-in. dowels. Screw cleats to the front and back of the drawer, 2-1/4 in. from the top, to support the rack.

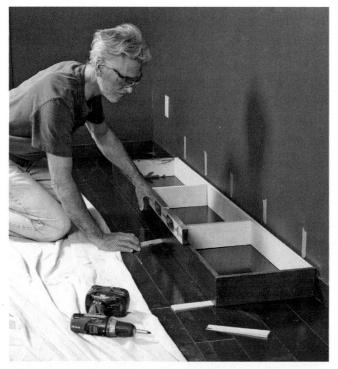

24 Level the base. Installing the towers is much easier if you start out with a level base. If your floor isn't level, slide shims under the base to level it. Then screw it to the studs. Cut off the shims and cover the gap with molding if necessary. You can make your own molding by ripping 3/8-in.-wide strips from 3/4-in. maple, or you can buy base-shoe molding.

25 Assemble the towers. Arrange the cabinets and side panels on the floor. We built simple 2x4 supports to hold the cabinets and side panels in place while we screwed them together. Drill holes through the cabinet sides a few inches from each corner. Then carefully line up the panels so the tops and bottoms are flush with the cabinets, and attach them with 1-1/4-in. screws.

26 Attach the towers to the wall. Transfer the stud locations to the inside of the cabinet and drive 2-1/2-in. screws into the studs to secure the towers. Use the 12-in.-wide shoe shelves as spacers at the top and bottom to position the second tower.

27 Finish it up by adding the tops, drawers and shelves. Tilt the top into place and attach it with 1-1/2-in. screws from inside the base cabinet. Then clip the doors onto the hinge plates and slide the drawers into the drawer slides to finish the job.

Closet Design Tips

Looking to make space in your closet, or just make it look nicer? Either way, these tips will help you create a closet that works for you.

A. HANG PANTS ABOVE SHIRTS

It may feel topsy-turvy, but hanging folded pants above shirts and coats makes everything easier to see.

B. BROWSE FOR YOUR ACCESSORIES ONLINE

Home centers will have a limited choice of accessories. Go online for a wider selection, including valet rods, pullout hampers and jewelry inserts..

C. USE SHOE SHELVES, NOT SHOE CUBBIES

It's hard to fit a pair of shoes into a narrow cubbie (especially men's shoes). Open shelf organizers allow air to circulate and also make better use of the available floor space below the long hanging section of clothes.

D. BEYOND PLAIN WHITE WIRE

Affordable ready-made storage components have come a long way throughout the years. They feature better hardware, new finishes and accessories that were once available only on high-end systems. Now your bedroom closet can look great and work like a professionally installed custom closet—at less than half the price.

E. GET EASY ACCESS TO HIDDEN SPACES

If your closet has a deep return wall (more than 24 in.), you can take advantage of that hard-to-use space by installing a hanging rod that runs the depth of the closet.

A.

B.

C.

D.

E.

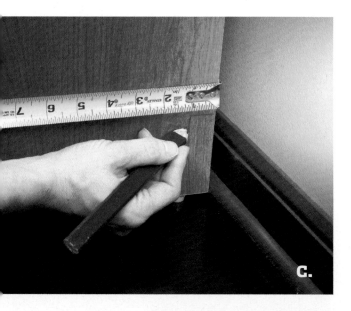

C.

D.

E.

Closet Assembly Tips

Putting together your closet is easier than you think with these tips.

A. ADD FLEXIBILITY WITH PANELS

Attach an extra tower panel to the closet side walls and cut your shelving 1/2 in. shorter to attach to the panel. The predrilled holes in the panels will allow you to easily move or add shelves and accessories to customize the closet now and in the future.

B. USE ADJUSTABLE SYSTEMS FOR FLEXIBILITY

Their movable shelf brackets make adjustable wall-mounted systems a good choice for storage areas that require frequent reorganization, such as kids' closets, pantries and the garage.

C. NOTCH THE BASE FOR A CUSTOM FIT

To achieve a "built-in" look with laminate, notch the bottom of the base tower panel sections so the tower hugs the closet wall. This will also stabilize the entire system.

D. BUY YOUR OWN DRYWALL ANCHORS

Instead of using the toggle bolts or drywall anchors included with most kits, buy your own screw-type drywall anchors (EZ Ancor is one brand) to attach shelf brackets and posts. That will give you the strongest hold.

E. PUTTY FIXES CHIPS AND SCRATCHES

If the melamine coating gets chipped or scratched, dab on spackle (for white melamine) or a matching wood putty for nearly invisible repairs. This will also fill a "whoops" drill hole in a shelf or cabinet.

Custom Clutter Buster

From anarchy to order in a weekend! (Melamine panels make it easy.)

Walk through the closet aisle at any home center and you'll see lots of closet organizers—everything from wire shelving systems to ones that look like real wood cabinetry with all kinds of fancy accessories. And while these systems are designed to work in just about any type of closet, you can get a fully custom closet organizer—and possibly even save a few bucks—by building one yourself. Here's how we built ours using melamine panels, plus some tips on building your own.

WHAT IS MELAMINE?

While real wood is strong and beautiful, building a closet organizer with it is expensive and time-consuming. Melamine products are an attractive and inexpensive alternative to wood or plywood. These boards, panels and sheets are made of particleboard with a tough, factory-applied melamine finish similar in appearance to plastic laminate. A 4 x 8-ft. melamine sheet is about half the cost of cabinet-grade plywood and available in a variety of colors. Be warned, however: Most home centers stock it only in white, which is what we used for our project.

PREDRILLED PANELS SAVE YOU TIME

At most home centers, you'll find 4 x 8-ft. melamine sheets. These full sheets are by far the most economical choice, but we bought 15-3/4-in. x 97-in. panels instead. These smaller panels come with banding on one or two edges and they are available with or without predrilled shelf pin holes.

So although we spent about three times as much as we would have on full sheets of melamine, we avoided hours of hard work drilling and edge banding—plus we eliminated the strain of transporting, lugging and cutting big, heavy sheets. Some home centers carry small melamine panels, but you might end up having to special-order them or shop online. Plan to cut 1/2 in. off each end to remove the ragged edges.

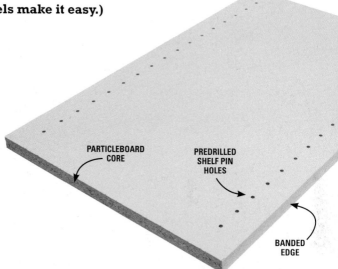

PARTICLEBOARD CORE

PREDRILLED SHELF PIN HOLES

BANDED EDGE

1 Choose your hardware first. If you're planning to install accessories similar to the ones we used for our project, be sure to buy them before you build the cabinets. Our wire baskets required a 24-in. opening, while the shoe shelf rails needed a 29-1/2-in. opening to allow for the width of the shoe shelves (with rails installed) plus the shelf pins.

WHAT IT TAKES	
TIME 1-2 days	**SKILL LEVEL** Beginner

TOOLS & MATERIALS
Circular saw, driver/drill, clamps, 6-ft. level, hacksaw, steam iron, edge-banding trimmer

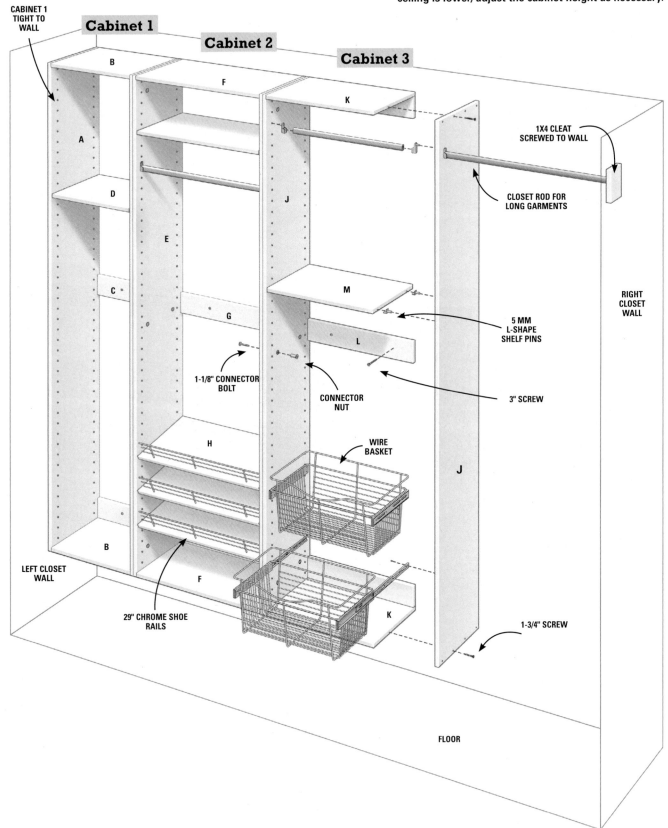

FIGURE A.

Overall dimensions: 77-1/4" wide x 96" tall x 15-3/4" deep

Our closet had a 9-ft. ceiling, so we built 8-ft. cabinets. If your ceiling is lower, adjust the cabinet height as necessary.

CABINET 1 TIGHT TO WALL

Cabinet 1

Cabinet 2

Cabinet 3

B

F

K

A

D

1X4 CLEAT SCREWED TO WALL

CLOSET ROD FOR LONG GARMENTS

J

E

C

G

M

RIGHT CLOSET WALL

5 MM L-SHAPE SHELF PINS

L

1-1/8" CONNECTOR BOLT

CONNECTOR NUT

3" SCREW

H

WIRE BASKET

J

B

F

K

LEFT CLOSET WALL

29" CHROME SHOE RAILS

1-3/4" SCREW

FLOOR

2 Prevent chip-out. You can cut melamine with a circular saw and a regular woodcutting blade, but its brittle faces are prone to chipping out. To minimize this problem, use a 60-tooth carbide-tipped blade and apply masking tape to the top side of your workpiece wherever you make a cut.

WEAR GLOVES!
Wear snug-fitting rubber-coated gloves while working with sharp-edged melamine.

3 Make perfect cuts every time. One of the challenges of using a handheld circular saw is making perfectly straight and square cuts. For our project, we used a self-squaring crosscut jig for cuts across panels, and a longer jig for cutting long, narrow pieces like the hanging strips. These jigs also help reduce chip-out. The jig shown here is just a narrow piece of 3/4-in. plywood glued on top of a wider piece of 1/4-in. plywood, and it has a squaring fence on the bottom. To see how to make similar jigs, go to familyhandyman.com and search for "saw cutting guides."

EDGE BANDING

4 Edge banding hides the ugly. The finished faces of melamine panels look great, but the raw edges don't. You might be able to build your organizer without having to apply any edge banding at all if you orient the raw edges so that they're not visible once the organizer is installed. If that's not possible, you'll need to apply iron-on edge banding, which is available at any home center. Be sure to buy an edge trimmer. For edge-banding tips, go to familyhandyman.com.

5 Drill pilot holes. We assembled each of the three cabinet boxes for our closet organizer by first drilling pilot holes with countersinks and then driving 1-3/4-in. coarse-thread screws. These screws are designed to be self-drilling, but the particleboard in melamine has a tendency to crumble and blow out. Drilling pilot holes is worth the effort.

Cutting List

KEY	QTY.	DIMENSIONS	DESCRIPTION
Cabinet 1			
A	2	15-3/4" x 96"	Sides
B	2	15-3/4" x 19-1/4"	Top and bottom
C	3	4" x 19-1/4"	Hanging strips
D	7	15-3/4" x 18-7/8"	Adjustable shelves
Cabinet 2			
E	2	15-3/4" x 96"	Sides
F	2	15-3/4" x 29-1/2"	Top and bottom
G	3	4" x 29-1/2"	Hanging strips
H	4	15-3/4" x 29-1/8"	Shoe shelves; adjustable shelves
Cabinet 3			
J	2	15-3/4" x 96"	Sides
K	2	15-3/4" x 24"	Top and bottom
L	3	4" x 24"	Hanging strips
M	3	15-3/4" x 23-5/8"	Adjustable shelves

Materials List

ITEM	QTY.
3/4" x 15-3/4" x 97" melamine panels (one banded edge with 5 mm shelf pin holes already drilled)	6
3/4" x 15-3/4" x 97" melamine panels one banded edge; no shelf pin holes)	7
Rev-A-Shelf 29" chrome Page P rails	3-pk.
Rev-A-Shelf 24" chrome wire baskets with full-extension slides	2
Rev-A-Shelf 14" valet rod	1
1-3/4" coarse-thread screws and plastic caps	102
3" No. 10 cabinet installation screws	6
1x4 ledger board	1
5 mm L-shape shelf pins	56
1-1/8" connector bolts and nuts	12
36" oval closet rod (cut to length with hacksaw)	1
24" oval closet rods (cut to length with hacksaw)	2

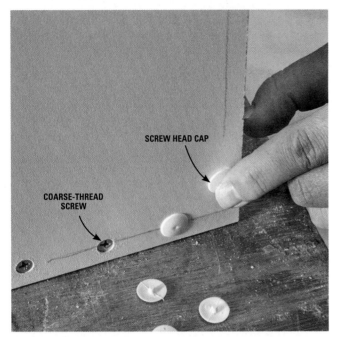

6 Hide the screw heads. The home center where we bought our melamine panels sells small bags of screws—labeled "melamine screws"—that are packaged with white plastic caps to hide the screw heads. You just press them on with a finger, then give each one a light tap with a hammer.

SCREW HEAD CAP

COARSE-THREAD SCREW

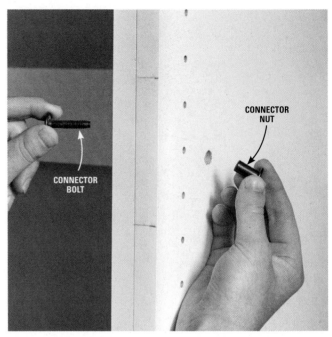

7 Connector bolts tie it all together. With the boxes screwed to the wall, drill holes and use connector bolts and nuts to join the sides of the cabinets. This will close any gaps between the boxes and stiffen up the entire assembly. Be sure the front edges of the cabinets are flush with each other before joining. If they're not, loosen the wall screws and adjust as needed.

CONNECTOR NUT

CONNECTOR BOLT

8 A ledger board makes installation easy. Once assembled, each cabinet box weighs about 100 lbs. To make hanging them easier, screw a 1x4 or 2x4—called a ledger board—to the back wall of the closet down near the floor. Make sure it's perfectly straight and level. Mark the stud locations with masking tape. Then get somebody to help you lift each box onto the ledger board, which will hold it in position until you can screw it to the wall. Drive 3-in. washer-head screws through the hanging strips of all three boxes and into the wall studs.

STUD LOCATION

1X4 LEDGER BOARD

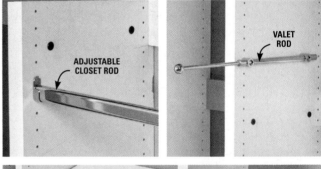
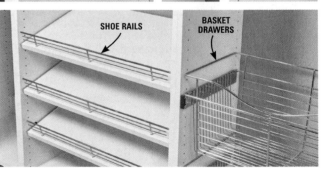

ADJUSTABLE CLOSET ROD

VALET ROD

SHOE RAILS

BASKET DRAWERS

9 Accessorize! Instead of building drawers for our closet organizer, we decided to purchase Rev-A-Shelf wire baskets with full-extension slides. This company makes lots of different closet accessories. Other companies make similar accessories. Search for "closet accessories" or "closet hardware" online and you'll find a huge variety. We also installed oval closet rods with brackets that you insert into the cabinets' shelf-pin holes, which makes for super easy height adjustments.

Handsome Closet Organizer

Save your overstuffed closet by building this storage system.

Is your closet too small and overstuffed? Do your cluttered shelves, packed and sagging clothes rods and jumbled shoes all cry out for more space? Of course, the coolest solution would be to expand the existing closet, but that's usually impossible. Instead, you can organize your existing closet with this attractive system, to make every cubic inch count and get more dresser space to boot.

It's surprisingly easy and economical to squeeze more storage out of limited space. You'll learn how to remodel a standard 8-ft.-long, 30-in.-deep closet, a size that's found in millions of homes. Here's what you can do to maximize your closet's storage.

Cabinet module: The 2-ft.-wide, 23-in.-deep, 78-in.- tall cabinet module is designed to provide extra drawer and shelving space. The unit is mounted 6 in. above the floor for easy cleaning. The mounting height also

WHAT IT TAKES	
TIME 2 weekends	**SKILL LEVEL** Intermediate

TOOLS & MATERIALS
Circular saw with cutting guide, driver/drill, clamps, brad nailer, steam iron, edge-banding trimmer

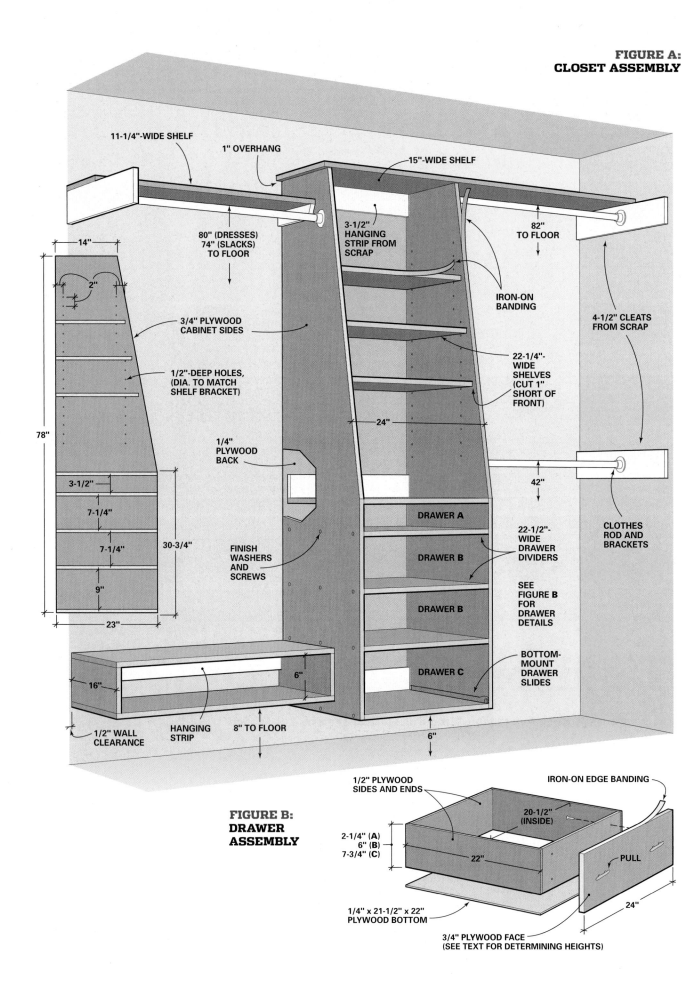

FIGURE A:
CLOSET ASSEMBLY

11-1/4"-WIDE SHELF

1" OVERHANG

15"-WIDE SHELF

3-1/2" HANGING STRIP FROM SCRAP

82" TO FLOOR

80" (DRESSES)
74" (SLACKS)
TO FLOOR

IRON-ON BANDING

4-1/2" CLEATS FROM SCRAP

14"

2"

3/4" PLYWOOD CABINET SIDES

1/2"-DEEP HOLES, (DIA. TO MATCH SHELF BRACKET)

22-1/4"- WIDE SHELVES (CUT 1" SHORT OF FRONT)

78"

1/4" PLYWOOD BACK

24"

3-1/2"

7-1/4"

7-1/4"

30-3/4"

42"

9"

FINISH WASHERS AND SCREWS

DRAWER A

CLOTHES ROD AND BRACKETS

DRAWER B

22-1/2"- WIDE DRAWER DIVIDERS

23"

DRAWER B

SEE FIGURE B FOR DRAWER DETAILS

6"

16"

DRAWER C

BOTTOM- MOUNT DRAWER SLIDES

1/2" WALL CLEARANCE

HANGING STRIP

8" TO FLOOR

6"

FIGURE B:
DRAWER ASSEMBLY

1/2" PLYWOOD SIDES AND ENDS

IRON-ON EDGE BANDING

20-1/2" (INSIDE)

2-1/4" (A)
6" (B)
7-3/4" (C)

22"

PULL

1/4" x 21-1/2" x 22" PLYWOOD BOTTOM

24"

3/4" PLYWOOD FACE (SEE TEXT FOR DETERMINING HEIGHTS)

makes installation easier because you don't have to fool with removing and reinstalling carpeting or baseboards.

Clothes rods: Rod capacity is maximized because the rods are double-stacked at one end of the closet for shorter clothes like shirts and skirts. The single rod at the other end of the closet is for slacks and dresses.

Shoe shelves: To tame shoe scatter, we've designed a two-tier shoe shelf. Including the space under the shelves, you'll have nine luxurious feet of shoe storage—enough for even those beat-up, knockabout shoes you can't bear to throw out.

CUSTOM-BUILD YOUR OWN CLOSET SYSTEM

It's easy to upgrade the typical single rod and shelf found in standard closets for more efficient "closetry." Home centers offer several lines of mix-and-match closet cabinets and organizers so you can design and install a custom closet system. Those systems look inexpensive—until you start adding up all the parts! A similar-size melamine cabinet module alone can cost hundreds of dollars. There is a more handsome, lower-cost alternative: Custom-build your own. For those same hundreds of dollars, you'll have a closet full of cabinetry that's so doggone good-looking that you'll want to leave the closet doors open.

This project doesn't call for any fancy woodworking joints. All the parts are end-cut and simply screwed together. While that makes for easy construction, it means you'll have to use

1 Cut the sides to length and width using a ripping jig. Rip the drawer dividers to width only. Cut the angles on the front edge of each cabinet side.

PRO TIP

When to Edge-band

You'll save a lot of time simply by edge-banding all the parts after ripping them to width and before cutting them to length. Then you won't have so many individual parts to edge-band, or those pesky short drawer front ends to deal with. Pay attention to the simple clamping tip using a shelf bracket shown in Photo 2.

Materials List

ITEM	QTY.
3/4" plywood	3 sheets
1/2" plywood (buy a 4x4 sheet if it's available)	1 sheet
1/4" plywood	1 sheet
Iron-on edge banding	3 rolls
Construction adhesive	1 tube
Woodworking glue	
8' chrome closet rods	1
6' chrome closet rods	1
Closet rod end brackets	3 sets
No. 8 finish washers	50
No. 8 2" oval head screws	40
No. 8 3" oval head screws	12
22" bottom-mount drawer slides	4 sets
Drawer pulls	4 (or 8)
Shelf brackets	12

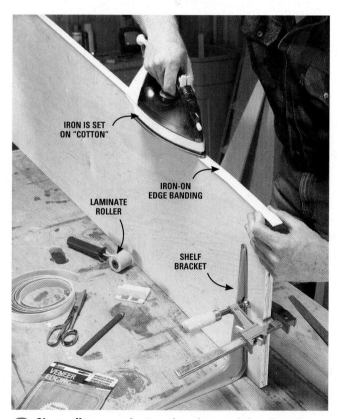

2 Clean off any sawdust on the edges and then iron the edge banding onto the outside edges of the sides and the two lengths of drawer-divider stock.

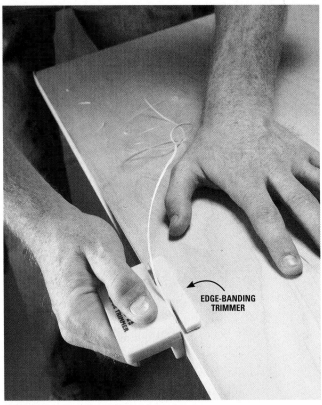

3 Trim the overhanging edges of the edge banding with a trimming tool, then file and sand the edges smooth and flush with the edge.

EDGE-BANDING TRIMMER

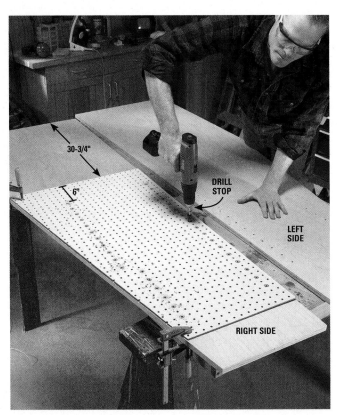

4 Mark the shelf bracket-hole locations on pegboard and use it as a drilling template. Flip the pegboard to drill the other side.

30-3/4"

6"

DRILL STOP

LEFT SIDE

RIGHT SIDE

5 Cut the five edge-banded drawer dividers to length with the crosscutting jig, four from one length and one from the other.

5TH DRAWER DIVIDER

EDGE-BAND ONE EDGE

22-1/2"

DRAWER DIVIDERS

CROSSCUT JIG

6 Screw a scrap to the top of the cabinet, spacing the sides 22-1/2 in. apart; clamp the bottom drawer divider between the sides. Predrill and fasten.

SCRAP

22-1/2"

BOTTOM DRAWER DIVIDER

plywood-core, veneered plywood because it'll hold screws and has a smooth, even surface ready for finishing. If you want to use particleboard-core sheets, plan on joining parts with biscuits, dowels or any other fastening system that is familiar to you. Birch plywood was used here to match the bedroom's existing woodwork. All of the materials shown are found at any well-stocked home center.

As for tools, you don't need much aside from a good circular saw, a screw gun, a carpenter's square and two 30-in. bar clamps. You'll also have to blow the dust off the clothes iron and use it to apply the edge banding **(Photo 2)**. There are a few other optional tools you'll find useful. While it is possible to hand-nail the parts together, a brad nailer **(Photo 8)** will speed up construction. (Since you can buy a brad nailer for less than $100, this project is a good excuse to add it to your tool collection.) Also pick up an edge-banding trimmer for quick, accurate edge trimming **(Photo 3)**.

BUILDING THE CABINET BOX

Start the project by cutting the cabinet box sides and five 22-1/2-in.-wide lengths for the drawer dividers; see **Photos 1 and 5**. Consult **Figure A**, Page 150, for all of the cutting dimensions. Before you cut the drawer dividers to length, edge-band one edge. That way the exposed edges will be finished before they're cut to length.

7 Stand the cabinet upright and rip spacer blocks from scrap to space and support the other drawer dividers as you screw them into place.

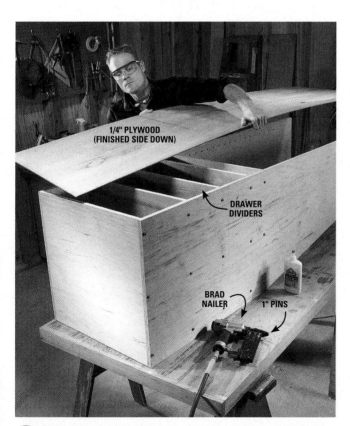

8 Glue and pin the cabinet back to the sides and dividers to square the cabinet. Then glue and pin the hanging strips to the back and sides.

9 Glue and pin the drawer sides together with 1-in. brads. Before the glue sets, square each drawer by gluing and pinning the bottom in place.

10 Screw the drawer slides into the cabinet and bottom edges of the drawer boxes. Slide each drawer into place to check the fit.

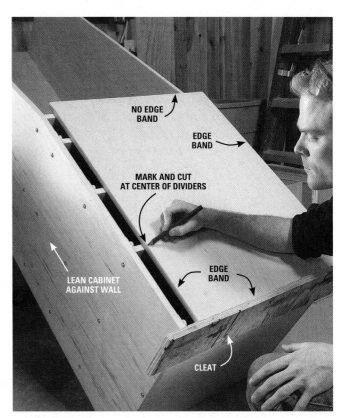

11 Set the drawer front panel (edge-banded on three sides) on a cleat screwed to the cabinet bottom. Mark and cut lowest drawer front. Edge-band raw edges.

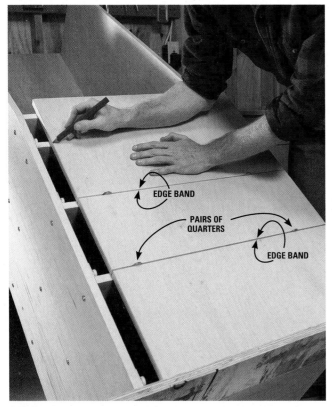

12 Space each panel two coin (quarters) thicknesses apart, then measure and cut the next. Edge-band the two raw edges that meet, then repeat the procedure.

13 Place crumpled newspaper behind each drawer and replace the drawers. They should stick out about 1/2 in. beyond the cabinet front.

Before you assemble the cabinet, drill the holes for the adjustable shelving. The old trick of using a pegboard jig for consistent hole spacing is used here **(Photo 4)**. Because the sides taper, you'll have to shift over a row or two of holes to keep the narrower top shelf brackets within a few inches of the front. Try to keep the front and rear holes about 2 in. from the edge. Buy a drill bit that matches the shaft on the shelving brackets that you chose. It's best to use a brad point drill bit to prevent splintering the veneer. Either use a depth stop or mark the drill bit with a piece of tape to keep from drilling through the plywood.

Begin assembling the cabinet on its back by attaching a spacer strip at the top, then screwing the bottom drawer divider into place **(Photo 6)**. Predrill with a 1/8-in. bit and drive 2-in.-long No. 8 oval-head screws with finish washers. Stand the cabinet; using spacer blocks ripped from scraps, position and hold drawer dividers in place while you screw them to the sides. Keeping dividers tight to the spacers as you screw them in place is vital for the drawers to work properly.

EDGE-BANDING BASICS

If you've never used iron-on edge banding, it'll only take a couple of attempts to achieve proficiency. Don't worry if you make a mistake; run the iron over it and the heat-sensitive glue will release so you can adjust the piece. Using sharp scissors, cut

14 Apply four beads of construction adhesive to the drawer boxes and restack the drawer fronts, spacing them with a pair of quarters.

15 Lay a board across each edge of the fronts and clamp overnight. Then drive four 1-in. screws through each box into the fronts.

16 Set cabinet on blocks and center it in the closet. Plumb it, shimming as needed, and drill 1/8-in. pilot holes through the cleats into studs or drywall.

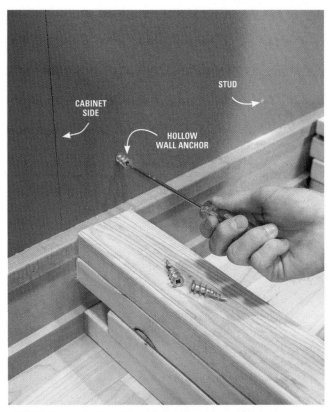

17 Remove the cabinet and screw drywall anchors into the holes without stud backing. Reposition the cabinet and screw it to the wall.

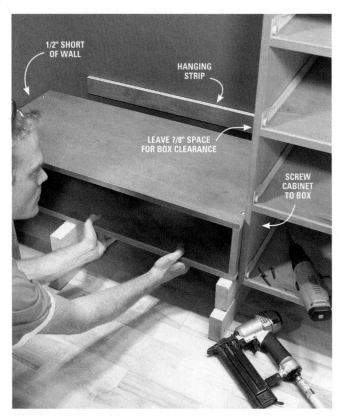

18 Build the shoebox about 1/2 in. short of the wall. Screw a cleat to the wall, then screw the box to the cabinet and nail it to the cleat.

19 Screw the closet rod brackets to the cleats and the cabinet, then install the clothes rods. Cut the top shelves and fasten them to cleats (Figure A).

20 Add the drawer pulls and adjustable shelves, then fill it up. Still not enough space? Donate whatever doesn't fit to charity.

each strip of banding about 1 in. longer than you need. Leave 1/2 in. or more of banding overhanging the starting corner because it tends to creep when you iron it. Move the iron (set on "cotton") along at about 1 in. per second all the way to the other end, guiding it with your other hand as you go. As you guide it, make sure the banding edges hang over each side of the plywood. Before it cools, push a block or roller over it to embed the banding. Then let the edge banding cool for about 30 seconds or so and check for voids. Re-iron and embed any loose spots.

Cut the ends as close to the plywood as possible with the scissors and then run the edge-band trimmer down both sides to trim off the overhang. You'll have to make multiple passes to get all of the spots flush. The trimmer works best if you trim with the grain. Sometimes that means reversing direction in the middle of trimming. Use a file held at a 45-degree angle to remove oozed-out glue and banding that's still sticking out, then sand all the joints smooth with a sanding block and 100-grit paper.

DRAWER CONSTRUCTION

Building drawers isn't all that hard. The key is to build the cabinet and the drawer boxes square. If you're using drawer slides other than the ones called for, make sure to read the directions before building the drawers. They'll tell you the necessary height and side-to-side clearances.

Building a square drawer is easy if you pin together the sides and then square them up with the plywood bottom **(Photo 9)**. Accurate side-to-side dimensions are crucial **(Figure B**, Page 150). You can shim out the drawer slides if the drawers are narrow, but if they're too wide, rebuild them.

Now is a good time to finish ripping and edge-banding your adjustable and fixed shelves. Don't cut them to final width until the cabinet is mounted so you can measure and cut exact widths to fit their selected positions. Stain and finish everything at the same time, prior to installation. We used an oil-based honey maple stain and a topcoat of two coats of satin polyurethane.

MAKING IT FIT IN YOUR CLOSET

The cabinet unit is 78 in. tall, so it will fit in any closet with 8-ft. walls, even with the 6-in. gap at the floor. Alter the height if you have a lower ceiling.

You'll have to set the cabinet aside before mounting it to install drywall anchors unless you're lucky enough to have the cabinet fall in front of two studs. Position the cabinet in the closet, then plumb and mark the wall **(Photo 17)** so the pilot holes line up with the anchors after you reset it. Then measure to the wall to determine the final length for the top shelf—don't forget to add 1 in. for the left-side overhang. Place the cleats and shelves anywhere you wish.

Making It Fit Your Space

Build the cabinet taller, wider or with more drawers. Drawer sizes can be easily altered, too—make deeper ones for sweaters or shallower ones for socks. The how-to steps shown here will work for whatever configuration best suits your needs.

Triple Your Closet Space!

All it takes is a little elbow grease to expand your storage space and eliminate closet clutter.

If you have to dig through a mountain of clothes to find your favorite sweatshirt, it's definitely time to take on that messy closet. This simple-to-build system organizes your closet with shelf, drawer and hanging space for your clothes, shoes and accessories. Going to a store and buying a closet system like this would cost you at least $500—you can build this one for less than that.

This system is really just four plywood boxes outfitted with shelf standards, closet rods or drawers. Here it is built for an 8-ft.-wide closet with an 8-ft. ceiling, but it'll work in any reach-in closet that's at least 6 ft. wide if you adjust the shelf width between the boxes or change the box dimensions.

TIME, MONEY AND MATERIALS

You can complete this project in a weekend. Spend Saturday cutting the lumber, ironing on the edge banding and applying the finish. Use your Saturday date night to clean everything out of the closet. That leaves you Sunday to build and install the new system.

This entire system was built with birch plywood. The cost, including the hardware for the drawers, shelves and closet rods, was around $300 (see Materials List). You could use MDF or oak plywood instead of birch. Everything you need for this project is available at home centers.

WHAT IT TAKES	
TIME 1 weekend	**SKILL LEVEL** Beginner

TOOLS & MATERIALS
Circular saw, driver/drill, jigsaw, steam iron, edge-banding trimmer, clamps, framing square

1 Finish now, save time later. Prefinishing gives you a faster, neater finish because you'll have fewer corners to mess with. Apply two coats of polyurethane quickly and smoothly with a disposable paint pad.

PAINT PAD

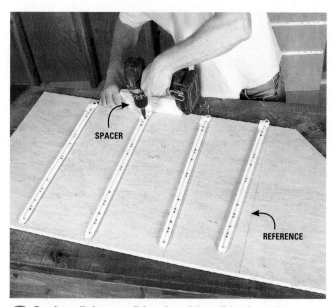

SPACER

REFERENCE

2 Pre-install drawer slides. Attaching slides is easier before the boxes are assembled. Position the slides using reference lines and a spacer. Remember that there are left- and right-hand slides, usually marked "CL" and "CR."

FIGURE A.
CLOSET STORAGE SYSTEM

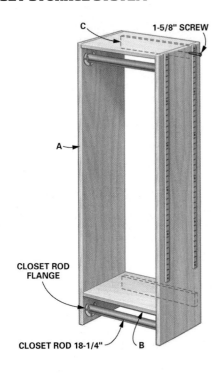

1-5/8" SCREW

C

A

CLOSET ROD FLANGE

CLOSET ROD 18-1/4"   B

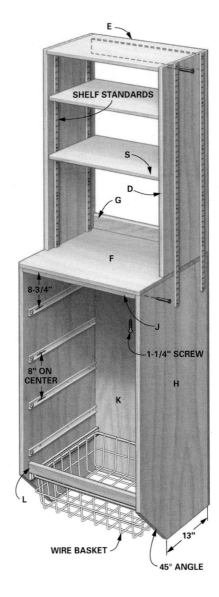

E

SHELF STANDARDS

S

D

G

F

8-3/4"

J

8" ON CENTER

1-1/4" SCREW

K

H

L

WIRE BASKET

13"

45° ANGLE

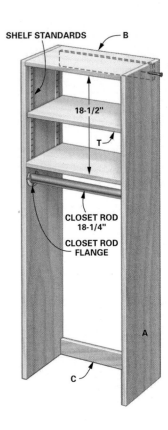

SHELF STANDARDS   B

18-1/2"

T

CLOSET ROD 18-1/4"

CLOSET ROD FLANGE

A

C

FIGURE B.
DRAWER CONSTRUCTION

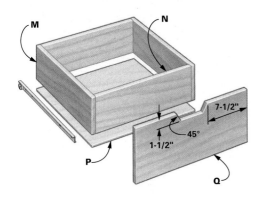

M

N

7-1/2"

45°

1-1/2"

P

Q

Cutting List

KEY	QTY.	DIMENSIONS	DESCRIPTION
A	4	3/4" x 11-7/8" x 52"	corner box sides
B	4	3/4" x 11-7/8" x 18-1/2"	corner box tops and bottom
C	4	3/4" x 2-1/2" x 18-1/2"	corner box screw strips
D	2	3/4" x 13-7/8" x 34"	shelf unit sides
E	1	3/4" x 13-7/8" x 22-1/2"	shelf unit top
F	1	3/4" x 21" x 24"	shelf unit bottom
G	2	3/4" x 2-1/2" x 22-1/2"	shelf unit screw strips
H	1	3/4" x 20-3/4" x 44"	drawer unit sides
J	1	3/4" x 20-3/4" x 22-1/2"	drawer unit top
K	1	1/4" x 24" x 44"	drawer unit back
L	1	3/4" x 2" x 22-1/2"	drawer unit cleat
M	8	1/2" x 6" x 20"	drawer sides
N	8	1/2" x 6" x 20-1/2"	drawer fronts and backs
P	4	1/4" x 20" x 21-1/2"	drawer bottoms
Q	4	3/4" x 8" x 22-1/4"	drawer face
R	8	3/4" x 11-7/8"	adjustable shelves, cut to length (not shown)
S	2	3/4" x 13-7/8" x 22"	adjustable shelves for shelf unit
T	1	3/4" x 11-7/8" x 18"	right corner box adjustable shelf
U	1	3/4" x 14-1/4" x 96"	top shelf (not shown)

Materials List

ITEM	QTY.
4' x 8' x 3/4" plywood	3
4' x 8' x 1/2" plywood	1
4' x 8' x 1/4" plywood	1
8' closet rod	1
Edge banding (iron-on veneer)	2 pkgs.
20" drawer slides	4 prs.
6' shelf standards	10
Closet rod flanges	10
Wire basket	1
2-1/2" screws	1 box
1-5/8" trim screws	1 box
1-1/4" screws	1 box
1" screws	1 box
Wipe-on poly	1 pint

CUT AND PREFINISH THE PARTS

Start by cutting all the parts to size following **Figure C** on Page 162 and the Cutting List on Page 160. The corner box sides are slightly narrower than 12 in., so you can cut off dings and dents and still cut four sides from a sheet of plywood.

You won't be able to cut the shelves that fit between the boxes to length until the boxes are installed (the shelves need to be cut to fit), but you can rip plywood to 11-7/8 in. and cut the shelves to length later.

Once the parts are cut, apply edge banding (iron-on veneer) to all the edges that will be exposed after the boxes are assembled **(Figure A)**. Build a jig to hold the parts upright. Place a part in the jig. Then cut the edge banding so it overhangs each end of the plywood by 1/2 in. Run an iron (on the cotton setting) slowly over the edge banding. Then press a scrap piece of wood over the edge banding to make sure it's fully adhered. Trim the edges with a veneer edge trimmer. Visit familyhandyman.com and search "edge banding" for instructions.

Lightly sand the wood and your closet rod with 120-grit sandpaper. Wipe away the dust with a tack cloth, then use a paint pad to apply a coat of polyurethane on everything except the drawer parts **(Photo 1)**. This inexpensive pad will let you finish each part in about 20 seconds. Let the finish dry, then apply a second coat.

ATTACH THE HARDWARE

It's easier to install the drawer slides and the shelf standards that go inside the boxes before you assemble the boxes. Use a framing square to draw reference lines on the drawer unit sides for your drawer slides (see **Figure A**). The slides are spaced 8 in. apart, centered 8-3/4 in. down from the top of the box. Keep the slides 3/4 in. from the front edge (this is where the drawer faces will go). Use a 7/64-in. self-centering drill bit to drill pilot holes and screw the slides into place **(Photo 2)**.

You'll need the wire basket now (they are available at home centers). Attach the glides for the basket 3 in. below the drawer slides. If your basket is narrower than 22-1/2 in., screw a cleat to the box side so the basket will fit. Now attach the shelf standards. You can cut them with a hacksaw, but an easier way is to use a metal blade in a jigsaw. Place two or more standards together so the numbers are oriented the same way and the standards are aligned at the ends. Tape the standards together where you're going to make the cut, then gang-cut them with a jigsaw **(Photo 3)**.

Screw the standards to the inside of the box sides, 1 in. from the edges. Keep the standards 3/4 in. from the top (that's where the box tops go). Be sure the numbers on the standards are facing the same way when you install them —this ensures the shelves will be level.

3 Gang-cut the standards. Cutting 16 standards one by one with a hacksaw would take hours. Instead, bundle two or more together with tape; cut them with a jigsaw.

SHELF STANDARDS

METAL BLADE

4 Nail first, then screw. Nail boxes together first to hold the parts in position. Then add screws for strength.

FIGURE C.
CLOSET SYSTEM CUTTING DIAGRAMS

This shows only the 3/4-in. plywood.

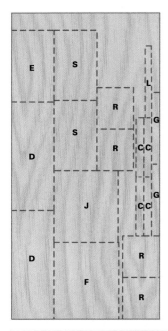
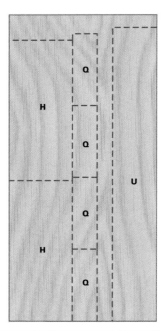

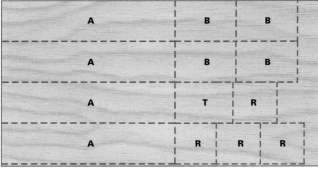

5 Square the drawer boxes. If the boxes aren't square, the drawers won't fit right or glide smoothly. Drawers take a beating; assemble them with nails and glue.

ASSEMBLE THE BOXES

Use a brad nailer to tack the boxes together following **Figure A** and **Photo 4**. If you don't have a brad nailer, use clamps. Then screw the boxes together. Use 1-5/8-in. trim screws because the screw heads are small and unobtrusive (you can leave the screw heads exposed). Here are some tips for assembling the boxes:

- Attach the screw strips to the box tops first, then add one side, then the bottom shelf, and then the second side.
- Drill 1/8-in. pilot holes to prevent splitting. Stay 1 in. from edges.
- If your cuts are slightly off and the top, bottom and sides aren't exactly the same width, align the front edges.
- The boxes will be slightly wobbly until they're installed in the closet, so handle them with care.
- The middle bottom box has a back. Square the box with the back, then glue and tack the back in place.
- After the corner boxes are assembled, screw shelf standards to the side that doesn't abut the wall (it's easier to install the standards before the boxes are installed).

6 Center the drawer faces perfectly. Stick the faces to the boxes with double-sided tape. Then pull out the drawer and drive screws from inside the box.

STUD LOCATION

LEVEL LINE

7 Plumb the shelf boxes. The corners of your closet may not be plumb, so check the box with a level before screwing it to the studs. Mark stud locations with masking tape.

8 Install the center unit in two parts. The center unit is clumsy, so install the shelf unit first, then prop up the drawer unit with spacers and screw it to the shelf.

BUILD THE DRAWERS

Cut the drawer sides and bottoms (see Cutting List, Page 160). Assemble the sides with glue and 1-in. screws. To square the drawers, set adjacent sides against a framing square that's clamped to your work surface. Glue and tack the drawer bottom into place **(Photo 5)**. Then set the drawer slides on the drawers, drill pilot holes and screw the slides into place.

Install the drawers in the box. Getting the drawer faces in their perfect position is tricky business. If the faces are even slightly off-center, the drawer won't close properly. To align them, place double-sided tape over the drawer front. Starting with the top drawer, center the drawer face in the opening **(Photo 6)**. You should have about a 1/8-in. gap on both sides and the top. Press the face into the tape. Take out the drawer and clamp the face to the drawer to keep it stationary. Drive two 1-in. screws through the inside of the drawer into the face.

HANG THE BOXES IN THE CLOSET

Now install the boxes. Start by drawing a level line in the closet, 11 in. down from the ceiling. This will give you just over 10 in. of storage space above the closet system after the top shelf is installed. Then mark the stud locations on the wall with tape.

Your closet walls are probably not plumb. So you can't just place a box in a corner without checking for alignment. Hanging the boxes is a two-person job, so get a helper. Start with the corner boxes. Align the top of the box with your level line on the wall. Have your helper plumb the box with a level while you drive 2-1/2-in. screws through the screw strip into the wall at the stud locations **(Photo 7)**. Attach the other corner box the same way.

Find the center of the wall, then make a mark 12 in. on one side of the center mark. That's where your shelf unit will go. Again, have your helper plumb the box while you align it with your marks and screw it to the wall.

Prop up the drawer unit on spacers so it's tight against the shelf unit. Align the edges, then clamp the boxes and screw them together **(Photo 8)**. Drive screws through the screw strip into the wall.

Then place the top shelf over the boxes. This shelf barely fit into place. If yours won't fit, you'll have to cut it and install it as two pieces. Make the cut near one end, over a corner box, so it's not noticeable. Screw the shelf to the box tops with 1-1/4-in. screws.

Then attach shelf standards along the sides of the shelf and drawer units **(Figure A)**. Cut the adjustable shelves to length to fit between the corner boxes and the middle boxes. Finally, screw the closet rod flanges into place, cut the closet rod to size and install the rods.

Cutting List

KEY	QTY.	DIMENSIONS	DESCRIPTION
A	1	42" x 30-1/2"	top
B	2	42" x 6"	front and back
C	4	33" x 6"	sides
D	1	42" x 4"	fixed top
E	1	37" x 33"	base
F	2	33" x 3/4" x 3/4"	side nailers
G	3	35-1/2" x 3/4" x 3/4"	front and back nailers
H	4	4-3/4" x 3/4" x 3/4"	corner nailers
J	2	33" x 1-1/2"	filler strips
K	4	3-5/8" x 1-1/2" x 5-1/2"	caster supports

Note: All 1/2" plywood

WHAT IT TAKES	
TIME 1 day	**SKILL LEVEL** Beginner

TOOLS & MATERIALS
Circular saw (or table saw), driver/drill

Under-Bed Rollout Drawer

Take advantage of some of the most abundant —and underutilized—space in the house.

Some of the most useful and rarely used storage space in your home is right under the bed, and you can take advantage of it with this durable rollout drawer4 made from a single sheet of plywood. Plastic versions are also available, but wood looks better, lasts longer and lets you custom-size your rollout.

Measure the distance between the floor and the bottom of the bed. Subtract 1/2 in. for clearance under the bed and 1/2 in. (on bare wood) to 1 in. (on thick carpet) for casters. Subtract another 1/2 in. for the hinged top to arrive at the maximum height for the storage box sides.

Mark all the pieces on a sheet of plywood and cut them with a table saw or a circular saw. Fasten 3/4-in. square nailers to the edges of the base with glue and finish nails or screws (1/2-in. plywood is too thin to nail into on edge). Attach the sides to the base, adding square nailers at the corners. Fasten the caster supports to the sides, then nail the outer side pieces to the caster supports.

Attach the front and back. Add the filler strips on top of the caster supports and the last nailer along the top edge of the back. Finally, nail on the fixed top, set the hinged top against it and screw on the hinges. Attach the hinges using 1/2-in. screws so the screws don't stick through the top.

FIGURE A.
ROLLOUT CONSTRUCTION

Overall dimensions:
7" H x 42" W x 34-1/2" D

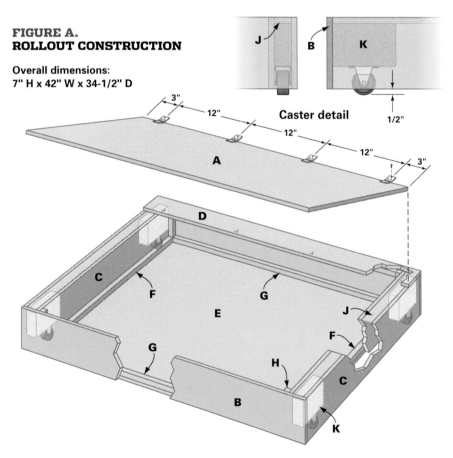

Materials List

ITEM	QTY.
AC-grade 4' x 8' x 1/2" plywood	1
3' x 3/4" x 3/4" square dowels	6
2x6 x 2' pine	1
2" fixed caster wheels	4
1-1/2" hinges	4
1" and 1-1/2" brad nails	

Note: All materials and dimensions listed are for a 7-1/2-in.-tall under-bed space. If you have more or less space, adjust these measurements.

Clutter-Free Laundry Room

These fast and easy projects create a pleasant, efficient work area.

A. PAPER TOWEL HOLDER

In a cramped laundry area, paper towels always fall into the sink. Solve the problem by slipping a bungee cord through the roll and hanging it from wire shelving. Works great!

B. INSTANT LAUNDRY ROOM CUBBIES

If you have a small laundry room without cabinets or shelves, buy a few inexpensive plastic crates at a discount store and create your own wall of cubbies. Just screw them to the wall studs using a fender washer in the upper corner of each crate for extra strength. The crates hold a lot of supplies, and they keep tippy things like irons from falling over.

C. SPONGE HOLDER

Wet sponges never dry properly, and they become moldy and smelly. To give your nose a break, screw a sieve to the back of the sink to hold the sponges. They dry nicely, they're out of the way, and they last forever.

D. SUPER SIMPLE SHELF

Make laundry day easier with this nifty shelf for all of your detergents, stain removers and other supplies. Build this simple organizer from 1x10 and 1x3 boards. If you have a basement laundry room, you may need to cut an access through the shelves for your dryer exhaust.

E. SKINNY LAUNDRY ROOM CART

To take advantage of oft-wasted space between or next to the washing machine and dryer (and stop socks from falling into it), build a simple plywood cart on fixed casters to hold detergents and other laundry supplies.

F. UTILITY SINK SHELF

To make paint cleanup easier, cut a section of leftover wire shelving and set it over the front of your utility sink. It's the perfect place to dry sponges, foam brushes and roller covers. Hang the paintbrushes from S-hooks so they can drip into the sink. When you're done with the shelf, hang it over the side of the tub so it's ready for your next painting project.

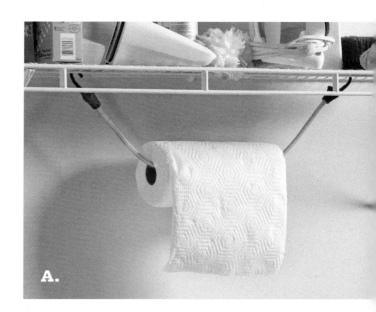

A.

B.

C.

D.

1x10 SHELF

1-5/8" SCREW WITH FINISH WASHER

1x3 MOUNTING STRIP SCREWED TO WALL

1x10 SIDE

E.

F.

Fold-Away Folding Table

There is no need to find a place to put a folding table—with this project, you can build one that's easy to store. Best of all, it's done in less than a day.

This 2 x 5-ft. table is a handy option for any laundry room. Located right across from the washer and dryer, it's the perfect place for sorting colors before washing, and folding the clothes as soon as they're dry. This project uses heavy-duty brackets that will hold more than 100 lbs. and neatly fold the top down (preventing future clutter).

Buy the countertop (and end cap) at a home center or salvage one from a friend who's getting new countertops. Also buy three 8-ft. pine boards—a 1x2, a 1x3 and a 1x4—as well as some wood screws. Buy 1-1/4-in. and 2-1/2-in. wood screws for mounting the wall cleats and the countertop stiffeners. Follow **Photos 1–6** for clear step-by-step instructions.

WHAT IT TAKES

TIME	SKILL LEVEL
Half a day	Beginner

TOOLS & MATERIALS
Circular saw, driver/drill, aviator snips, steam iron, wood glue

1 Buy a 6-ft. plastic laminate countertop blank from a home center. Measure in 1-1/2 in. from the back side, and draw a straight line. Cut this section away with a circular saw equipped with a sharp blade. Trim the countertop to length, cutting from the back side. Longer tables will sag without an additional bracket. Space the brackets no farther than 32 in. apart.

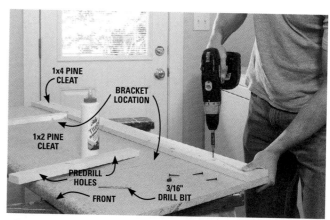

2 Glue and screw 3/4-in.-thick pine supports to the underside of the countertop. Use a 1x4 along the back and 1x2s at the bracket sites. The supports will stiffen the countertop and give better backing to the bracket screws.

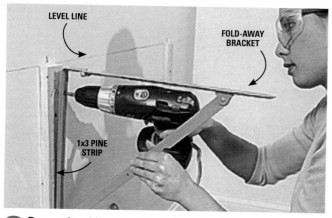

3 Draw a level line 1-1/2 in. below the finished height of the laundry table. This one is 33 in. high including the thickness of the top. Screw 1x3 pine strips to the wall into the studs behind. For concrete walls, predrill holes for anchors and then screw the steel laundry table brackets to the strips and wall with 2-1/2-in. screws.

4 Set the top onto the brackets and screw them into the pine supports (use 1-1/4-in. screws) under the table. Remember to keep about 1/8-in. clearance between the wall and the end for wiggle room when you lift and close the table. This will keep the wall from scarring each time the tabletop is lifted and closed.

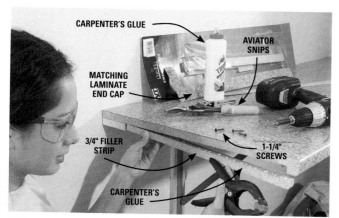

5 Glue and screw the 3/4-in.-thick filler strips to the exposed bottom edge of the counter. Align the filler strip so it's flush with the edge of the top.

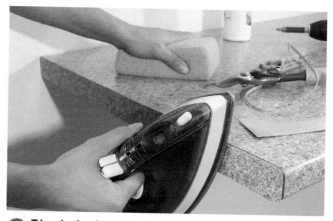

6 Trim the laminate end cap with aviation snips to fit the size of the end panel. Set the iron on medium heat and slide it across the whole end panel until the glue bonds. Ease any sharp edges with a smooth-cutting metal file.

Laundry Room Wall Cabinet

Here's how to make the most of the unused space above your washer and dryer.

Turn that wall space above the washer and dryer into a valuable dust-free storage space by adding a utility wall cabinet. This project shows a 54-in.-wide, 24-in.-high and 12-in.-deep cabinet that's available at home centers. It's prefinished inside and out, so it'll be easy to clean.

Chances are, a dryer vent or some other obstruction exists right where you'll want to put the new cabinet. To solve this problem, simply cut away the back and insert a 4-in. galvanized duct as a liner to give the cabinet a 1-in. clearance from the dryer vent, preventing heat from building up inside the cabinet. With the liner, the vent is isolated behind the cabinet, keeping everything inside cool and clean. Follow the step-by-step how-to in **Photos 1–5**.

WHAT IT TAKES	
TIME Half a day	**SKILL LEVEL** Beginner

TOOLS & MATERIALS
Circular saw, jigsaw, driver/drill, needle-nose pliers, framing square, step ladder

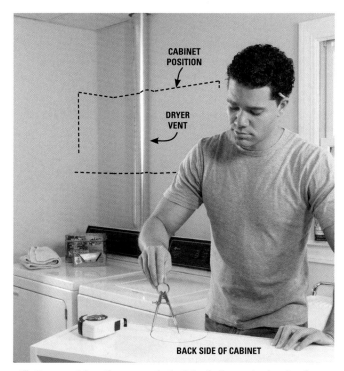

1 Draw a 6-in.-diameter circle 2 in. in from the back edge of the cabinet to correspond with the location of the dryer vent. Flip the cabinet upside down and draw the same circle to correspond with the top.

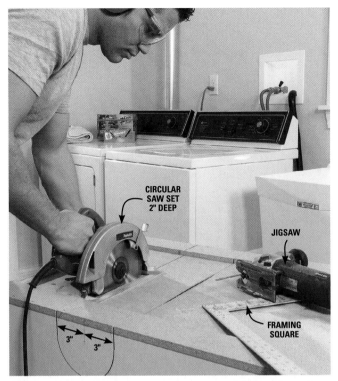

2 Cut slots 6 in. apart on the back side of the cabinet that align with the edges of the semicircles. Set the circular saw for a 2-in. depth of cut. Once the back is cut, then use a jigsaw to cut along the circles at the top and bottom of the cabinet.

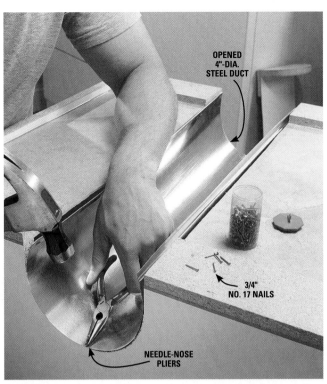

3 Nail a 4-in. steel duct pipe to the cabinet to act as a heat shield for the dryer vent. Use 3/4-in.-long, No. 17 wire nails. This shield will prevent heat buildup inside the cabinet and allow the contents of the cabinet to stay cool.

4 Level and screw a temporary 1x4 cleat to the wall studs with 2-1/2-in. drywall screws. The cabinet will rest on the cleat and a partner will be able to slide the cabinet left or right to align it. Once the cabinet is in place, screw it to the studs with the cabinet screws provided.

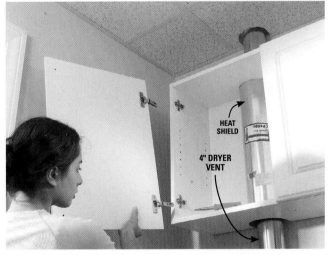

5 Reattach the cabinet doors and drill holes for the door pulls. Cut the shelves for the cabinet with a jigsaw to fit around the new heat shield.

PRO TIP

No Painting Required

Buy an easy-to-clean melamine wall cabinet from a local home center—you won't have to paint it, and it'll likely cost around $100.

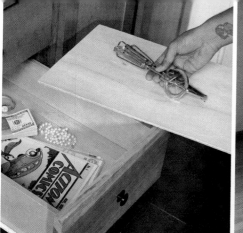

CHAPTER **FOUR**

AROUND THE HOUSE

Entry Organizer

If you would love to have a mudroom but just don't have the space, this compact bench and shoe shelf is the solution.

It's easy to keep your home decluttered with this organizer, which boasts plenty of storage space and room for just about anything you might need. Mount it near the garage service door and you'll have a convenient spot to remove and store shoes or boots before going inside. There's even a hollow bench with a flip-up lid to store hats and gloves.

All of the parts for this project are cut from standard pine boards, so you don't need to haul big sheets of plywood home or worry about finishing exposed plywood edges. Choose your lumber carefully, though. The wide pine planks tend to cup and warp, so look for boards that are flat and straight. And plan to build the project soon after buying the lumber. If you leave the lumber sitting around for weeks, it may begin to warp or twist.

CUT OUT THE PARTS

Start by choosing the four straightest, best-looking 1x12s for the shelf sides. Cut these to 72 in. Then use the Cutting List on Page 177 to cut the remaining parts **(Photo 1)**. If you're lucky enough to own a sliding miter saw, you can use it to cut the parts to length. Otherwise a circular saw will work fine. The boards for three sides of the bench and one of the bench bottoms have to be ripped a little narrower. Use a circular saw or table saw for this. After cutting the lumber, sand it with 100-grit sandpaper to remove any marks and smooth out any ripples left from the milling process. A random orbital sander works great for this, but you could hand-sand if you don't own a power sander.

ASSEMBLE THE PARTS WITH SCREWS

We joined the parts with 2-in. trim-head screws, recessing them slightly to make room for the wood filler. But you can substitute regular screws if you don't mind the look of screw

1 Cut the parts. Cut the boards to length, following the Cutting List on Page 177. Running your circular saw along a large square ensures straight, square cuts. Parts F, G and N also have to be ripped to width. You can do this with a circular saw or on a table saw.

2 Mark the screw locations. On the inside of the shelf sides, mark the middle shelf location. On the outside, make light pencil lines at the center and 3/8 in. from both ends. These light marks will help you position the screws. Drill 1/8-in. pilot holes at the screw locations to avoid splitting the boards.

WHAT IT TAKES	
TIME 1-2 days	**SKILL LEVEL** Intermediate

TOOLS & MATERIALS
Circular saw (or table saw), large square, driver/drill, clamps, sandpaper (optional: sliding miter saw)

heads. Even though our screws had self-drilling tips, for extra insurance against splitting the wood we drilled 1/8-in. pilot holes for the screws.

Clamping the parts together before driving in the screws makes it easier to keep the parts aligned. And if the wood is a little twisted or cupped, flatten it with clamps before driving the screws. We also added three cleats to the bottom of the seat board to hold it flat. Spread wood glue on these cleats and attach them with 1-1/4-in. screws.

We chose a continuous hinge for the lid. Cut the hinge to 35-5/8 in. with a hacksaw. Since you'll also have to cut all the metal shelf standards to fit, buy a sharp, new 32-tooth blade. Photo 6 shows how to attach the hinge. Finish up the assembly by cutting and attaching the metal shelf standards **(Photo 7)**.

HANG THE PROJECT ON THE WALL

First, locate the wall studs. An electronic stud finder makes it easy. Mark the stud locations with strips of painter's tape. Now choose a position for the project that will allow you to attach each of the 12-in.-wide shelf units to at least one stud. Next, screw the temporary 1x2 ledger to the studs, making sure it's level and the top is located 7-1/2 in. from the floor **(Photo 8)**. The ledger supports the shelf units and bench while you attach them to the wall. **Photos 9–13** show the installation steps. Finish up by choosing the locations for the adjustable shelves and installing them with the shelf clips. We prefinished the project with Behr Semi-Transparent Waterproofing Wood Stain.

4 Build the bench frame. Drill pilot holes in the sides of the bench frame and clamp the parts together. The wide part (E) is the front of the bench, so face the best-looking side out.

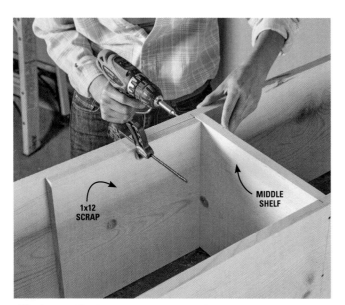

3 Assemble the shelves. Arrange the parts on a flat surface and clamp them together. Clamp a scrap along the centerline to help you position the middle shelf. Then drive trim-head screws through the pilot holes to connect the parts. If you want to fill the screw holes later, recess the screws slightly.

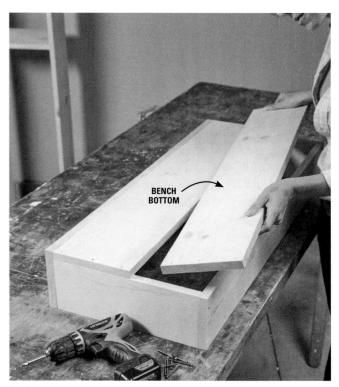

5 Attach the bench bottom. To make sure the bench frame is square, measure diagonally from opposite corners. Adjust the frame until the two diagonal measurements are equal. Then screw the bottom boards to the frame.

FIGURE A.
ENTRY ORGANIZER

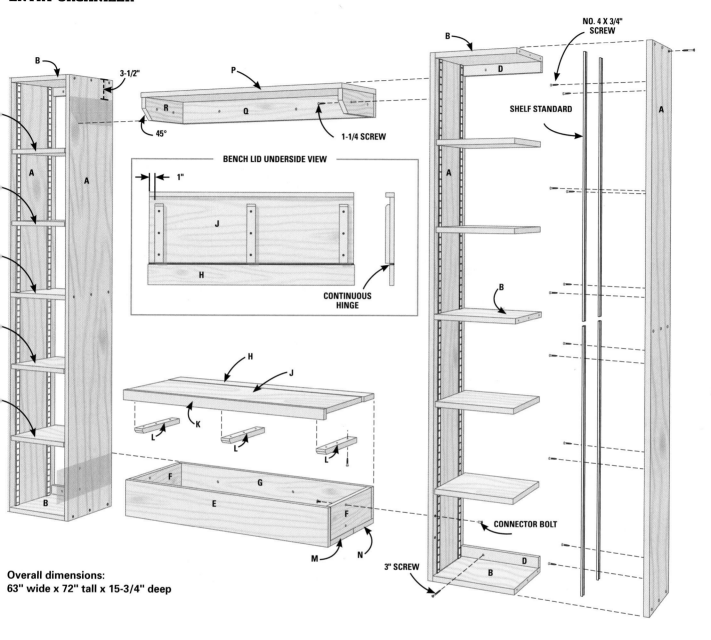

3-1/2"

45°

1-1/4 SCREW

P

R

Q

BENCH LID UNDERSIDE VIEW

1"

J

H

CONTINUOUS
HINGE

H

J

K

L

L

L

F

G

E

F

M

N

B

A

A

B

Overall dimensions:
63" wide x 72" tall x 15-3/4" deep

NO. 4 X 3/4"
SCREW

B

D

SHELF STANDARD

A

B

A

CONNECTOR BOLT

3" SCREW

D

B

Materials List

ITEM	QTY.
1x12 x 8' standard pine boards	6
1x8 x 6' standard pine boards	1
1x6 x 10' standard pine boards	1
1x4 x 8' standard pine boards	1
1x2 x 10' standard pine boards	1
Hardware	
2" trim-head screws	100
1-1/4" screws	14
3" cabinet screws	10
No. 4 x 3/4" screws (for shelf standards)	Sm. box
1-1/2" connector bolts	4
1-1/2" x 36" continuous hinge	1
72" shelf standards	8
Shelf clips	32
Coat hooks	
Wood filler and 100-grit sandpaper	

Cutting List

KEY	QTY.	DIMENSIONS	DESCRIPTION
A	4	3/4" x 11-1/4" x 72"	Sides
B	6	3/4" x 11-1/4" x 12"	Top, bottom, middle shelf
C	8	3/4" x 11-1/4" x 11-5/8"	Shelves
D	4	3/4" x 1-1/2" x 12"	Hanging strips
E	1	3/4" x 5-1/2" x 36"	Bench front
F	2	3/4" x 4-3/4" x 13-1/4"	Bench sides
G	1	3/4" x 4-3/4" x 36"	Bench back
H	1	3/4" x 3-1/2" x 36"	Bench top (back)
J	1	3/4" x 11-1/4" x 35-5/8"	Bench top lid
K	1	3/4" x 1-1/2" x 35-5/8"	Bench lid nosing
L	3	3/4" x 1-1/2" x 10"	Bench seat cleats
M	1	3/4" x 7-1/4" x 36"	Bench bottom
N	1	3/4" x 6-3/4" x 36"	Bench bottom
P	1	3/4" x 11-1/4" x 36"	Top shelf
Q	1	3/4" x 3-1/2" x 36"	Top shelf back rail
R	2	3/4" x 3-1/2" x 10-1/4"	Top shelf side rail

6 Mount the seat hinge. Clamp the lid and the back rail together as shown. Center the hinge on the two lid parts and attach it with four screws, two on each end. Then drill 5/64-in. pilot holes and drive in the remaining screws

7 Install the shelf standards. Cut each of the 72-in. shelf standards into two 34-3/4 in. pieces using a hacksaw. Measure from the ends to the centers in order to retain factory ends on each piece. We spray-painted the standards to match the finish.

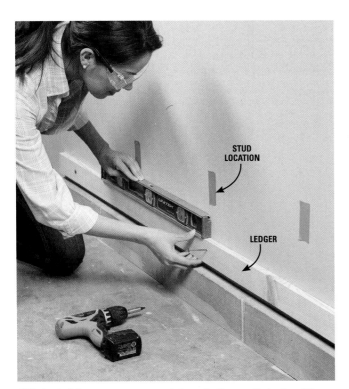

8 Install temporary support. Locate the wall studs with a stud finder and mark them with strips of painter's tape. Install a 1x2 ledger with the top edge 7-1/2 in. above the floor to support the shelves and seat during installation.

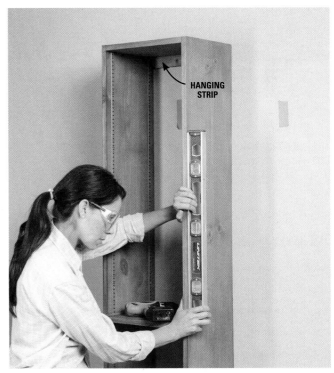

9 Install the first shelf unit. Rest the shelf on the ledger. Drive a screw through the top hanging strip into a stud. Then use a level to make sure the sides of the shelf unit are plumb. If necessary, push the bottom one way or the other to plumb the sides. Drive a screw through the lower hanging strip into a stud to secure the shelf unit.

10 Install the coat-hook shelf. Screw the coat-hook shelf to the studs, making sure it's level. Then level the shelf from front to back and attach it to the side of the tall shelf with 1-1/4-in. screws. Attach the opposite side after installing the second shelf unit.

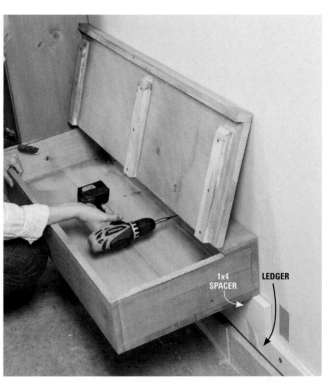

1x4 SPACER

LEDGER

11 Mount the bench. Rest a scrap of 1x4 spacer on top of the temporary ledger to elevate the bench to the correct height. Set the bench on the spacer. Then drive screws through the back of the bench into the studs.

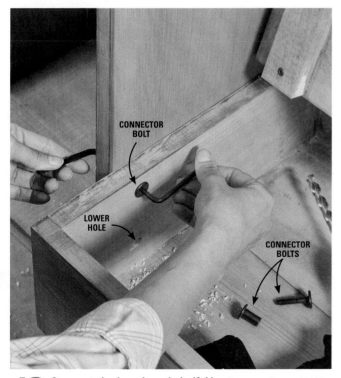

CONNECTOR BOLT

LOWER HOLE

CONNECTOR BOLTS

12 Connect the bench and shelf. Use two-part connector bolts to connect the front of the bench to the shelves on each side (connect the second side later after the second shelf is mounted). These bolts provide more support than screws to ensure the bench will be safe to sit on. The bolts we used required two Allen wrenches to tighten.

13 Finish up with the second tall shelf. Rest the second shelf unit on the ledger and tip it up into place, then attach it to the wall by driving 3-in. screws through the top and bottom hanging strips and into the stud. Then connect the bench with the connector bolts and attach the other side of the upper shelf with 1-1/4-in. screws.

Hide-the-Mess Lockers

Build simple boxes and add store-bought doors.

Here's a common scenario for new homeowners: You recently bought a house with a nice big coat closet by the front door. The problem is, since the garage is in the back, everyone—including the dog—uses the back door.

We designed and built these lockers with homeowners who frequently use the back door in mind. Each locker is big enough to stash a coat, backpack, boots, hats, and odds and ends that normally wind up on the floor. Since they're modular and space efficient, you can build one for each member of the family—including the dog. Now everyone has a personal place for stashing stuff—and the responsibility for keeping it organized.

The louvered door is made from one of a pair of closet bifold doors, which you can buy at almost any home center. Since the doors come in pairs and you can get two locker "boxes" from each sheet of plywood, you'll make the best use of materials by building them in twos. Here's how to do it.

MONEY, MATERIALS AND TOOLS

Our total materials cost was just under $100 per locker. Since we were planning to paint the lockers, we used inexpensive "AC" plywood. If you plan to stain your lockers, and use hardwood plywood such as oak or birch and hardwood doors, you'll spend about $150 per locker. On a row of lockers, only the outer sides of the end lockers show, so you can use inexpensive plywood for the inner parts and more expensive

WHAT IT TAKES	
TIME 2 days	**SKILL LEVEL** Intermediate

TOOLS & MATERIALS
Table saw (or circular saw with cutting guide), miter saw, driver/drill, clamps, sandpaper (optional: finish nailer)

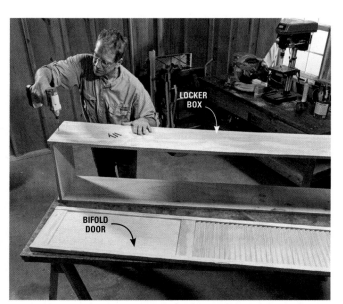

1 Build a simple box. Cut the plywood parts and assemble them with trim-head screws. Make sure the box opening is 1/4 in. taller and wider than the door itself.

2 Square it up. Take measurements diagonally, corner-to-corner, and then adjust the box until the measurements are equal and the box is square. Install the back, using one edge of the back to straighten the box side as you fasten it. Check once again for squareness, then secure the other edges of the back.

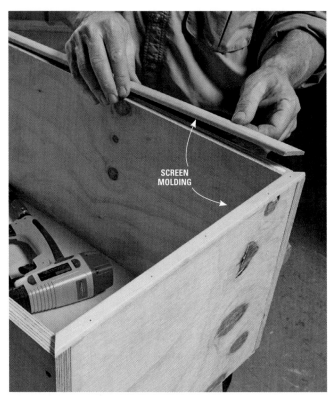

3 Cover the plywood edges. Install screen molding over the front edges of the box. Apply wood glue lightly and use just enough nails to "clamp" the molding in place while the glue dries.

4 Build slatted shelves. Plywood shelves would work fine, but slatted shelves allow better ventilation so wet clothes and shoes can dry. Space the slats with a pair of wood scraps.

material for the outer parts. Expect to spend at least a day buying materials, rounding up tools and building a pair of lockers. Set aside another day for finishing.

A table saw is handy for cutting up plywood, but a circular saw with a guide will provide the same results. To see how to build a guide, search for "cutting guides" at familyhandyman.com. You'll also need a miter saw to cut the screen molding. A finish nailer will help you work faster, but hand-nailing will work as long as you drill holes to prevent splitting.

BUY THE DOORS FIRST

There are a variety of bifold doors available. If you need more ventilation, use full louvered doors; if ventilation isn't an issue, use solid doors. The doors you buy may not be exactly the same size as ours, so you may have to alter the dimensions of the boxes you build. Here are two key points to keep in mind when planning the project:

■ You want a 1/8-in. gap surrounding the door. So to determine the size of the box opening, add 1/4 in. to the height and width of the door. Since our bifold doors measured 14-3/4 x 78-3/4 in., we made the opening 15 x 79 in.

■ To determine the shelf depth, subtract the door thickness from the width of the sides (including the 1/4-in. screen molding). Our doors were 1-1/8 in. thick, so we made the shelves 10-7/8 in. deep (12 minus 1-1/8 equals 10-7/8 in.). When the doors are closed, they'll rest against the shelves inside and flush with the screen molding outside.

GET BUILDING!

Use a table saw or straight-cutting guide to cut the plywood sides (A) and top and bottom (B). The Cutting List on Page 183 gives the parts dimensions for our lockers. If you plan to paint or stain the lockers, it's a good idea to prefinish the inside of the parts. Once the lockers are assembled, brushing a finish on the inside is slow and difficult.

Assemble the boxes with 2-in. trim-head screws **(Photo 1)**. Trim-head screws have smaller heads than standard screws and are easier to hide with filler. Cut the 1/4-in. plywood back (C) to size. Make certain the box is square by taking diagonal measurements (they should be equal; see **Photo 2**), and then secure the back using 1-in. nails. Use the edges of the back as a guide to straighten the edges of the box as you nail the back into place.

Cut 1/4 x 3/4-in. screen molding and use glue and 1-in. finish nails or brads to secure it to the exposed front edges of the plywood **(Photo 3)**. Cut the shelf front and back (D), sides (E) and slats (F) to length, then assemble the three slatted shelf units **(Photo 4)**. With the locker box standing upright, position the shelves and hold them temporarily in place with clamps or a couple of screws. Adjust the shelf spacing based on the height of the locker's user and the stuff that will go inside. Once you have a suitable arrangement,

FIGURE A
LOCKER CONSTRUCTION

Overall Dimensions:
16-1/2" wide x 81" tall x 12-1/4" deep

Cutting List

For one locker. These locker parts suit a door measuring 14-3/4 x 78-3/4 in. Verify the exact size of the doors before building.

KEY	QTY.	DIMENSIONS DESCRIPTION
A	2	11-3/4" x 80-7/8" sides (3/4" plywood)
B	2	11-3/4" x 15" top/bottom (3/4" plywood)
C	1	16-1/2" x 80-1/2" back (1/4" plywood)
D	2	3/4" x 1-1/2" x 15" shelf front/back (solid wood)
E	2	3/4" x 1-1/2" x 9-3/8" shelf sides (solid wood)
F	6	3/4" x 1-1/2" x 15" shelf slats (solid wood)

Materials List

For two lockers. Because bifold doors are sold in pairs, and one sheet of 3/4-in. plywood yields two lockers, you can make the best use of materials by building an even number of lockers.

ITEM	QTY.
30" bifold door pack (2 doors)	1
3/4" x 4' x 8' plywood	1
1/4" x 4' x 8' plywood	1
1/4" x 3/4" x 8' screen molding	5
3/4" x 1-1/2" x 8' solid wood	9

2" trim-head screws, 1-1/4" screws, 1" nails, 1-1/2" nails, wood glue, no-mortise hinges, door handles and magnetic catches.

FIGURE B
CUTTING DIAGRAMS

3/4" plywood

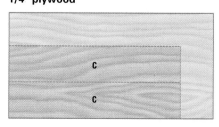

1/4" plywood

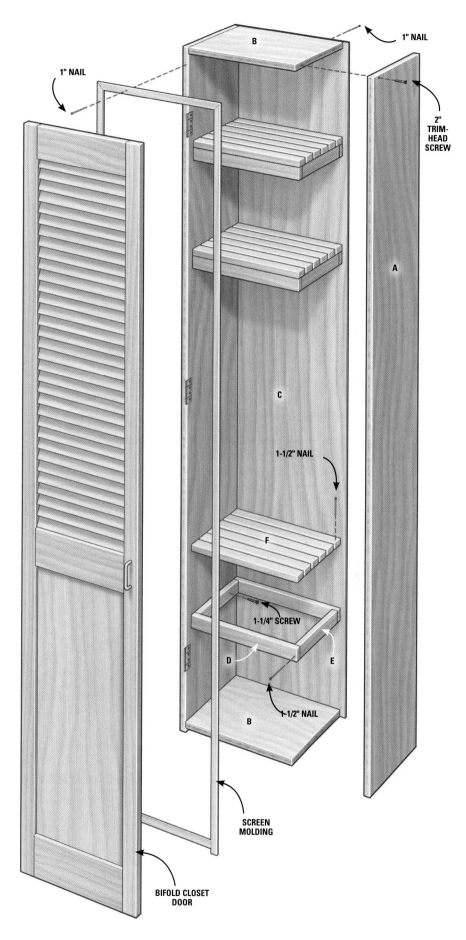

THICKNESS OF
DOOR

5 Install the shelves. Stand the locker up and position the shelves to suit the stuff that will go in it. Mark the shelf locations, lay the locker on its back and screw the shelves into place. Make sure the shelves are inset far enough to allow for the door.

"NO-MORTISE"
HINGE

6 Mount the hinges. Remove the hinges from the doors (they'll be pointed the wrong way) and reinstall them on the door based on the direction you want it to swing. Prop up the door alongside the box and align the door so there will be a 1/8-in. Gap at the top and bottom of the box. Then screw the hinges to the box.

lay the locker on its back and screw the shelves into place **(Photo 5)**. The shelves are easy to reposition in the future as needs change.

ADD HARDWARE AND FINISH, THEN INSTALL

Remove the hinges that hold the bifold doors to each other. Determine which way you want the door to swing, then mount the hinges onto the door accordingly. (Note: You'll need to buy another set of hinges if you're building two lockers.) Remember, you want the louvers to point downward on the outside! With the locker on its back, position the door and secure the hinges to the plywood side **(Photo 6)**. Install door handles and magnetic catches to hold them closed.

Remove the doors (don't finish them yet!) and install the locker boxes. Your lockers can stand against baseboard, leaving a small gap between the backs of the lockers and the wall. Or—if you remove the baseboard—they can stand tight against the wall. Either way, installing them is a lot like installing cabinets: Fasten all the boxes together by driving 1-1/4-in. screws through the side of one locker into the next. Then screw the entire assembly to wall studs.

Install the unfinished doors to make sure they all fit properly, then remove them again. This may seem like a waste of time, but there's a good reason for it: The locker boxes may have shifted a little during installation, and the doors may not fit properly. If a door or two need some edge sanding, you want to do that before finishing.

When you've checked the fit of all the doors, remove them one last time for finishing. Whether you're using paint or a natural finish, louvered doors are a real pain. If the plans include a clear coat, consider polyurethane or lacquer in spray cans: They'll give better results in far less time, though you'll spend an extra $5 to $10 per door. After finishing, install the doors and load up those lockers!

Stackable Shelving

A simple board-and-channel design allows you to easily adapt this shelving to any wall space.

To maximize the storage on a wall, consider this stackable option. These shelves are easy to build, stylish enough to display collections of favorite things, yet strong enough to hold plenty of books. In addition, you can easily customize the versatile system to fit around windows, doors, desks and other features and make every inch of wall space count.

In this project, we'll show how to make these handsome shelves with plywood and iron-on edge veneer. Then we'll show how to mount them in simple grooved 1x2 uprights that fasten to the walls.

Cutting the groove in the uprights **(Figure B)** and making square, splinter-free crosscuts on the plywood are the only tricky parts of the project, and we'll show foolproof methods for you to do both. Even though the shelves are simple, you will be cutting out a lot of parts, so you should plan to spend a weekend on this project. Allow a few more days for staining and finishing.

You'll need a circular saw with a sharp 40-tooth carbide blade for cutting the plywood. To cut the groove in the 1x2, you'll need a table saw and standard blade. You'll also need a drill and countersink bit, a level and a clothes iron to melt the glue on the iron-on edging. An edge-trimming tool like the one we show isn't mandatory (a sharp utility knife and patience give good results), but it simplifies the job.

You'll need 1-1/2 sheets of 3/4-in. plywood to build the 8-ft.-long section shown. Add the edging, 1x2s and hardware,

WHAT IT TAKES	
TIME 2 weekends	**SKILL LEVEL** Intermediate

TOOLS & MATERIALS
Circular saw, table saw, driver/drill, countersink bit, level, clothes iron (optional: edge trimmer, stud finder)

FIGURE B.
SHELF DETAILS

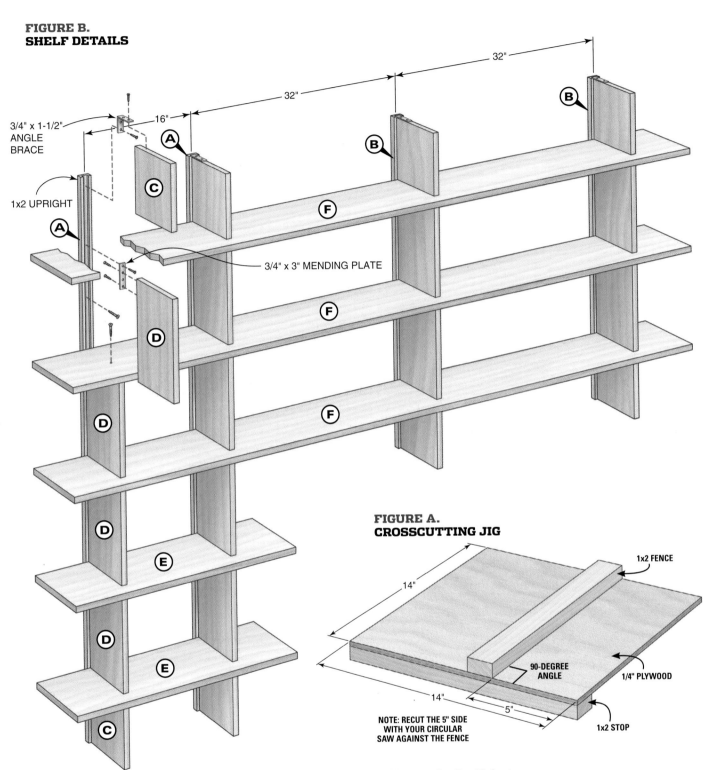

3/4" x 1-1/2" ANGLE BRACE

1x2 UPRIGHT

16"

32"

32"

3/4" x 3" MENDING PLATE

FIGURE A.
CROSSCUTTING JIG

14"

14"

5"

1x2 FENCE

90-DEGREE ANGLE

1/4" PLYWOOD

1x2 STOP

NOTE: RECUT THE 5" SIDE WITH YOUR CIRCULAR SAW AGAINST THE FENCE

Materials List

ITEM	QTY.
3/4" x 4' x 8' A1 grade plywood	1
3/4" x 4' x 4' A1 grade plywood	1
1x2 x 6' oak	3
1x2 x 4' oak	1
3/4" or 7/8" iron-on veneer tape	60 ft.
1-5/8" flathead screws	32
2-1/2" flathead screws	20
1-1/4" trim head screws	4
3/4" x 3" mending plates	12
3/4" x 1-1/2" angle braces	4
3/4" x No. 6 flathead screws	52

Cutting List

KEY	QTY.	DIMENSIONS	DESCRIPTION
A	2	3/4" x 1-1/2" x 72"	(cut to length) supports
B	2	3/4" x 1-1/2" x 48"	(cut to length) supports
C	8	3/4" x 8" x 8" plywood	uprights
D	12	3/4" x 8" x 11-7/8"	plywood uprights
E	2	3/4" x 10" x 32"	plywood shelves
F	3	3/4" x 10" x 96"	plywood shelves

FIGURE C.
SHEET LAYOUT

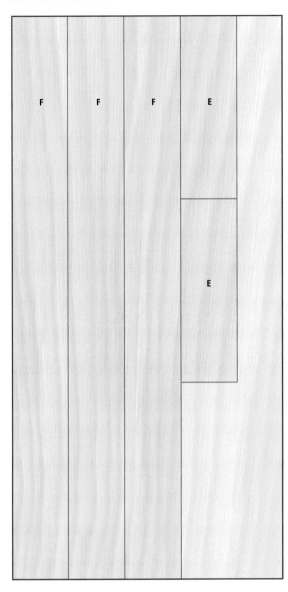

FIGURE D.
GROOVED
UPRIGHTS

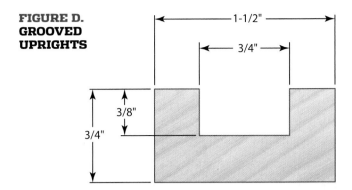

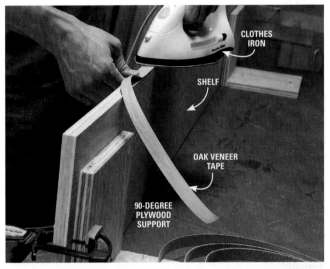

1 Rip the plywood to width and iron on the veneer tape. Align one edge with the plywood edge, set the iron to "cotton" and move it slowly along the veneer to melt the glue.

and the cost of these shelves comes to about $150. We purchased 3/4-in. veneer-core oak plywood with two good faces. Less-expensive plywood may just have one good side, but since only the uprights require two good sides, you may be able to work around any defects on the less desirable side. For a contemporary look, we stained these oak shelves black and applied two coats of sealer, but you can choose any paint or stain color to match your decor.

CUT THE PLYWOOD AND IRON ON THE EDGE VENEER

Start by cutting the 4 x 8-ft. sheet of plywood into four 10-in.-wide strips **(Figure C)**. Cut the 4 x 4-ft. sheet into five 8-in.-wide strips. We used a table saw, but clamping an 8-ft. straightedge to the plywood as an edge guide for a circular saw will also work. Sand any saw marks from the edge of the plywood strips, being careful not to round over the corners. Then vacuum the edges to remove the sawdust.

The next step is to cover one long edge of each plywood strip with veneer tape **(Photo 1)**. Iron-on veneer tape is

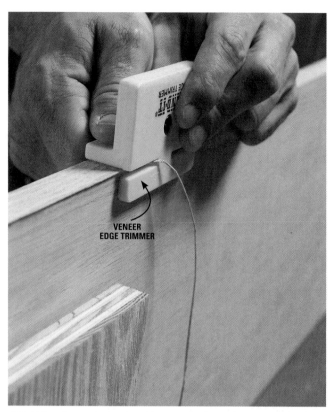

2 Trim the ends flush with a utility knife. Then trim the long edges flush with a special trimming tool. Finish by lightly sanding the edges flush with 220-grit paper.

VENEER
EDGE TRIMMER

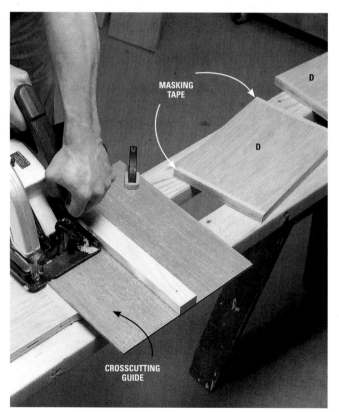

MASKING
TAPE

D

D

CROSSCUTTING
GUIDE

3 Crosscut the 8-in.-wide strips of plywood. Use a crosscutting jig with a circular saw to get perfectly square cuts. Masking tape minimizes splintering.

available at woodworking stores and home centers. Start by cutting strips of veneer tape a few inches longer than the plywood. Then align one edge of the tape with the face of the plywood and press the tape into place with a hot iron. Move the iron slowly enough to melt the glue, but fast enough to avoid scorching the veneer. An 8-ft. strip should take about 10 seconds. While the glue is still hot, rub a small chunk of wood along the tape to press and seal it to the plywood. Inspect the seam between the tape and the plywood for gaps, and reheat and press any loose areas. Use a sharp utility knife to trim the ends of the tape flush. Then use a special trimmer **(Photo 2)**, a utility knife or a block plane to trim the long edges flush. Finish by sanding the edges of the tape flush to the plywood. Wrap 220-grit sandpaper around a small block of wood and angle it slightly when sanding to avoid scuffing through the thin veneer on the plywood face. Cover the ends of the shelves with veneer tape later, after you cut the short shelves (E) to length.

BUILD A JIG FOR ACCURATE CROSSCUTTING

It may take a half hour to build, but an accurate crosscutting jig is essential for perfectly square, splinter-free cuts **(Figure A)**. Start by cutting a 14-in. square of 1/4-in. plywood on your table saw. Align a 1x2 stop with the edge of the plywood and attach it with 3/4-in. screws. Keep the screws 3 in. from the ends to avoid sawing through them. Countersink the screw heads.

On the opposite side, attach another 1x2 perpendicular to the first one and about 5 in. from the edge of the plywood. Use a speed square or combination square to align this 1x2 90 degrees to the first one. Clamp the jig to a scrap of plywood. With the saw's base tight to the fence, saw through the jig and plywood (check for screws in the path of the blade before cutting). Check the test cut on the plywood with a framing square. If it's not perfectly square, adjust the position of the stop slightly. You'll have to make new screw holes for each adjustment. You can also use the jig as a measuring guide for the longer uprights by cutting the jig to 11-7/8 in. wide on the table saw. For repetitive cuts without measuring, line up one end of the jig with the end of the plywood and cut along the opposite end.

To avoid splintering the plywood, press high-adhesive masking tape over the cutting path **(Photo 3)** and cut slowly with a sharp, thin-kerf 40-tooth carbide blade.

USE TABLE SAW TO CUT A GROOVE FOR THE UPRIGHTS

There are many ways to cut the grooves in the 1x2s. We'll show you how to do it with a table saw and a standard blade. Of course, if you own a set of dado blades for the table saw, cutting the groove will take less time. You could also use a

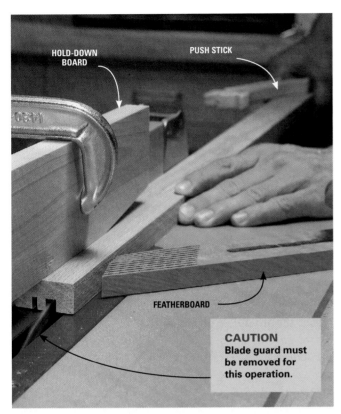

HOLD-DOWN BOARD

PUSH STICK

FEATHERBOARD

CAUTION
Blade guard must be removed for this operation.

4 Cut 3/4-in.-wide grooves in the 1x2s by making a series of passes on the table saw. Practice on a scrap to set the exact width and depth of the cut.

1-5/8" FLATHEAD SCREWS

A

C

PILOT HOLE AND COUNTERSINK BIT

5 Predrill and glue and screw one 8-in.-square upright piece to each 1x2, making sure to keep the bottom of the upright aligned with the bottom of the 1x2.

STUD LOCATION

A

4' LEVEL

C

2-1/2" FLATHEAD SCREWS

6 Cut the 1x2s to length. Then locate the studs, plumb the first 1x2 support and screw it to a stud. Predrill and space the screws every 16 in.

router mounted in a router table to cut the groove, but we won't show this technique.

The first step is to use a scrap of wood to set the exact width of the groove. Cut a 16-in. length from one of the 6-ft. 1x2s as a practice piece. Adjust the height of the blade to 3/8 in. above the saw's table and set the fence 11/16 in. from the blade. Set up a featherboard and clamp a hold-down board to the fence (**Photo 4**). Run the 1x2 through the saw. Use a push stick when the board gets within 6 in. of the blade. Rotate it end-for-end and run it through again. There should be a groove that's about 1/8 in. wide. Move the fence about 1/8 in. closer to the blade and make two more cuts on the 1x2. Repeat this process to make the groove progressively wider. When the groove gets close to 3/4 in. wide, make finer adjustments with the fence. Test after each pair of passes until the 1x2 fits snugly over the edge of the plywood. Make sure the mending plates also fit in the groove (**Photo 10**). With the width of the cut perfectly set, cut the grooves on the 1x2 uprights in reverse, starting from the outer edges and moving in (**Photo 4**). Run each 1x2 through the saw twice, once in each direction. Then move the fence about 1/8 in. farther from the blade and repeat the process until the groove is complete. Remove slivers of wood from the grooves with a sharp chisel.

PREPARE THE 1x2s AND MOUNT THEM ON THE WALL

First attach the 8-in.-tall plywood uprights to the low end of the 1x2s (**Photo 5**). Determine the length of each 1x2 by literally stacking uprights and scraps of plywood in the groove to simulate the shelving system you want. Then cut the 1x2s to length.

Photos 6–8 show the process for mounting the 1x2s to the wall. Start by locating the studs with a stud finder. Mark the studs with a strip of masking tape centered about 80 in. from the floor. Then screw the long 1x2s to the studs (**Photos 6 and 7**).

If the wall has a stud that's bowed, the 1x2 will be crooked and the shelves won't fit well. To avoid having to deal with this problem, hold a straightedge against the face of the 1x2 after you've screwed it to the wall. If it's crooked, back out the screw near the low spot and add washers to shim the 1x2 straight (**Photo 8**).

With the long 1x2s in place, add shelves and uprights until you get to the level of the first long shelf. **Photo 11** shows how to make sure the long shelf will be straight when you mount the short 1x2s. The rest is simple.

Stack the parts and screw them together until you reach the top. **Photo 12** shows how to anchor the top shelf with an angle brace. To anchor the bottom of the final upright, drive a trim screw at an angle through the shelf from underneath.

7 Level the top of the next 1x2 support to the first 1x2 and fasten it near the top. Then use the level to plumb the sides and screw it to the stud every 16 in.

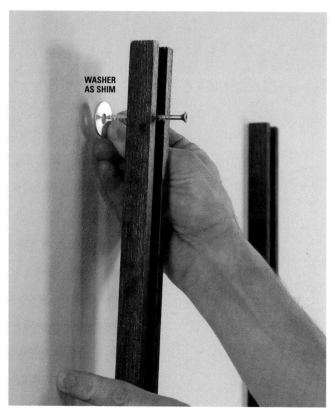

8 Check the 1x2 supports for dips and bows with a straightedge. Remove screws and shim behind the 1x2s with 1-in.-diameter washers to straighten them if necessary.

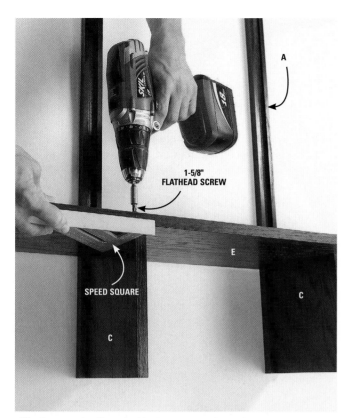

9 Center the first shelf with an equal overhang at each end. Square the uprights (C) to the front of the shelf. Predrill and drive a 1-5/8-in. screw through the shelf into the uprights.

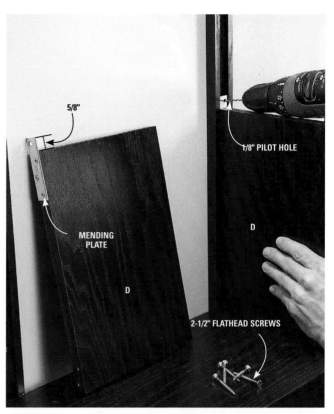

10 Screw a mending plate to the back of each upright. Set the uprights into the groove, predrill and drive a screw through the mending plate and 1x2 into the stud.

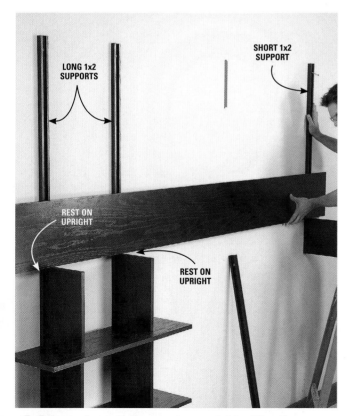

11 Rest a long shelf across two uprights. Align the bottom short 1x2 supports with the shelf, plumb them and screw the supports to studs.

12 Stack the remaining shelves and uprights following the procedure in Photos 9 and 10. Secure the top upright to the 1x2 with a metal angle brace.

Ultimate Office Organizer

Convert a spare closet into super organized office storage

Is your home office a mess? Do you need a spot to organize the kids' schoolwork and projects? Or do you just want to get the office stuff out of sight when guests are coming? We'll demonstrate how to solve all these problems by converting a spare closet into a super organized space.

In this story, we'll show how to build and install wall shelf cabinets, a countertop and under-mount drawers, and how to adjust the dimensions to fit these projects in your closet. We'll also show an easy way to conceal all those cords that usually dangle down behind the desk. We've included a Materials List on Page 196, but be sure to adjust the quantities to fit your closet. The project shown here is constructed with birch plywood and boards and is great for any intermediate to advanced DIYer.

WHAT IT TAKES	
TIME 1-2 weekends	**SKILL LEVEL** Advanced

TOOLS & MATERIALS
Table saw (or circular saw), driver/drill, (optional: nailer) clamps, wood glue

CABINET SIDE

COUNTERTOP SUPPORT

1 Mark the walls and attach the countertop supports. Draw level lines for the bottom of the countertop and cabinets. Draw vertical lines to indicate the sides of the cabinets, then screw countertop supports to studs at the back and sides of the closet.

There's no complicated joinery to deal with in this project—the wall shelves and drawers are just wooden boxes that are screwed together. We used a table saw to cut the plywood, a narrow-crown staple gun to attach the shelf backs and drawer bottoms, and an 18-gauge nailer to attach the face frames. If you don't have these tools, use a circular saw and straightedge guide to cut the plywood, and a good old-fashioned hammer and nails. The work will just take a little longer.

ADJUST THE DIMENSIONS TO FIT YOUR CLOSET

Start by measuring the distance between the side walls. Keeping in mind that 32 in. is about the maximum width for a plywood shelf, decide how many shelf units you need. To figure out exactly how wide each cabinet should be, subtract 1-1/2 in. from the total measurement and divide the remainder by the number of cabinets. This will leave a 3/4-in. space between the cabinet and the wall at each end that you'll cover with the face frame. This space makes it easy to install the shelf cabinets in the closet without worrying about an exact fit. We needed three

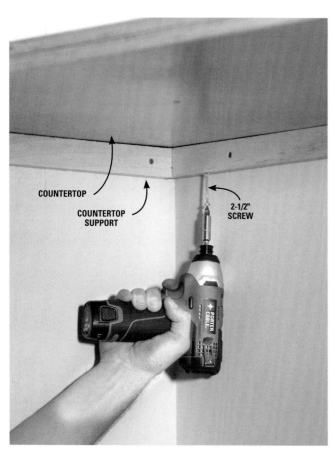

COUNTERTOP

COUNTERTOP SUPPORT

2-1/2" SCREW

2 Fasten the countertop. Screw through the countertop supports into the countertop. Lay something heavy on top, or ask a helper to press down on the countertop while you drive the screws.

FACE BOARD

3 Cap the front edge. Glue and nail a board to the front edge to cover the plywood and add strength. Wipe off glue squeeze-out with a damp rag.

FIGURE A.
OFFICE ORGANIZER

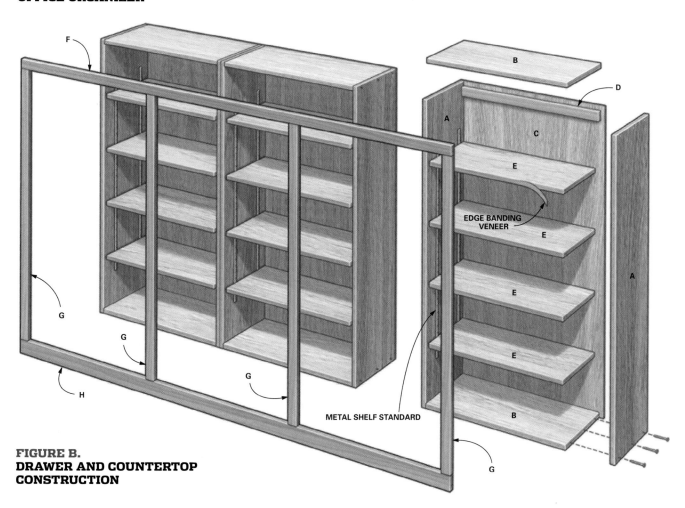

EDGE BANDING VENEER

METAL SHELF STANDARD

FIGURE B.
DRAWER AND COUNTERTOP CONSTRUCTION

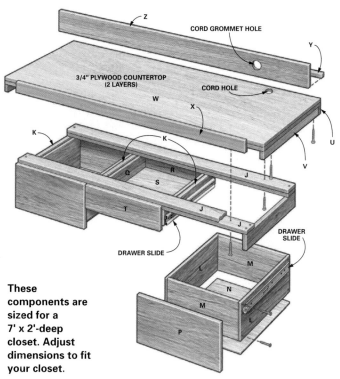

CORD GROMMET HOLE

3/4" PLYWOOD COUNTERTOP (2 LAYERS)

CORD HOLE

DRAWER SLIDE

DRAWER SLIDE

These components are sized for a 7' x 2'-deep closet. Adjust dimensions to fit your closet.

Cutting List

KEY	QTY.	DIMENSIONS	DESCRIPTION
SHELF CABINET			
A	6	11-1/4" x 47-3/4" x 3/4"	plywood sides
B	6	11-1/4" x 26" x 3/4"	plywood top, bottom*
C	3	27-1/2" x 47-3/4" x 1/4"	plywood back
D	3	1-1/2" x 3/4" x 26"	hanging strip
E	12	11-1/4" x 25-5/8" x 3/4"	plywood shelves*
F	1	1-1/2" x 84" x 3/4"	face frame
G	4	1-1/2" x 48" x 3/4"	face frame **
H	1	2-1/2" x 84" x 3/4"	face frame
DRAWER FRAME			
J	4	3" x 57" x 3/4"	plywood stringers
K	4	3" x 20" x 3/4"	plywood dividers
DRAWERS			
L	4	7-1/4" x 20" x 3/4"	plywood sides
M	4	7-1/4" x 15-1/2" x 3/4"	back and front*
N	2	17" x 20" x 1/4"	plywood bottoms*
P	2	18-7/8" x 9" x 3/4"	plywood fronts*
Q	2	2-1/4" x 20" x 3/4"	plywood sides
R	2	2-1/4" x 15-1/2" x 3/4"	back and front*
S	1	17" x 20" x 1/4"	plywood bottom*
T	1	18-7/8" x 3/4" x 4"	plywood front*
COUNTERTOP			
U	1	1-1/2" x 3/4" x 84"	back support
V	2	1-1/2" x 3/4" x 23-1/4"	side supports
W	2	24" x 84" x 3/4"	plywood countertop **
X	1	1/4" x 32"	opening width x face
Y	1	1" x 3/4" x 84"	cleat
Z	1	4-3/8" x 84" x 3/4"	backsplash

* Based on full 3/4" plywood. Adjust if your plywood is slightly thinner.
** Cut to fit.

27-1/2-in.-wide cabinets to fit our 84-in.-wide closet. We built the cabinets 47-3/4 in. tall. If you have standard 8-ft.-tall walls, the cabinets will reach the ceiling. After doing the calculations, double-check the math by drawing lines on the closet wall. Draw a level line 28-1/2 in. from the floor to mark the bottom of the 1-1/2-in.-thick countertop. Then draw another line 47-1/2 in. from the floor for the bottom of the wall cabinets. Finally, draw vertical lines for the sides of the cabinets.

You'll also have to decide how wide to make the drawers. You can use the technique we show here to build drawers in a size and configuration that will work best in the closet. The key is to build the frame and mount the drawer slides before building the drawers. Then measure between the slides **(Photo 8)** and build the drawers to fit.

MOUNT THE COUNTERTOP

The countertop is two layers of plywood that are glued and screwed together. It rests on cleats that are screwed to the wall studs. Start by measuring the closet interior at the level of the countertop. Use a framing square to check the corners. Deduct 1/4 in. from the length and depth to allow for the top to fit easily. You can cover any gaps with the backsplash. Transfer these measurements to your plywood and cut out the two pieces. Use less expensive plywood for the bottom if you like. Screw 1x2 cleats to the back, side and front walls to support the top **(Photo 1)**. Then drop the top into place and attach it from underneath with 2-1/2-in. screws **(Photo 2)**. Finish the front edge with a 2-1/4-in.-wide board **(Photo 3)**.

BUILD THE WALL SHELF CABINETS

Start by cutting the parts from the 4 x 8-ft. sheets of plywood. If using a table saw, keep the good side of the plywood facing up as you cut the parts. If using a circular saw, face the good side down so that any splintering or

Wiring Your Closet—Get Help Online!

We're not showing how to wire your closet office here, but chances are you'll want to add multiple electrical outlets and possibly cable, phone or network wiring. We've got tons of how-to information on our website to help you with these projects. Go to familyhandyman.com and enter one of the search terms below.

To add an outlet, search for "electrical outlet." But note that the National Electrical Code requires that branch circuit extensions or modifications be arc-fault protected. This means you'll have to either connect to or add a circuit that's protected by an arc-fault-circuit-interrupter (AFCI). While you're adding wiring, don't forget about closet lighting (search for "lighting"). And for more information on how to install coax, phone and Cat6 cable, search for "communication cable."

chipping won't show. We think it's easier to finish the parts before you assemble them.

It's also easier to install the shelf standards to the cabinet sides before putting the cabinet together. Make sure the shelf standards are oriented the right way. We put a piece of painter's tape on the top of each side to keep track. Here's a building tip for the cabinet and drawer boxes: Nail the cabinet sides to the top and bottom before drilling pilot holes for the screws. The nails hold the parts in perfect alignment while you drill the holes and drive the 1-5/8-in. screws. Screw the sides to the top and bottom **(Photo 4)**. Then nail on the back. If you were careful to cut the 1/4-in. plywood back accurately, you can square the cabinet by aligning it with the back before nailing it on **(Photo 5)**. Cover the front edge of the cabinets with a wood face frame after they're mounted **(Photo 7)**. Finish the front edge of the plywood shelves with iron-on edge banding. For complete instructions on installing edge banding, go to familyhandyman.com and search for "edge banding."

Start the cabinet installation by screwing a 1x2 ledger to the wall to support the wall cabinets. Align the top edge of the board with the 47-1/2-in.-high level line and drive a screw at each stud location. Next, measure from the vertical lines to the center of the wall studs, and transfer these measurements to the hanging strip at the top of each wall cabinet so you'll know where to drive the cabinet installation screws. Hang the cabinets by resting the bottom edge on the ledger, tipping them up against the wall, and driving 3-in. screws through the hanging strip into the studs **(Photo 6)**. Secure the bottom of the cabinets by driving

Materials List

ITEM	QTY.
4' x 8' x 3/4" plywood	4
4' x 8' x 1/4" plywood	2
1x2 x 8' boards	7
1x3 x 8' board	1
1x3 x 6' board (rip to 2-1/4")	1
1x6 x 8' board (rip to 4-3/8" for parts Y and Z)	
Shelf standards	6
Shelf clips	48
20" full-extension drawer slide sets	3
Iron-on veneer edging	48 ft.
1-1/4" screws	
1-5/8" screws	
2-1/2" screws	
3" screws	
Finish nails or nail gun pins	
Wood glue	
Cord grommets	

4 Assemble the wall cabinets. Mount shelf standards on the cabinet sides before assembly. Then screw the sides to the bottom and top with 1-5/8-in. screws. Drill pilot holes to prevent the plywood from splitting.

SHELF STANDARD

5 Square the cabinet with the plywood back. Use the plywood back as a guide for squaring the cabinet. Apply a bead of glue. Then nail one edge of the plywood back to the cabinet side. Then adjust the cabinet box as needed to align the remaining edges and nail these.

6 Install the cabinets. Rest the bottom of the cabinet on ledger and tilt the cabinet up. Drive 3-in. screws through the hanging strip at the top of the cabinet into the studs.

1x2 LEDGER

7 Finish the fronts. Nail a 1x3 to the lower cabinet edge to create a valance for under-cabinet lighting. Nail 1x2s to the cabinet top and sides to cover the raw plywood edges.

1x2

1x3

a nail or screw down into the ledger. Connect the fronts of the cabinets by hiding 1-1/4-in. screws under the shelf standards. Complete the installation by nailing on the face frames **(Photo 7)**. We used a 1x3 for the bottom face frame to hide the under-cabinet lighting.

BUILD THE DRAWERS

Drawer slides that mount directly to the underside of a desk or countertop are available, but we'll show a method that allows you to use high-quality, side-mounted drawer slides. We bought these full-extension ball-bearing slides at the local home center. They cost about $15 per drawer. But you can substitute less-expensive epoxy-coated slides to save some money. You'll have to measure your closet to figure out the drawer sizes. Just make sure the drawers clear the open closet doors.

Building the drawer support frame is straightforward. Start by laying two of the stringers (J) side by side and marking the location of the drawer dividers (K) on them. Ball-bearing slides are not very forgiving, so measure and attach the drawer dividers carefully so the dividers are perfectly parallel when the frame is assembled.

For our 24-in.-deep countertop, we used 20-in. drawer slides. We cut the drawer dividers (K) 20 in. long and built

8 Build the drawer frame and measure for drawers. Make sure the drawers fit perfectly by building the drawer frame first. Then measure between the slides and build the drawers to exactly this width.

9 Mount the drawer slides. Draw a line parallel to the top of the drawer to indicate the center of the drawer slide. Line up the slide by centering the line in screw holes. Attach the slide with the screws provided.

10 Hang the frame under the countertop. Make center marks on the frame and the underside of the counter and align them. Then use a spacer to set the frame 3/4 in. back from the countertop edging and drive the screws.

the drawer boxes 20 in. deep. If the closet is shallower, use shorter slides and adjust dimensions to match. The drawer slides have two parts. One mounts to the dividers and the other to the drawer. Remove the part that attaches to the drawer according to the included instructions. Then screw the part of the slide with the ball bearings to the dividers, aligning the bottom edges. The center dividers will have drawer slides on both sides. Screw through the stringers (J) into the drawer dividers (K) to build the frame. Be careful to keep the front of the drawer slides facing forward. Then add the second layer of stringers (J). Check the frame against a framing square as you screw it together to make sure it's square. When the frame is complete, measure between the slides to determine drawer sizes **(Photo 8)**.

Build the drawers by screwing through the sides into the fronts and backs, and then gluing and nailing on the plywood bottom. Nail one edge of the bottom to the drawer box. Then use a framing square to square the drawer box before nailing the other three edges. To attach the drawer slide to the drawers, we first drew lines 1-7/8 in. down from the top edges of the drawers **(Photo 9)**. (You may have to adjust this distance to match your drawer slides. The dimension isn't critical as long as there's about a 1/4-in. clearance between the drawer and the stringer when the drawer is mounted.) Then sight through the screw holes in the slides to center them on the line before attaching them with the included screws.

Finish the drawer installation by attaching the frame to the underside of the countertop **(Photo 10)** and installing the fronts. Hold the drawer frame back 3/4 in. from the back of the countertop edging. Install the drawers by lining up the slides and pushing them in. **Photo 11** shows a tip for aligning the drawer fronts. The hot-melt glue holds the fronts temporarily. Attach them permanently by opening the drawers and driving four 1-1/4-in. screws through the drawer box into the drawer front from the inside.

FINISH IT OFF WITH A CORD-CONCEALING BACKSPLASH

Here's a handy method to hide cords and still have easy access to them. Simply mount a backsplash board about 4 in. from the back wall to create a cord trough. **Figure B** shows how we used a cleat to attach the backsplash. Drill holes through the face and install cord grommets to allow cords to pass through. We found 2-in. cord grommets at the home center, but since they were a loose fit in the 2-in. hole, we held them in place with a dab of silicone caulk. Lay a multi-outlet power strip behind the backsplash for extra outlets. We drilled a hole through the countertop so that we could plug the power strip into a wall outlet. You can also nail backsplash boards to the end walls for a more finished look.

11 Glue on the drawer front. Starting with the center drawer front, dab on hot-melt glue and press it against the drawer. Quickly center the drawer front 1/4 in. below the countertop edge. Hold it still for about 10 seconds until the glue cools. Now position the other two drawer fronts. Drive screws from the inside.

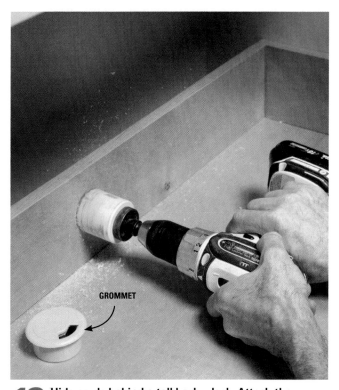

12 Hide cords behind a tall backsplash. Attach the backsplash with cleats, holding it about 4 in. from the wall. Then drill holes where you'll have cords and install cord grommets.

Suspended Shelf

Steel cable and shaft collars add style & strength.

This wall-hung bookshelf is one of the easiest we've ever built. If you can stack blocks, you can build it. And installing the cable doesn't require any more skill than drilling a hole. Things will go a lot quicker with a table saw, a miter saw and a pneumatic nailer, but you could easily build this project with just basic hand tools and a circular saw. We used a router to bevel the shelf edges, but this is optional.

If you use a penetrating oil finish, you can complete this in a day. For a urethane or painted finish, allow a few extra days—you'll need to prefinish the parts before assembly.

CUT THE PARTS

Start by ripping the shelves to the widths given in the Cutting List (Page 202). We used a full-width 1x10 for the bottom shelf and successively narrower boards as we went up. Making all the shelves the same width would be OK, too. While you're at it, rip two 1-in.-wide strips from the 1x2s for the support cleats. Next, cut the boards to length. We used a 45-degree chamfer bit and router to bevel the ends and front edges of the shelves, but you could leave them square. After the parts are cut and prefinished, you're ready to assemble the shelf.

ASSEMBLE THE SHELVES

The shelves are too big to build on a normal workbench. If you're young and nimble, you could put them together on the floor. Otherwise, save your back and line up a few old doors on a pair of sawhorses.

Assembly is straightforward; follow **Photos 1–6** and the details shown in **Figures A and B**. Here are a few tips:

WHAT IT TAKES	
TIME 1-3 days	**SKILL LEVEL** Beginner
TOOLS & MATERIALS Circular saw (or table saw), driver/drill (optional: miter saw, nailer, router)	

TOP CLEAT

CABLE HOLE

1 Drill an angled hole for the cable. Start by drilling straight down about 1/8 in. Then tilt the drill to about a 45-degree angle and use the starter hole to keep the bit in place as you start to drill. The angle of the hole isn't critical.

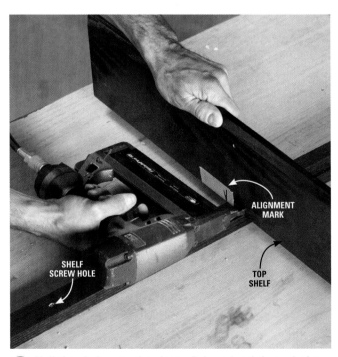

ALIGNMENT MARK

SHELF SCREW HOLE

TOP SHELF

2 Nail the shelves to the cleats. Drive a brad through the shelf into the support cleat. These brads just hold the shelves in place when you flip the bookshelf over to drive in the shelf screws (Photo 5) and secure the cable (Photo 6).

- Mark the back of the shelves 13 in. from the ends so you'll know where to line them up with the standards **(Photo 2)**.
- Keep the shelves and standards at a right angle to each other as you attach the cleats. That will ensure that the cleats fit tight to the shelves.
- Don't drive nails where you'll be drilling holes.
- Drill mounting screw holes after all cleats are installed. It's easier to do it before you mount the shelves on the wall.

STRING THE CABLE

The cable is flexible and easy to cut, so it's a breeze to install. Just remember to put two collars on the cable, between each pair of shelves, as you thread the cable through the holes. Leave about 4 in. of cable sticking out the top and an extra foot or so on the bottom. The extra cable on the bottom lets you use our "cable pedal" method for removing slack **(Photo 8)**. After stringing the cable, flip the whole entire works over so you can drive the shelf screws **(Photo 5)** and anchor the top of the cable **(Photo 6)**. Take a coffee break while the epoxy sets up.

Materials List

ITEM	QTY.
1x10 x 5' board	2
1x8 x 5' board	2
1x6 x 5' board	1
1x2 x 6' board	4
1-1/4" wood screws	10
3" wood screws	10
No. 10 finish washers	10
3/8" steel washers	2
3/4" wood screws	2
Five-minute epoxy	1
No. 10-32 cap nuts	2
Set screw shaft collars (6432K17)	22
Extra-flexible wire rope (3450T38)	14

Cable and collars are available from McMaster-Carr (mcmaster.com). Enter the product numbers into the search box to find the items listed. Cable may also be available at home centers or hardware stores.

Cutting List

KEY	QTY.	DIMENSIONS	DESCRIPTION
A	1	3/4" x 5-1/4" x 59-1/2"	shelf
B	1	3/4" x 6-1/4" x 59-1/2"	shelf
C	1	3/4" x 7-1/4" x 59-1/2"	shelf
D	1	3/4" x 8-1/4" x 59-1/2"	shelf
E	1	3/4" x 9-1/4" x 59-1/2"	shelf
F	2	3/4" x 1-1/2" x 68-1/4"	standards
G	10	3/4" x 1" x 11-1/4"	cleats
H	2	3/4" x 1" x 7-3/4"	cleats

CLEAT

3 Assemble the shelves. Add a cleat under the shelf and nail it in. Then add another shelf and tack it to the cleat. Continue like this until you get to the bottom. Now do the same thing on the other side.

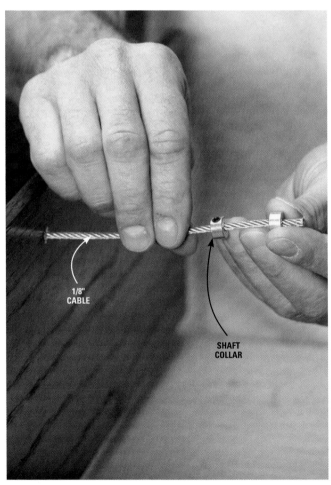

1/8" CABLE

SHAFT COLLAR

4 Thread the cable. Start at the bottom shelf and run the cable through the collars and shelves. Add two collars between each pair of shelves. At the top, thread the cable through the angled hole.

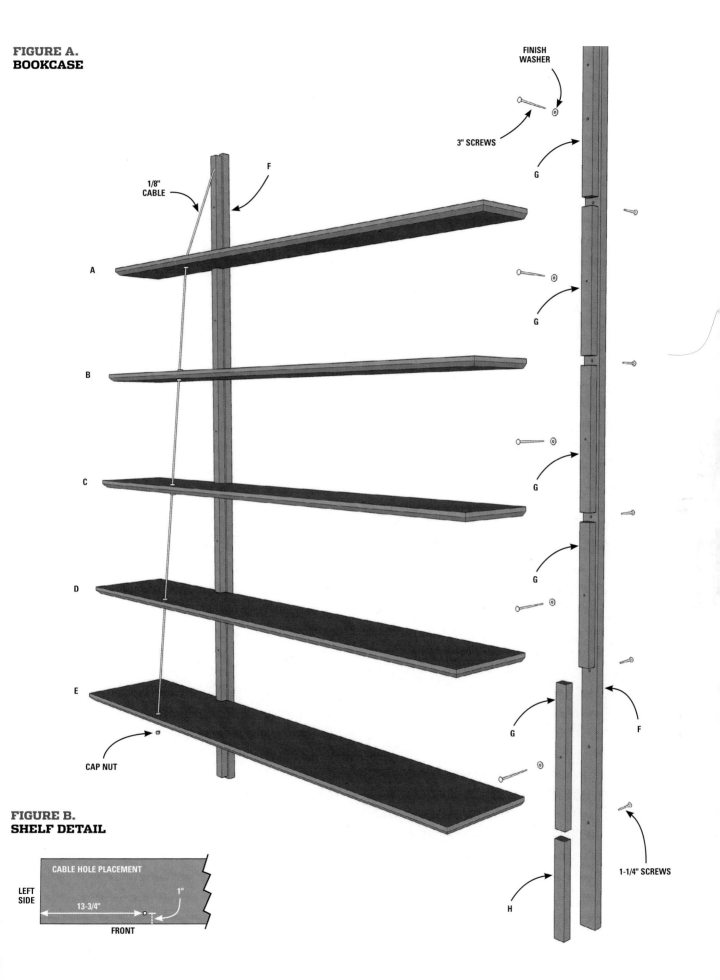

FIGURE A.
BOOKCASE

FINISH
WASHER

3" SCREWS

G

1/8"
CABLE

F

A

B

C

D

E

CAP NUT

G

G

G

G

F

FIGURE B.
SHELF DETAIL

CABLE HOLE PLACEMENT

LEFT
SIDE

1"

13-3/4"

FRONT

H

1-1/4" SCREWS

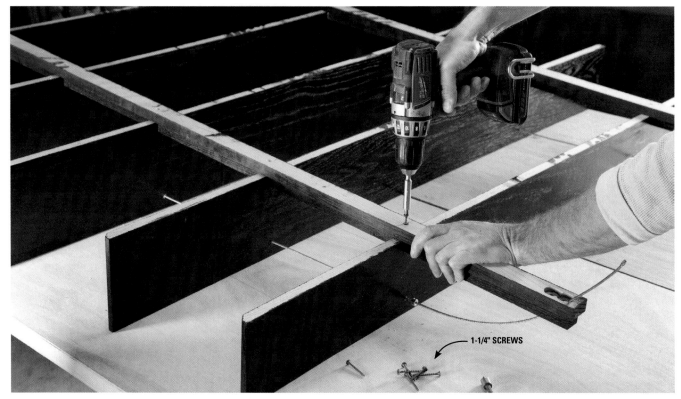

1-1/4" SCREWS

5 Fasten the shelves. Flip the bookshelf over and drive screws into the back of each shelf through the holes in the standards.

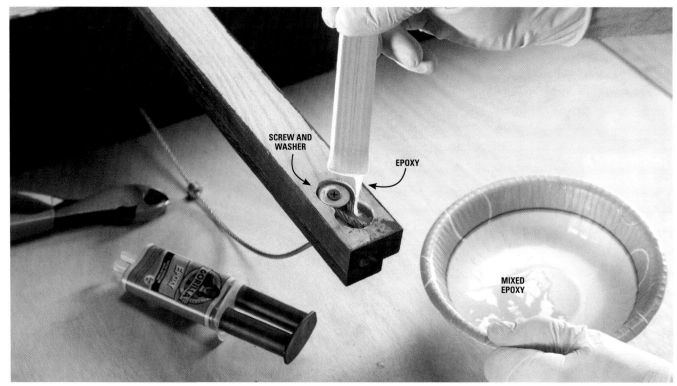

SCREW AND WASHER

EPOXY

MIXED EPOXY

6 Anchor the cable with epoxy. Loop the cable in the recess and hold it down with a washer and screw. Then mix five-minute epoxy and fill the recess with it.

MOUNT THE SHELVES

The shelf standards are spaced 32 in. on center to align with studs. So all you have to do is locate two studs where you want the shelves to go and mark them with painter's tape. Setting the shelves on blocks **(Photo 7)** is a handy way to hold them up while driving the first few screws. Start by driving one of the top screws. Before you drive the top screw in the second standard, check to make sure the shelves are level. After the two top screws are in place, make sure the standards are plumb before driving the remaining screws. We used No. 10 finish washers under the screws for a decorative effect.

TIGHTEN THE CABLE

At this point, the cable is slack and the collars are still loose. Your goal is to take the slack out of the cable and then adjust each shelf so it's level from front to back while you tighten the collars **(Photo 8)**. Use an Allen wrench to tighten the setscrews. Remember, you don't need too much tension on the cable, just enough to remove the slack. Finish up by cutting the cable and then covering the end with a cap nut **(Photo 9)**. Then you're done—all that's left to do is figure out what to put on the brand-new shelves!

7 Mount the bookshelf. Locate two studs that are 32 in. apart with a stud finder. Screw the standards to the studs, making sure the shelves are level and the standards are plumb.

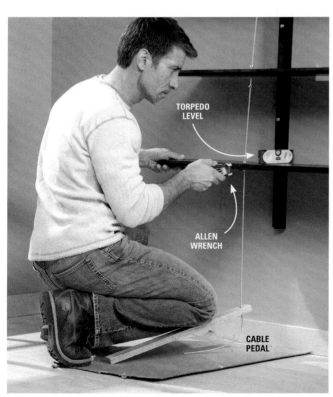

8 Tension the cables. Tighten the cable using a scrap of wood with a hole in it to put tension on the cable while you tighten the setscrew on the collar below the lowest shelf. Then snug the remaining collars to the top and bottom of the shelves and tighten the collars.

9 Trim and cap the cable. Use a side-cutting pliers or lineman's pliers to cut the cable. Leave 1/4 in. protruding. Cover the end of the cable with a cap nut. Use hot-melt glue or silicone caulk to hold the cap nut in place.

Floating Shelves

Customize them to suit any room!

You can buy inexpensive floating shelves in stores or online. But before you do that, consider building your own. For about the same cost, you can get the size, thickness and look you want. You can even finish them to match your trim or furniture. And homemade shelves will be sturdier than most store-bought shelves—ours can support about 50 lbs. each. Plus, you'll earn serious bragging rights when you're done.

MONEY, TIME AND TOOLS

A pair of shelves cost us about $150 to build. We were able to make two shelves from a single 4 x 8-ft. sheet of 1/2-in.-thick red oak plywood. It can be tough to find locally, so call around before shopping, or choose different plywood.

Our shelves are 2-1/2 in. thick and 72 in. long, so finding veneer long enough on store shelves is also a challenge. You can special-order it at some home centers, however. We bought ours online from Rockler Woodworking and Hardware (rockler.com). There is less expensive veneer available, but we love this stuff because you don't have to heat it or apply any glue—it's just peel and stick! Expect to spend about $20 on stain and other assorted materials.

It took us a couple of hours to build each shelf, including sanding, staining and mounting on the wall. We made ours

using a circular saw and cutting guide, but you can make them much faster with a table saw. And you can certainly hand-drive small nails, but it's much faster and easier to use a pneumatic brad nailer. You'll need a small compressor

CUTTING GUIDE

1 Cut the parts. Using a 60-tooth blade in the circular saw and a cutting guide, cut all the parts to size (see "Build Cutting Guides for Perfect Cuts," Page 211.) A 4 x 8-ft. sheet of plywood will yield enough parts for two shelves.

WHAT IT TAKES	
TIME 1 day	**SKILL LEVEL** Beginner

TOOLS & MATERIALS
Circular saw (or table saw), driver/drill, edge trimmer, stud finder (optional: random orbit sander, belt sander, nailer)

2 Glue and nail the frame together. Apply carpenter's glue to the edges of the rails and fillers and nail on the first panel with 1-in. brads. Then flip the shelf over and nail on the other panel.

3 Sand the front and sides flush. Using a random orbit sander and 100-grit sandpaper, sand the front and sides of the shelf so that the rails and panels are flush with each other. This will give you a flat, smooth surface on which to apply the veneer.

to power it. It also helps to have a random orbit sander, especially for sanding the sides flush before applying the veneer. Bonus points if you own a belt sander for scribing!

CUT AND ASSEMBLE THE PARTS

Set a full sheet of 1/2-in. plywood on three or four 2x4s laid across sawhorses (**Photo 1**). Measure and mark the plywood for each of the shelf parts and use a circular saw and cutting guide (see "Build Cutting Guides for Perfect Cuts" on Page 211) to make the cuts. The cutting guide will help keep cuts perfectly straight and minimize chip-out.

Next, glue and nail all the parts together (**Photo 2**). It helps to draw pencil lines on the top and bottom panels first so you'll know where to drive the nails for the fillers after you cover them with the top and bottom panels. With all eight parts cut to size, it's fairly easy to assemble the shelf with glue and nails. Start by laying the front rail (C) on end on top of your worktable (an old hollow-core door or plywood scrap on sawhorses works great), plus a couple of short support blocks cut from a 2x4. These blocks will support the top panel (A) while you glue and nail it onto the front rail. Carefully align the top and front pieces and use an 18-gauge pneumatic brad nailer to drive 1-in. brads.

Now stand the side rails (D) on end and glue and nail them to the top panel. Flip the whole thing over and install the fillers (E) with glue and brads. The fillers should be evenly spaced, but don't be too fussy because they'll be hidden once you install the bottom panel (B). Nail through the front rail into each of the fillers.

Then flip the whole thing over again and nail through the top panel into each of the fillers. Now flip the whole works over one more time and nail through the bottom panel into the fillers.

APPLY THE WOOD VENEER

The top and bottom panels have exposed plywood edges that get covered with veneer. If those edges aren't perfectly smooth and flush with the faces of the front and side rails, the veneer won't stick properly. Sand everything flush with a random orbit sander and 100-grit sandpaper (**Photo 3**). Lay out the roll, veneer side down, and draw a straight line using a marker and straightedge at 3 in. wide along the entire length of the roll. This will give you 1/4 in. of overhang when you apply the veneer to the front and sides of the shelf.

Cut along the line with a pair of scissors and then cut the strip of veneer into three pieces for the front and two sides, leaving them long enough so there's 1/4 in. of overhang on each end (**Photo 4**). Apply the veneer to the sides first, being careful to keep the veneer aligned with the shelf (**Photo 5**). Don't peel and stick more than a few inches at a time, and rub a block of wood over the veneer to press it on. Cutting the pieces slightly oversize helps in case you don't get it on perfectly straight.

Overall dimensions: 72" long x 11" deep (after scribing 1/8" off the back) x 2-1/2" thick

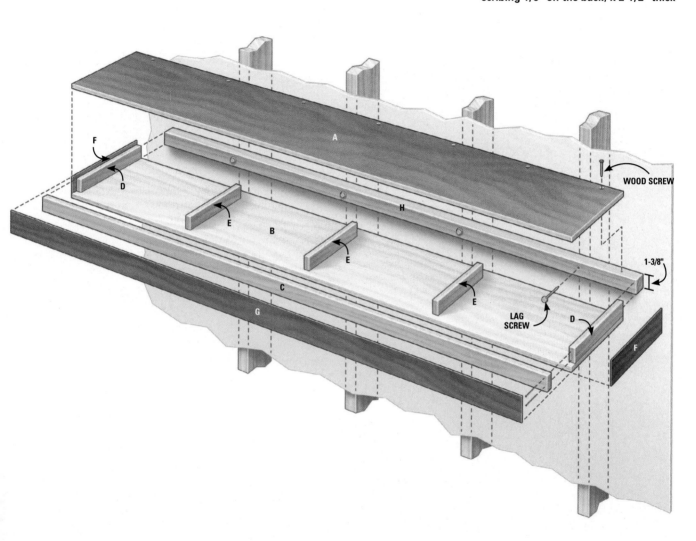

Materials List

for 2 shelves

ITEM	QTY.
4' x 8' sheet of 1/2" red oak plywood	1
24" x 96" roll of peel-and-stick veneer (enough for seven or eight shelves)	1
2x4	1
Non-hardening wood putty	
Tack cloths	
1-5/8" (No. 8) wood screws	
4" lag screws	
Stainable wood filler	
Wood stain	
Cotton rags	
Disposable foam paintbrushes	
1" brad nails (18 gauge)	
Carpenter's glue	

Cutting List

for 2 shelves

KEY	QTY.	DIMENSIONS	DESCRIPTION
A	1	11-1/8" x 72"	Top panel
B	1	11-1/8" x 72"	Bottom panel
C	1	1-1/2" x 72"	Front rail
D	2	10-5/8" x 1-1/2"	Side rails
E	3	8-1/2" x 1-1/2"	Fillers
F	2	3" x 11-5/8" (trimmed to fit)	Side veneer
G	1	3" x 72-1/2" (trimmed to fit)	Front veneer
H	1	1-3/8" x 1-1/2" x 70-3/4"	Wall cleat

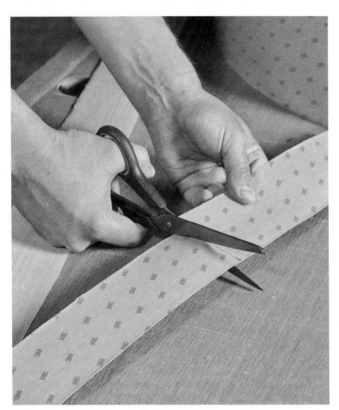

4 Cut the veneer to size. Using scissors, cut three pieces of oak veneer big enough to cover the front and sides of the shelf. Make them 3 in. wide so there is 1/4 in. of overhang on each side.

VENEER

5 Stick on the veneer. Peel off the back and stick on the veneer, leaving a little bit of overhang on all four edges. Press the veneer on firmly with a block of wood.

Pull an edge-banding trimmer apart and use one of the two sides to trim the veneer flush with the shelf **(Photo 6)**. This method works well going with the grain of the veneer, but not when trimming across it. For the short cuts across the grain, back the veneer up with a block of wood and trim the veneer flush (on the sticky side) with a sharp utility knife. A handheld router with a flush-trimming bit also works well. Install the front veneer piece after the sides. Then drill several countersink holes in the back of the shelf for some No. 8 wood screws **(Photo 7)**. Space the holes about 12 in. apart and 3/4 in. from the back edge.

MAKE A WALL CLEAT

Cut a wall cleat (H) out of a straight 2x4 and make it 1-1/2 in. x 1-3/8 in. x 70-3/4 in. **(Photo 8)**. Use a circular saw and the same cutting guide you used to cut the plywood pieces to width (set another 2x4 under the guide to keep it from tipping). Rip the cleat to width and then crosscut it to length. The narrow part of the cleat should slip into the hollow opening in the shelf with just a bit of wiggle room.

Using an electronic stud finder and painter's tape, find and mark the stud locations on the wall. Transfer the stud locations to the wall cleat and predrill holes in the cleat slightly smaller than the diameter of the shanks of the lag screws. Hold the cleat to the wall and drill pilot holes in the wall using the cleat as a drilling guide.

Drive 4-in. lag screws through the cleat and into the wall **(Photo 9)**. Start by driving a lag screw on one end of the cleat, check for level, then screw down the other end before driving the middle screws.

FIT THE SHELF TO THE WALL

Slip the shelf onto the cleat and tight to the wall. If your wall isn't perfectly flat, you'll see some small gaps between the shelf and the wall. You can eliminate those gaps by "scribing" the shelf to fit the contours of the wall **(Photo 10)**, but this step is optional—skip it if you don't mind the gaps. To scribe, drag a pencil against the wall and trace a line onto the top of the shelf. The line follows the contours of the wall.

Now use a belt sander to sand up to the pencil line **(Photo 11)**. Trying to sand freehand with the belt sander can be pretty tricky because if you don't hold the sander perfectly perpendicular to the shelf, the scribe on the top and bottom panels won't match and the shelf won't end up fitting tight to the wall. For a better method, turn the belt sander on its side and clamp it on top of a temporary worktable like an old door or scrap of plywood. Turn it on and adjust the belt tracking so that the belt just barely disappears below the surface of the worktable (be advised that not all belt sanders let you do this). Run the shelf flat against your worktable and slowly sand up to the pencil line.

EDGE-BANDING TRIMMER

6 Trim the veneer flush. Using half of a handheld edge-banding trimmer, trim the veneer flush with the edges of the shelf. You can also use a router with a flush-trimming bit for this step.

COUNTERSINKING DRILL BIT

7 Drill holes for screws. Drill countersink pilot holes in the top of the shelf for some No. 8 wood screws. Drill them 3/4 in. from the "wall" edge. Space them about 12 in. apart.

8 Cut the cleat to size. Using a circular saw and a cutting guide, rip a wall cleat out of a 2x4. Make sure the 2x4 you're cutting from is dead straight.

Build Cutting Guides for Perfect Cuts

It's hard to get nice, straight cuts without something to help guide the circular saw. That's where a cutting guide comes in. We used a self-squaring crosscut guide for short cuts and a longer guide for "rip" cuts. The guide shown here is just a narrow piece of 3/4-in. plywood attached on top of a wider piece of 1/4-in. plywood, with a squaring fence on the bottom. The base of the saw rides against the guide's "fence." To see how to make one for yourself, go to familyhandyman.com and search for "saw cutting guide."

9 Screw the cleat to the wall. Drill pilot holes in the cleat and wall and secure the cleat with 4-in. lag screws. There's no need for fender washers if you use washer-head type screws like the ones shown.

SAND, STAIN AND INSTALL!

Using a fingertip or putty knife, push some "stainable" wood filler into each of the nail holes **(Photo 12)**. The filler might shrink when it dries, so leave a bit extra in each hole—enough that it sits proud of the plywood. Once it dries, sand all sides of the shelf using a random orbit sander and 100- and then 150-grit sandpaper. After sanding with the 100-grit, vacuum or wipe off the sawdust so loose granules don't scratch up the shelf when you sand with the 150-grit. Vacuum up the dust or wipe it off with a tack cloth and apply stain following the directions on the can **(Photo 13)**. If you want the shelf to look darker, wait a few hours and apply a second coat. Wait a day or two after staining and then brush on three coats of polyurethane for protection.

Holding the shelf over the cleat and tight to the wall, drive 1-5/8-in. wood screws through the pilot holes that you drilled earlier and into the wall cleat **(Photo 14)**. Drive one of the middle screws first to help hold the shelf in place while you drive the others.

With the shelf secured, cover the exposed screw heads with a "non-hardening" type of wood filler colored to match your stain **(Photo 15)**. This type of putty stays soft, allowing you to dig it out should you decide to remove the shelf someday.

10 Scribe for a tight fit. Hold the shelf over the cleat and firmly against the wall and drag a pencil along the wall to trace a scribe line onto the shelf. Scribing and sanding (next photo) allow shelves to fit perfectly against wall contours, but you can skip these steps if you don't mind a few gaps.

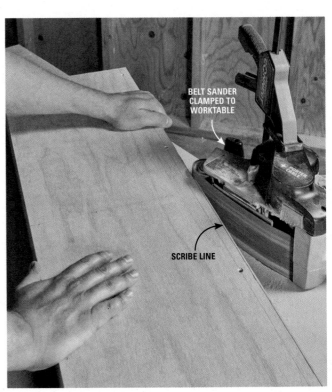

11 Sand to the scribe line. Using a belt sander clamped to a sacrificial worktable, sand up to the scribe line on the shelf.

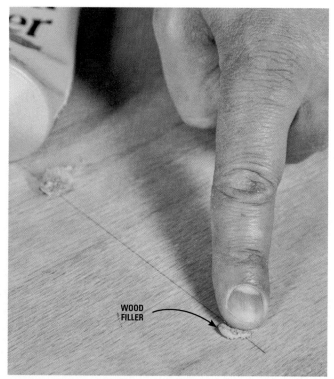

12 Fill nail holes. Push "stainable" wood filler into the nail holes, leaving it protruding slightly above the plywood in case of shrinkage.

WOOD FILLER

13 Sand and stain the shelf. Sand all the sides of the shelf using 100- and 150-grit sandpaper. Remove all dust after sanding with the 100-grit to prevent loose granules from scratching the plywood's surface.

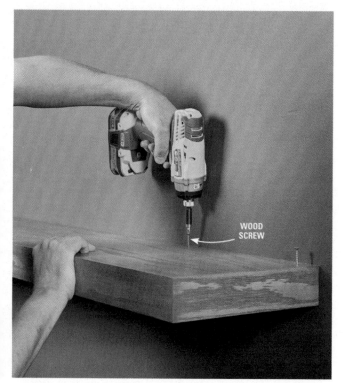

WOOD SCREW

14 Attach the shelf to the cleat. Hold the shelf against the wall and drive 1-5/8-in. wood screws through the shelf's pilot holes and into the wall cleat.

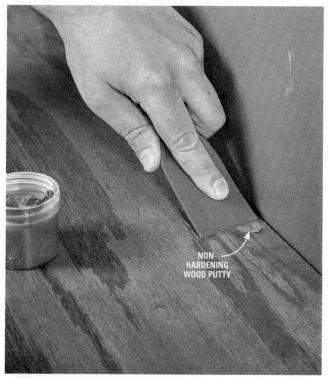

NON-HARDENING WOOD PUTTY

15 Hide the screw heads. Hide the screw heads with wood putty that matches the color of your stain. Use "non-hardening" putty so you can dig it out if you decide to remove the shelf someday.

Modular Masterpiece

A stunning wall unit that's infinitely flexible—customize it to suit your space and your stuff.

Faced with a need to store and display more stuff, we made plywood boxes in two sizes and mixed them up, adding doors to some and painting the inside backs of others the same color as the wall. The result was a truly stunning showcase that's adaptable to any situation while also including useful storage space.

CREATE YOUR OWN DESIGN

To plan the unit, we used Lego blocks to play around with a few different patterns **(Photo 1)**, but you could just use paper or cardboard. Before starting, note any outlets or vents along the wall (see "Dealing with Outlets and Vents," Page 216).

Once your design is set, figure out how much plywood is needed. Each box is composed of five parts: a back (A and E; see Cutting List, Page 217), top and bottom (B and F), and two ends (C and G). You can also add doors (D and H).

Count the number of single and double boxes in the design, then take a look at how many of these pieces you can get from one sheet of plywood **(Figure B)**. The sheet shown here yields two single boxes and one double box, but you could cut one sheet into all singles or all doubles or any mix of the two sizes. In addition to the boxes, you'll need more plywood to surround the unit on all four sides (J and K; Figure A). These pieces aren't essential, but they give the unit a clean, finished look by hiding all the seams. And they make all the members look equal in thickness.

You may also need plywood to build a base for the boxes to stand on (L–P; Figure D). This part isn't essential either (you could stack the boxes directly on the floor), but we definitely recommend it for a large unit like this one. Starting out with a level base—rather than an uneven floor—makes aligning the boxes much easier when you stack them.

CUT THE PLYWOOD TO ROUGH SIZE

Building plywood boxes is usually no big deal, but these have to fit together just right. Every square box has to be absolutely square—that is, its height must be exactly the same as its width. And a double box must be exactly twice as long as a single. If that level of precision sounds intimidating,

don't worry. We worked out a method of cutting, building and assembling the boxes that guarantees success.

Here's the best strategy for cutting the plywood: Break down the sheets into oversize backs, tops, bottoms and ends first, then cut each of these pieces to final size in batches. You'll be making "rip cuts" and "crosscuts." Rip cuts go along with the grain, and they determine a piece's width; crosscuts go across the grain and determine a piece's length.

Start by making three cardboard templates using the rough dimensions given in the Cutting List. Cut each piece of plywood into three 16-in.-wide strips, then use the templates to draw every crosscut you intend to make **(Photo 2)**. Label the parts and tally them to be sure you have enough of each kind. Add two extra single-box backs to the list. You'll need

these to build a pair of jigs that are essential for assembling the boxes **(Figure C)**.

Crosscut each strip using a sled on the table saw **(Photo 3)**. Use a 60-tooth or higher crosscut blade to avoid chipping out the face veneers. For tips on building and using a sled, go to familyhandyman.com and search for "table saw sled." Sort the parts into clearly marked piles.

The next step is to make one perfectly straight edge on each part, following the grain. The best method is to rip each part twice—the cut edge will become straighter, and smoother, with each cut you make. First, set the saw's fence to cut 15-3/4 in. wide, then rip all the pieces from their straightest side **(Photo 4)**. Mark these edges, then reset the fence to 15-1/2 in. and rip each piece again, running the

marked edge against the fence. Make a different mark on this new edge to indicate it's the best one.

Next, cut one square corner on each piece **(Photo 5)**. Make test cuts first to be sure the sled is cutting absolutely square (see "Super-Tune Your Sled," Page 218). Be fussy—accuracy will pay off when you assemble the boxes.

WHAT IT TAKES	
TIME 8 days	**SKILL LEVEL** Intermediate
TOOLS & MATERIALS Table saw, drill/driver, brad nailer, clamps, basic edge-banding tools	

1 Design with building blocks. Here's an easy way to design your wall unit: Use Lego blocks to represent single and double boxes. Take photos of various patterns, then compare the photos to decide which arrangement works best.

2 Lay out parts with templates. Your wall unit may require dozens of parts, but there are only three rough sizes. Cut full sheets of plywood into 16-in.-wide strips, then mark the parts using a set of three cardboard templates, based on the rough sizes given in the Cutting List.

3 Cut the rough-sized blanks. Crosscut the plywood strips using a table saw sled or guide for a circular saw.

CUT THE PARTS TO FINAL SIZE

The backs determine the overall size of each box, so make them first. Start with the smallest ones—the single-box backs. Begin by setting the saw's fence to 13-9/16 in., then make a rip cut from the good edge of each single-box back **(Photo 6)**. Rotate each piece 90 degrees and make a crosscut from the other good edge. This dimension—13-9/16 in.—is repeated in a number of other parts, so it's best to cut them all at the same time. Crosscut all the single-box tops and bottoms, then rip all the double-box backs at this setting.

Next, you'll need to cut all the double-box backs to length. It's better to use actual parts, rather than a ruler, to figure out this dimension (about 28-9/16 in.). The length of a double's back equals the sum of two single backs plus the thickness of two pieces of plywood.

Place these four parts next to the saw's blade, and then butt the saw's fence next to them. (Use two scraps to represent the plywood's thickness.) Crosscut all the backs to this length. Cut all the double-box tops and bottoms to this length as well.

Dealing With Outlets and Vents

Don't cover electrical outlets and air vents—work around them. Plan ahead so a box's edge won't cover an outlet. The outlet must sit "inside" a box, accessible through a hole in the box's back. Cut the hole when you're stacking the boxes to be sure you put it in the right place.

To allow airflow from a floor vent, add an elbow and extend the duct to the front of the base. Cut a hole in the front of the base to receive the duct and then fasten the vent cover to the base.

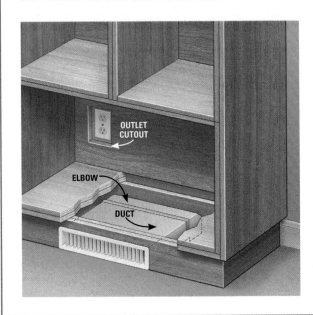

FIGURE A.
HOW PARTS FIT TOGETHER

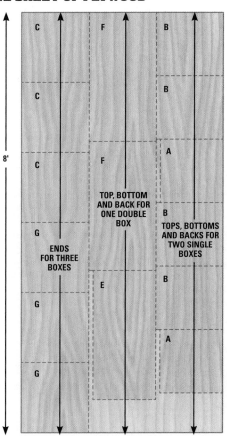

15-1/4"

1-1/4"
NO. 8
SCREW

15"

B

A

C

15"

K

1-1/4"
NO. 8
SCREW

EDGE TAPE

E

G

1-1/4" NO. 8
SCREW

F

J

FIGURE B.
A TYPICAL YIELD FROM ONE SHEET OF PLYWOOD

8'

C
C
C
G
G
G

F
F
E

B
B
A
B
B
A

TOP, BOTTOM
AND BACK FOR
ONE DOUBLE
BOX

ENDS
FOR THREE
BOXES

TOPS, BOTTOMS
AND BACKS FOR
TWO SINGLE
BOXES

Materials List

ITEM
3/4" birch plywood
Edging tape
1-1/4" deck screws
1-1/4" coarse-thread drywall screws
Electrical tape (for shimming)

Cutting List

PARTS	ROUGH WIDTH X LENGTH	FINAL WIDTH X LENGTH
Single box		
A - Back	16" x 14-1/2"	13-9/16" x 13-9/16" (a)
B - Top and bottom	same as A	15-1/4" x 13-9/16"
C - End	16" x 16"	15-1/4" x 15"
D - Door	Same as A	13-3/8" x 13-3/8" (b)
Double box		
E - Back	16" x 29-1/2"	13-9/16" x 28-9/16"
F - Top and bottom	Same as E	15-1/4" x 28-9/16"
G - End	Same as C	15-1/4" x 15"
H - Door	Same as E	13-3/8" x 28-3/8"
Surround		
J - Platform and top		15-1/4" wide (c)
K - End cap		15-1/4" wide (d)
Base		
L - Front and back		4" wide (e)
M - Cross members		4" x 11"
N - Skin, front		4-1/2" wide (f)
P - Skin, return		4-1/2" wide (f)

*Notes: ALL PARTS ARE CUT FROM 3/4" PLYWOOD. (a) All dimensions assume two layers of plywood equal 1-7/16" thick. (b) Final dimensions allow for a 3/32" gap all around the door and include edging on all four sides of the door. (c) Length equals one row of boxes. (d) Length equals height of column of boxes plus 1-7/16". (e) Length is 3-7/16" shorter than part J. (f) Width includes 1/2" for scribing.

FIGURE C.
SQUARING JIG

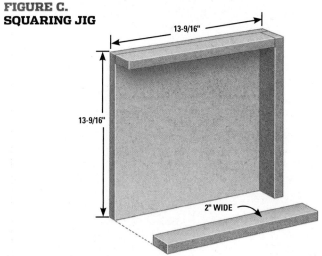

13-9/16"

13-9/16"

2" WIDE

FIGURE D.
THE BASE

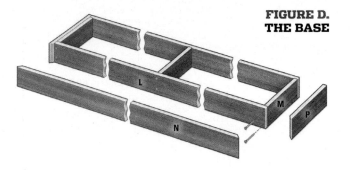

L

M

N

P

Super-Tune Your Sled

We always use a sled to cut plywood panels on our table saws. It's easy to build—to see how, search for "table saw sled" at familyhandyman.com.

A sled is supposed to guarantee a square cut, and truly square cuts are essential for the boxes of this wall unit to stack properly. Was our sled really that accurate? I've checked panels I've cut with a combination square and they seemed OK, but before building these boxes I put my sled to the ultimate test (**Photos 1 and 2**).

The result? Our sled was off just a teensy bit. The best solution is to readjust the sled's fence, but, in a hurry, we just shimmed it with a few layers of tape (**Photo 3**). Now it's dead-on perfect'

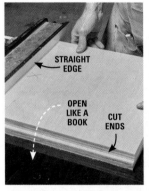

1 Cut two pieces. To check your sled's accuracy, cut two large pieces of plywood from the same side of the sled's fence. Stack the pieces on top of each other with the newly sawn edges facing the same way. Lay the stack against the table saw or other straight edge, then flip the top piece over—like opening a book.

STRAIGHT EDGE

OPEN LIKE A BOOK

CUT ENDS

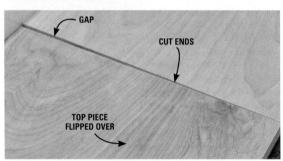

GAP

CUT ENDS

TOP PIECE FLIPPED OVER

2 Look for a gap. If there's no gap, your sled is producing perfect cuts. A gap shows twice the amount of error the cut deviates from 90 degrees.

3 Adjust with tape. To correct the angle, add tape to the sled's fence one piece at a time. Repeat the flip test and add or subtract tape until the gap disappears.

Use a similar method to figure out the precise length of all the end pieces (**Photo 7**). This dimension equals the width of a single-box back plus the thickness of two pieces of plywood. Place these pieces next to the saw's blade and butt the fence to them. Crosscut all the ends at this setting (about 15 in.).

The final cuts determine the outside depth of both boxes. Set the fence to 15-1/4 in. and rip the ends, tops and bottoms at this setting.

BUILD THE BOXES

Apply iron-on edging to the fronts of all parts. For tips on that, visit familyhandyman.com and search for "edge band."

It's much easier to finish the boxes before building them than after! We chose a dark stain to hide any small gaps between boxes; when you use a dark color, any gaps just look like shadows.

Build two jigs to help with assembly (**Figure C**). Start assembling the single and double boxes by attaching a top to a back (**Photo 8**). Support the top with the jigs. Butt the top up to two stops clamped to the back. Be sure both pieces are aligned side-to-side, then shoot three 1-1/2-in. brads to lock the pieces into place.

Next, drill three pilot holes and drive in screws. The nails prevent the pieces from shifting; the screws pull the parts together. (Tight joints are essential for the boxes to nest together properly.) We used deck screws that have a smooth shank right under the screw's head. To drill the pilot holes, we used a combination bit and countersank the holes halfway into the top piece of plywood so none of the screw's threads would engage it—that's the key to pulling parts tight.

Leave the jigs in place, then turn the assembly over and repeat the procedure for attaching the box's bottom piece.

Next, reverse the jigs and clamp the open end of the U-shape assembly (**Photo 9**). Nail and fasten the top of one end piece, making sure front edges are flush. Turn the assembly over. Use a clamp, if necessary, to nudge front edges flush again, then finish nailing and screwing the end. Repeat the procedure for the other end, then remove the jigs.

ASSEMBLE THE WALL UNIT

Much the same as building a house, the foundation of this wall unit must be level and straight before you go ahead and start stacking any boxes. The easiest way to do that is to make a ladder-like base (**Photo 10 and Figure D**).

Size the base so that the wall unit will overhang it by 1 in. on all four sides. Our base is 4 in. high—it is just tall enough to raise the wall unit above our baseboard molding. Our wall unit was so long that we had to make two bases and screw them together.

After leveling the base, make a "skin" of stained and finished plywood pieces to cover the screw holes in the base. Rip the skin pieces extra wide so you can scribe them to the

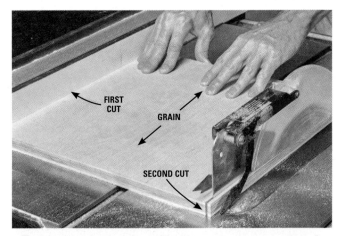

4 Cut twice for a perfect edge. To ensure that one edge of each blank is dead straight, rip it twice. Make one cut, rotate the piece 180 degrees, reset the fence and cut again. The second cut will result in a perfectly straight edge. Mark it.

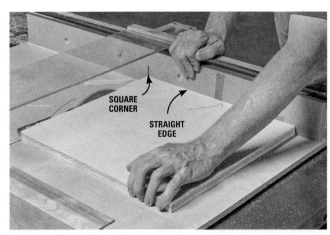

5 Cut one perfect corner. Place the marked straight edge of each blank against the sled's fence, then crosscut one end of the blank. Mark the square corner.

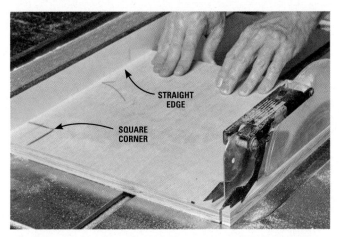

6 Two cuts make a square. Use the saw's fence to cut the single-box backs to final size. Make one rip cut, then rotate the piece 90 degrees and make a crosscut. The result will be a perfect square.

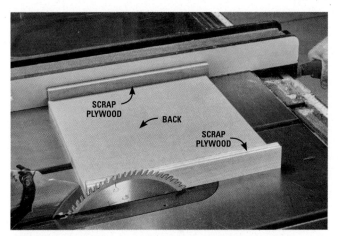

7 Set your fence to cut the ends. The length of each end piece equals a back plus two thicknesses of plywood. Unplug your saw and flip up the guard. Place these pieces next to the saw blade, then butt the fence up to them. Cut the remaining pieces to width and length using the fence as well.

8 Join the top and bottom to the back. Begin assembling each unit by fastening a top and bottom to a back. Use two simple jigs and a pair of stops to align the parts. Shoot three brads to lock the parts in place, then drill pilot holes and drive in screws.

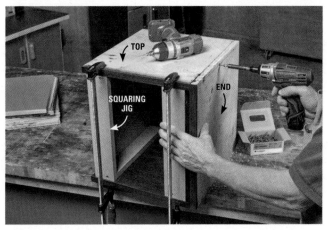

9 Add the ends. Use the jigs again to hold the parts square. Make sure all the front edges are flush before fastening the parts together.

floor, covering the gaps where the base is shimmed. The skin is mitered at the corners and nailed to the base.

Screw one plywood piece or pieces to the base to create a shelf for stacking the boxes. The length of this shelf must equal the length of the bottom row of boxes. To figure it out, temporarily clamp together a row of boxes and measure it.

Assemble the first couple of rows on the shelf (**Photo 11**). Use clamps to temporarily hold the boxes together, then shift individual boxes as needed to align their front edges. When things are looking good, go ahead and fasten the boxes together with your drywall screws. Their black heads will be almost invisible.

Complete stacking one end of the wall unit and add an end cap (**Photo 12**). Fasten the cap from inside the boxes.

Fill in the remaining boxes, working from the end cap over. You may need to shim here and there to keep edges aligned. I used rubber electrical tape for shimming. It's a hefty 1/32 in. thick, black all the way through, and sticks anywhere.

Fasten a few of the boxes to studs in your wall so there's no chance of the unit toppling forward. Top the boxes with another piece of plywood to preserve a "double wall" look throughout the unit. And that's it—you're done! You now have an eye-catching piece that's just as nice to look at as it useful for storing all of your stuff.

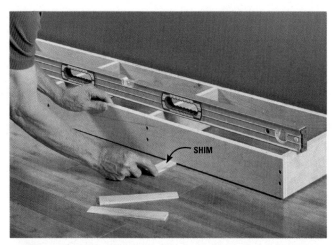

10 Build a level base. Build a base from plywood and level it with shims to ensure your wall unit will be plumb. Wrap the base with "skins" (parts N and P) and cover it with the platform (J).

SHIM

11 Clamp, then fasten. Use small clamps to assemble a couple of rows of boxes. Shift the boxes as needed to align them, then fasten them together from the inside.

END CAP

SUPPORT

12 Add end caps. Build up one side of the entire assembly first, then fasten end cap to cover the seams. Add the remaining boxes a couple of rows at a time before fastening them together. Then add the other end cap and top.

Easy, Invisible Hinges

To complement the units sleek, modern look, we wanted the door's hinges to be hidden from the outside. Euro-style hinges are the way to go.

Euro hinges may look complicated, but that's just because they're fully adjustable. After you install them, you can easily even up the gap around a door simply by turning some small screws on the hinges.

Installing Euro hinges is pretty darn simple, but you'll need a 35 mm (1-3/8-in.) Forstner bit. A template for locating the hinge holes is handy too. You can get both in one package at woodcraft.com (DrillRite Hinge Jig and Bit, No. 143958). We used Blum 110-degree soft-close hinges and Blum 9 mm clip mounting plates. Both are available online.

Basement, Laundry and Utility Rooms

Clutter and basements go together like lawn mowers and, well, grass — but they don't have to. Here's how to tidy up some of the most frequently messy areas of the house.

A. KEEP PAPERWORK ON HAND

Tired of ransacking the house to find paperwork related to your water heater, water softener and other mechanical systems? Use clear magnetic pouches sold at craft and office supply stores for manuals, receipts and other paperwork, and stick them right onto the water heater, fridge, washer and dryer, and furnace. No more digging around all over the house for important papers.

B. BASEMENT JUNK

Junk takes many forms—luggage, camping gear, the ugly vase Aunt Martha gave you for your wedding…stuff you need to keep but don't use all the time. If your house has a set of stairs with a sloped closet underneath, you have a huge amount of space that's mostly wasted. Here's how to get the most out of that black hole.

This one is built like a shelf unit and rides on fixed casters so it slides straight out to keep things organized and accessible. When Aunt Martha comes to visit, just roll it out, grab the vase and you're golden.

A.

B.

C.

C. HANGER SHELF

Sometimes you just need another place to hang clothes, such as on the shelf over the washer and dryer. Turn the edge of that shelf into a hanger rack by predrilling some 3/4-in. plastic pipe and screwing it to the top of the shelf along the edge.

Taming Tech Clutter

Streamline components and hide your wires.

A. TUCK AWAY WIRES IN SURFACE-MOUNT CHANNEL

This CordMate cord-cover kit by Wiremold is a nice solution for someone who's not quite up for cutting holes in walls and fishing wires. It's adhesive backed, so you don't need to make any screw holes in the wall, and there's room inside for several wires. To make the channel less visible, paint it the same color as your walls. Several kits are available at home centers and online depending how many feet of cord you need to cover—different options cover anywhere from 9 to 15 ft. of cords.

B. CONTROL CORDS WITH STICK-ON CLIPS

A quick search online turns up all manner of wire management systems. Simple wire clips are hard to beat for routing cords. We particularly like these adhesive-backed clips. They're low profile and have a small footprint, so they are easy to hide along the edge of a desk. Prices vary, but all are inexpensive. The eBoot clips shown on the desk are available online.

C. ADD A RECESSED OUTLET

The best way to get the TV as flat against the wall as possible and hide cords is to install an approved (listed) recessed outlet directly behind the TV. The plug for the TV often limits how close to the wall you can get, but this outlet solves that problem elegantly. Besides being recessed into the wall, the outlet is angled, allowing a clean, wall-hugging installation. This unit also has an opening for other cables to pass through. If you have an outlet lower on the wall, directly below the TV, all you need to do is cut a hole for the new unit and drop a cable to the existing outlet for power.

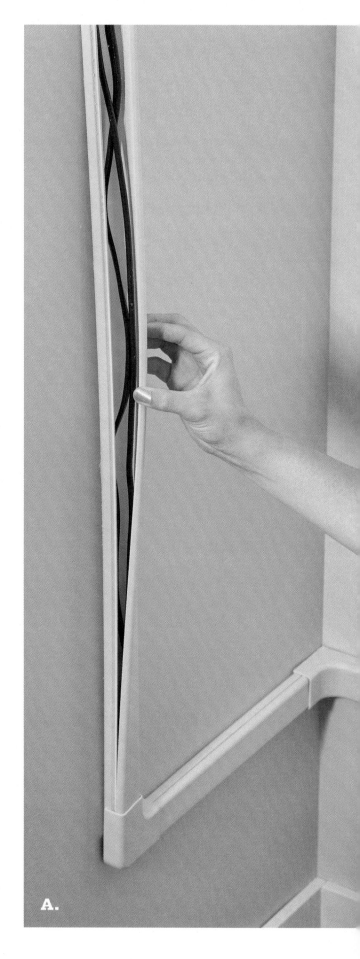

A.

B.

C.

Craft Center

Build a worktable with a huge surface, convenient storage and easy mobility by sandwiching three small storage units between a base with casters and a plywood top with hardwood edging.

First, cut the hardwood plywood for the top and base and install hardwood edging and iron-on edge banding as shown in **Step 1**. Position two Kallax shelving units back to back and fasten them to the base with flat-head sheet metal screws after drilling countersink pilot holes through the Kallax frames **(Step 2)**.

The frames are hollow panels, so be careful not to punch through their thin faces when drilling the countersinks. Make sure the screw heads seat flush.

Install the third Kallax unit across the front of the base, using the same method. Then tip the assembly over onto the top and fasten it as before **(Step 3)**. Install locking swivel casters **(Step 4)**. Then tip the assembly right-side up and round over all the top's sharp edges with a router and a round-over bit. Complete the job by installing Kallax drawer inserts and applying your favorite finish to the top **(Step 5)**.

WHAT IT TAKES	
TIME 1 day	**SKILL LEVEL** Beginner

TOOLS & MATERIALS
Circular saw (or table saw), clothes iron (optional: edge trimmer) driver/drill, countersink bit

1 Make the top and base

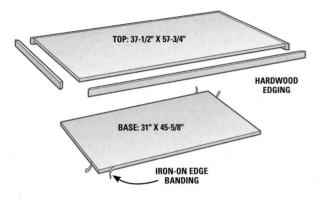

TOP: 37-1/2" X 57-3/4"

HARDWOOD EDGING

BASE: 31" X 45-5/8"

IRON-ON EDGE BANDING

2 Fasten units to base

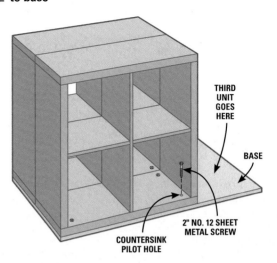

THIRD UNIT GOES HERE

BASE

2" NO. 12 SHEET METAL SCREW

COUNTERSINK PILOT HOLE

3 Fasten top

10-1/2"

TOP

4 Attach casters and flip over

LOCKING SWIVEL CASTERS

5 Round edges, install drawers

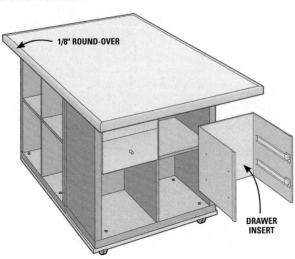

1/8" ROUND-OVER

DRAWER INSERT

Materials List

ITEM	QTY.
IKEA Kallax Shelving Unit No. 202.794.59	3
IKEA Kallax Insert with Two Drawers No. 702.866.50	2
4' x 8' x 3/4" birch plywood	2
Birch iron-on edge banding	25
3/4" x 1-1/2" birch or maple solid wood	20'
3" locking swivel casters	4
No. 12 x 2" flat-head sheet metal screws	24
Polyurethane, wood glue	

Secret Hiding Places

It's easy to fool would-be thieves by placing your valuables in unexpected places. Here's how.

A. FALSE-BOTTOM DRAWER

Pick a deep drawer so the depth change won't be obvious. Cut 1/4-in. plywood 1/16 in. smaller than the drawer opening and rest it on a couple of wood strips that are hot-glued to the drawer sides. Then hot-glue some item you'd expect to find in that drawer to the bottom so you have a handle to lift the false bottom and reveal the booty.

B. TOE-KICK HIDEAWAY

There's an enormous 4-in.-tall cavity under all those kitchen cabinets behind the toe-kicks. You can pull the toe-kicks free and make them removable. Most are 1/4-in. plywood held in place with 1-in. brads, and they're pretty easy to pull off. If you have a secondary 3/4-in. toe-kick, you'll have to cut it out at both ends. An oscillating tool works well for that task.

Stick both halves of round hook-and-loop self-adhesive tape to the toe-kick. Then push the toe-kick into place. The adhesive will stick to the cabinet base and leave half of the hook-and-loop tape in place when you pull it free.

C. BURIED TREASURE

Roll up some cash, stick it in a medicine bottle or any other watertight container, and bury it in a potted plant. For quicker access and to keep dirt from getting under your fingernails, place a stone or pine cone over it. Not many burglars are going to be excavating around your houseplants.

D. CABINET HIDEY-HOLE

Between almost every pair of upper cabinets, there will be a 1/2-in. gap. Take advantage of that gap by hanging a manila envelope containing, oh, how about two grand? Hang the cash with a set of binder clips too wide to fall through.

E. COUNTERFEIT CONTAINERS

Go online and type in "secret hiding places" and you'll be amazed by how many brand-name phony containers are available. But you can save some money and craft a homemade version. This mayonnaise jar had its interior spray-painted with cream-colored paint for plastic.

F. THE 'FAKE PIPE' TRICK

Put in a fake PVC pipe complete with a cleanout plug in your basement. Unscrew the plug, and there are the goods.

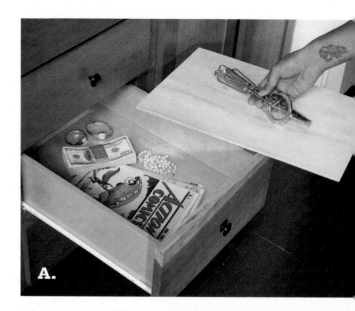

A.

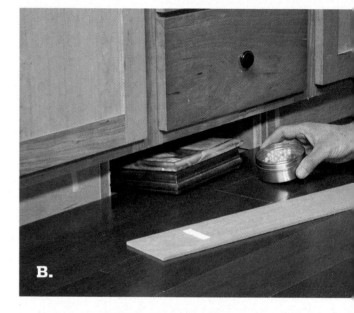

B.

C.

D.

E.

F.

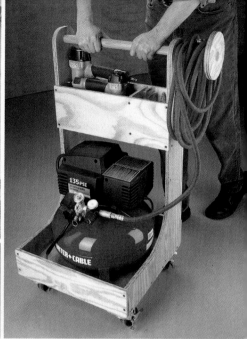

CHAPTER **FIVE**

WORKSHOP

Drill Dock

Keep your drills and drivers from contributing to workbench clutter with this simple, easily customizable organizer.

Cordless drills and drivers are our most-used tools. We couldn't work without them. But with their chargers and spare batteries, they're also a prime source of workbench clutter. What they need is a dedicated space that allows for easy organization and instant access—like this drill dock.

CUSTOMIZE IT!

If the drill dock shown here suits your needs perfectly, just go ahead and build it as detailed in **Figure A**. If you find those measurements won't work for you or you need to allot your space differently, you can easily alter the dock. Here are a few of our suggestions:

■ Three-inch PVC pipe is best for the holsters and accommodates most tools. A 10-ft. pipe costs less than $20. Many home centers also sell shorter lengths.
■ We made our holsters 12 in. long. Shorter is absolutely fine, but don't go so short that you'll have to remove bits in order to stow the tools. Cut the pipe with a miter saw or a handsaw.

■ Leave enough space between holsters so that you can comfortably grab the tool. We centered our holsters 6-1/2 in. apart.
■ Adjusting the width of the dock to suit your tools is easy; just change the length of the shelves and the back. But don't skimp. Leave space for future tools.
■ Get a power strip and park it on the bottom shelf so you can plug in all your chargers. Drill a hole in the side of the dock to accommodate the power strip cord.
■ Tools and batteries are heavy, so build the dock from 3/4-in. plywood. Ours required a 4 x 4-ft. sheet ($20).

WHAT IT TAKES	
TIME 2 hours	**SKILL LEVEL** Beginner

TOOLS & MATERIALS
Clamp (optional), jigsaw, circular saw, basic hand tools, drill

1 Measure with a clamp. To determine the width of the pipe slot, use a clamp to measure the width of the tool handle.

2 Mark the slot. Transfer the handle width to the pipe and mark out the slot. You should make the slot about 1/8 in. wider than the tool handle. The length of the slot isn't critical; 5 in. is about right for most drills.

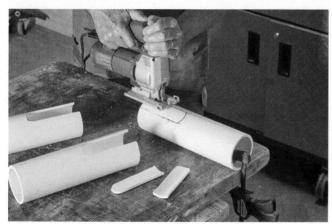

3 Cut the slot. A fine-tooth jigsaw blade, such as a metal-cutting blade, is best. After cutting, ease the sharp edges with a file or sandpaper.

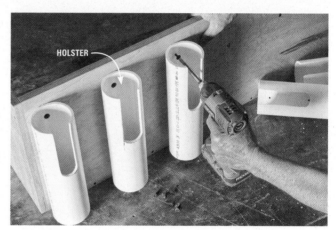

HOLSTER

4 Mount the holsters. Drill holes in the pipes and fasten each with at least two screws. You can mount the holsters on an existing shelf, or you can build the drill dock as shown below.

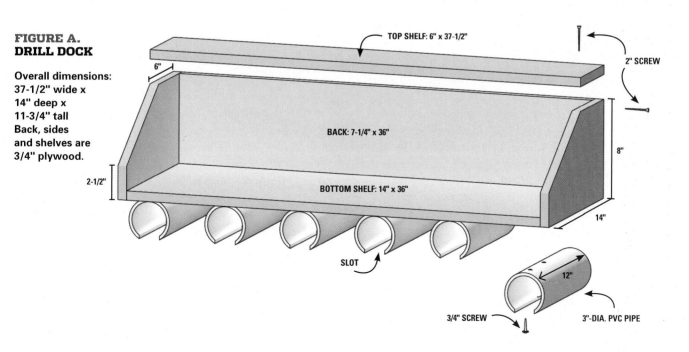

FIGURE A.
DRILL DOCK

Overall dimensions:
37-1/2" wide x
14" deep x
11-3/4" tall
Back, sides
and shelves are
3/4" plywood.

TOP SHELF: 6" x 37-1/2"

2" SCREW

6"

BACK: 7-1/4" x 36"

8"

2-1/2"

BOTTOM SHELF: 14" x 36"

14"

SLOT

12"

3/4" SCREW

3"-DIA. PVC PIPE

Benchtop Organizer

**Combine a few plastic bins with a simple plywood cabinet
to super-organize small stuff.**

A stack of plastic bins can organize thousands of small items, but it's not very convenient when the bin you need is at the bottom of the stack—then you have to take them all down, get what you need and put them all back. That's annoying. The point of this cabinet is to eliminate the bother: You can slide out any bin, anytime.

You can easily build a cabinet identical to this one. Or you can customize it, using larger or smaller bins, more bins or fewer. Whatever configuration you choose, this project is a great clutter solution for the garage, workshop or craft room.

SHOP BEFORE YOU BUILD

We bought our cabinet at a home center. Most discount stores and home centers carry similar bins. Whichever one you purchase, be sure the bins you choose have a sturdy rim that can rest on the runners. You'll also need a 2 x 4-ft. sheet of 1/2-in. plywood for the cabinet box. If you have a table saw, you can cut runners from any 3/4-in.-thick board. If not, check the millwork aisle at your home center. You'll find 1/4 x 3/4-in. stock like we used or other moldings that will work. When you're done shopping, just follow **Photos 1-3** and **Figure A** to build the cabinet.

WHAT IT TAKES	
TIME 2 hours	**SKILL LEVEL** Beginner
TOOLS & MATERIALS Table saw or circular saw, driver/drill, nail gun (optional)	

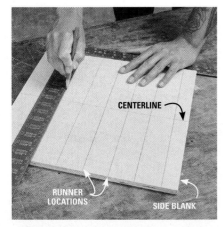

1 Mark both cabinet sides at once. Mark the centerline and the runner locations onto a single plywood blank. In Step 3, you'll cut the blank in half to make two identical cabinet sides.

2 Attach the runners. You can use brads, staples, nails or screws. Just be sure to keep the fasteners at least 1/2 in. away from the centerline so you don't hit them with your saw in Step 3.

3 Cut the blank in half. Set the table saw fence at 7-1/2 in. and cut the blank. Since the blank is slightly oversized, also trim the offcut side to 7-1/2 in. If you don't have a table saw, make the cuts with a circular saw or jigsaw. Join the two sides to the top, bottom and back as shown in Figure A.

FIGURE A.
BENCHTOP ORGANIZER

Overall dimensions: 15-1/4" tall x 11-3/4" wide x 8" deep

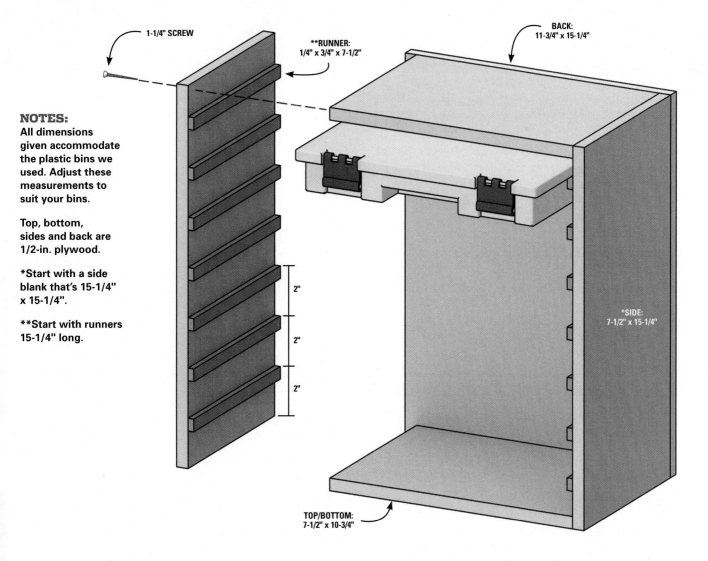

1-1/4" SCREW

**RUNNER:
1/4" x 3/4" x 7-1/2"

BACK:
11-3/4" x 15-1/4"

NOTES:

All dimensions given accommodate the plastic bins we used. Adjust these measurements to suit your bins.

Top, bottom, sides and back are 1/2-in. plywood.

*Start with a side blank that's 15-1/4" x 15-1/4".

**Start with runners 15-1/4" long.

2"

2"

2"

*SIDE:
7-1/2" x 15-1/4"

TOP/BOTTOM:
7-1/2" x 10-3/4"

Workshop Storage Tips

Take advantage of these inventive ways to organize your work space.

A.

A. UP, UP AND AWAY

Put joist spaces to use with this simple storage idea. Fasten eye screws to the joists and cut lengths of chain to keep odd lengths of trim and pipe out of the way but easy to find. Open one side of the eye screw with a pliers to slip the chain into place. Make the chain a bit longer for future expansion.

B. PVC PIPE CLAMP RACK

Are your pipe clamps missing in action right when you need them? Build this snap-in, snap-out storage rack from PVC pipe. For 1/2-in.-diameter iron pipe, use 3/4-in. PVC, and for 3/4-in.-diameter pipe, use 1-in. PVC.

To make the rack, cut 2-in. lengths of PVC, and with a hacksaw or band saw, slice them lengthwise about 3/16 in. past the diameter's centerline. This creates the gripping action to firmly hold the heavy iron pipe. Drill and countersink two holes in each PVC piece, then screw them to a pair of boards. Attach the upper board to your shop wall and snap a pipe clamp in each end to position the lower board for screwing to the wall.

C. STORE SHEET GOODS ON A LADDER

An old extension ladder is just right for holding leftover plywood, drywall, plastic laminate and spare boards. Take the ladder sections apart, lay one on the floor near a wall and then load it up. This handy rack will hold your sheet goods high and dry, and make it easier to find what you need.

D. ADJUSTABLE DRAWER DIVIDERS

You can restore order to messy shop drawers with 1/4-in. plywood partitions and self-stick weather stripping. For the strongest grip, use spongy "closed cell" weather stripping.

Apply weather stripping to the two sides of a drawer as shown, then cut the partitions long enough so they squish firmly into the rubber on both ends. A good rule of thumb is to make the partitions 1/4 in. longer than the inside measurement between the pieces of weather stripping.

B.

C.

D.

Ultimate Tool Corral

A cabinet designed with tools in mind.

This cabinet provides a home for all your tools. Park often-used power tools on the shelves and occasionally used tools in the deep drawers. The shallower drawers are perfect for hand tools, blades, bits and accessories. And the countertop is just large enough for tool setup or adjustments. We built a double-wide cabinet out of hardwoods. You could cut costs by using pine lumber.

EDGE THE PLYWOOD

Most home centers carry "screen molding," which works great for edging plywood. But we couldn't find it in birch, so we cut our own edging from birch boards. Start by ripping approximately 100 ft. of solid wood into 3/16-in. strips (LL). We used a simple (and safe!) setup to cut multiple thin strips: Just round the end of a 1x4 slightly and clamp it to the saw table **(Photo 1)**. Position this block slightly in front of the blade, not directly next to it.

Next, cut the plywood parts (B-G, N), but cut them extra long by 1/4 to 1/2 in. The extra length will allow you to trim the parts to final size after the edging is on.

Cut the edging strips to approximately the same length as the oversized plywood, and attach with glue and nails **(Photo 2)**. Make sure the edging overhangs the plywood as you tack it down. Also clamp the edging **(Photo 3)**.

After the glue dries, the protruding edging needs to be flushed up to the plywood. You could use a sander, but you run the risk of sanding through the thin veneer and ruining the part. Instead, use a trim router retrofitted with an offset base. Set the router on the plywood, lower the bit until it just touches and trim the edging flush to the plywood **(Photo 4)**. All that's left is a little hand sanding and you've got perfect edging.

WHAT IT TAKES	
TIME Two weekends	**SKILL LEVEL** Intermediate
TOOLS & MATERIALS Table saw, router, driver/drill, brad nailer or pin nailer, clamps	

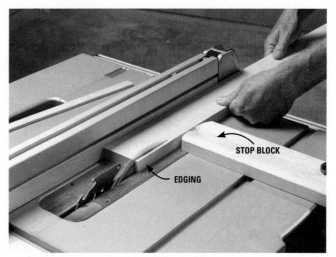

1 Cut the edging safely. Don't simply set the fence 3/16 in. from the blade to cut the edging strips. That can lead to kickbacks when the thin strips get pinched between the fence and the blade. Instead, clamp a stop block 3/16 in. from the blade. Set the stock against the stop block, position the fence against the stock and you're ready to rip. You'll need to reset the fence after each cut.

2 Tack on the edging. Spread a little glue and tack the edging onto the plywood parts with a pinner or brad nailer. Center the edging by "feel," allowing it to overhang slightly on both sides. The edging can also overhang the plywood at one end, but the other end should be flush with the plywood.

FIGURE A.
TOOL CABINET

Overall dimensions:
80" tall x 61-1/2" wide x 26" deep

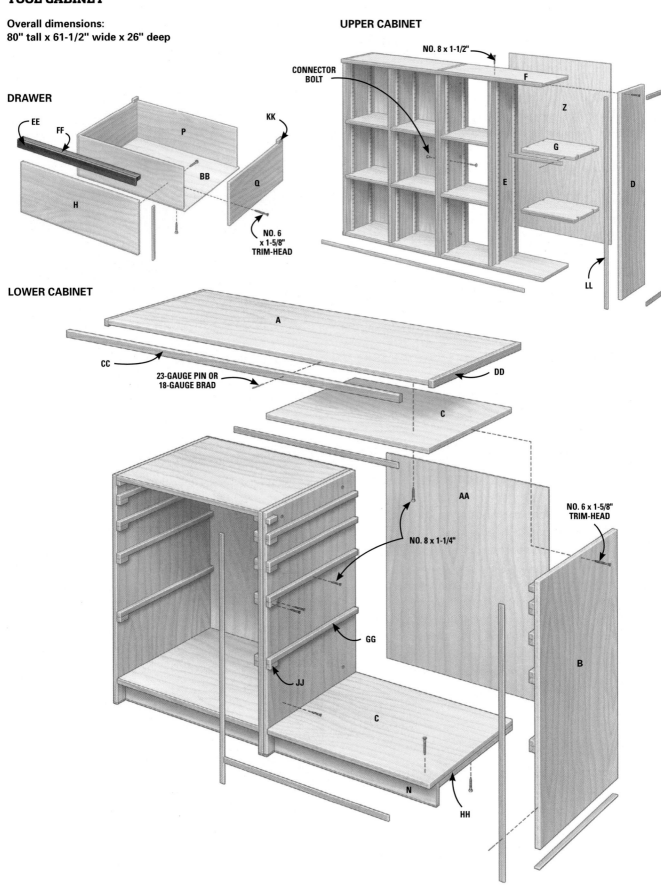

DRAWER

UPPER CABINET

NO. 8 x 1-1/2"

CONNECTOR
BOLT

EE
FF
P
KK
Z
F
G
D
BB
Q
E
H
NO. 6
x 1-5/8"
TRIM-HEAD
LL

LOWER CABINET

A
CC
DD
23-GAUGE PIN OR
18-GAUGE BRAD
C
AA
NO. 6 x 1-5/8"
TRIM-HEAD
NO. 8 x 1-1/4"
GG
B
JJ
C
N
HH

Trim the cabinet parts to their final length on the table saw. Set the fence a little long and use a miter gauge to cut one end. Then, set the fence to the final length and cut the opposite edge. This leaves your edging perfectly flush and square to the plywood on both ends.

BUILD THE CABINETS

Set the cleats (GG, HH) on the lower cabinet sides with screws. Use MDF spacers to ensure correct spacing **(Photo 5)**. Align the cleats flush with the front edge of the cabinet sides. Leave a 1/4-in. gap at the back to prevent dust accumulation that would interfere with the drawer closing.

Assemble the lower cabinets, using trim-head screws for the top shelf. The bottom shelf is fastened with regular wood screws through the bottom cleat **(Photo 6)**. Cut the backs (Z, AA) and attach them with just a few screws for now.

Assemble the upper cabinets with regular screws. They will be covered with trim later. The adjustable shelves are notched to prevent the shelves from accidentally pulling out when you drag your circular saw off the shelf. We notched

FIGURE B.
CLEAT POSITIONS

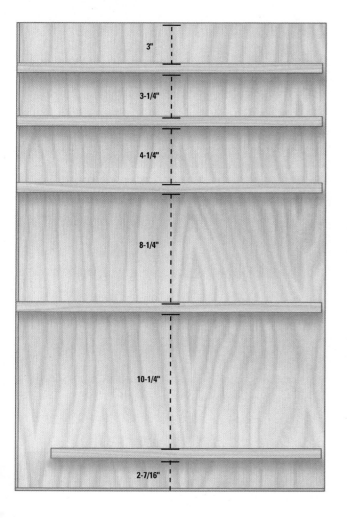

3"

3-1/4"

4-1/4"

8-1/4"

10-1/4"

2-7/16"

Materials List

ITEM	QTY.
4' x 8' x 3/4" birch plywood	4
4' x 8' x 1/2" birch plywood	2
4' x 8' x 1/4" birch plywood	4
1" x 6" x 3/4" birch or maple	60 lin. ft.
48" shelf standards	15
Shelf clips	32
Connector bolts	6

EDGING

CAUL

3 Clamp the edging. Clamps alone won't force the flimsy edging tight against the plywood, so use a thicker board or "caul" to distribute the pressure evenly.

RISER

4 Trim the edging flush. A straight router bit set at just the right depth will trim off the protruding edging without cutting into the plywood. Remove the plastic base plate from your router and mount the router on a "riser" scrap of MDF, plywood or melamine.

FIGURE C:
CUTTING DIAGRAMS

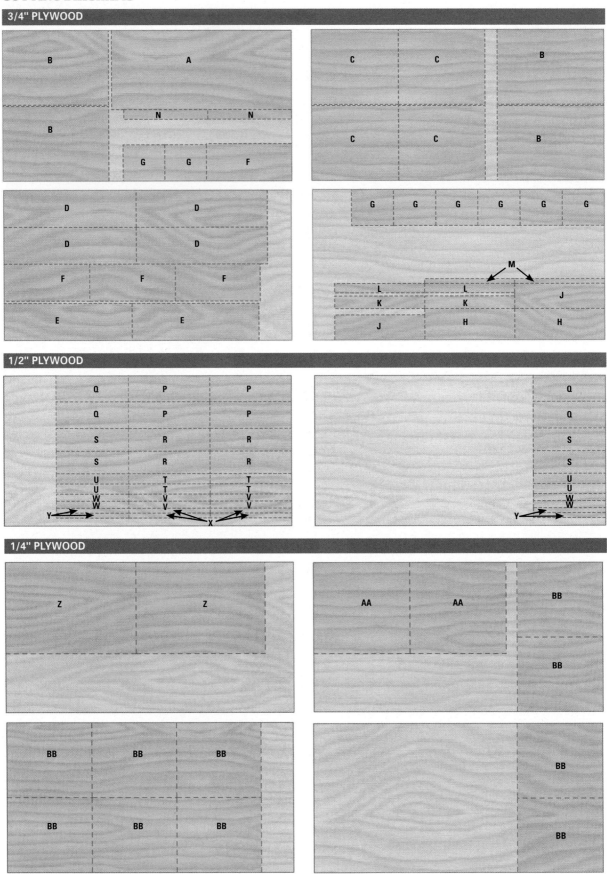

3/4" PLYWOOD

1/2" PLYWOOD

1/4" PLYWOOD

the shelves four at a time. Attach a wood sub-fence to your miter gauge. Clamp the shelves together, then clamp the set to your sub-fence to gang-cut the notches **(Photo 7)**. Shift the stack for each cut until the notch is cut full width. Lay out the notch locations on one shelf according to shelf standard spacing. We put ours 2 in. from the front and back. Make the notches 1/4 in. deep and 3/4 in. wide.

Attach the two base cabinets to each other with screws. Measure and cut the plywood top (A). Apply the edging (CC, DD) to the top with nails and glue, then clamp with cauls. Attach the top and set the upper cabinets. Join the upper cabinets with connector bolts.

BUILD THE DRAWERS

Cut the drawer parts (P-Y and BB). To start, build just one drawer box and check for fit. We used No. 6 x 1-5/8-in. trim-head screws to build the drawer boxes. Make sure the drawer is square, then secure the bottom with No. 6 x 1-in. screws. Test the drawer fit in its opening on both cabinets. If the drawer slides smoothly, go ahead and assemble the other drawers. If it's tight, trim the fronts and backs down a bit for a good fit. Countersink all the screw heads into the plywood bottom so they don't interfere with the sliding of the drawer on the cleats.

Remove the backs on the lower cabinets and set the drawers in their openings. Add a couple of short shims (KK) on the sides at the back of the cabinet to center the drawer when it's shut. Glue the shims to the sides with the tapered

Cutting List

KEY	QTY.	DIMENSIONS	DESCRIPTION
3/4" plywood			
A	1	25-1/4" x 60"	Top
B	4	23-13/16" x 35"	Lower cabinet sides
C	4	23-13/16" x 28-1/2"	Lower cabinet top and bottom
D	4	11-13/16" x 44"	Upper cabinet sides
E	2	11-13/16" x 42-1/2"	Upper cabinet dividers
F	4	11-13/16" x 28-1/2"	Upper cabinet top and bottom
G	8	11-1/2" x 13-7/8"	Upper cabinet adjustable shelves
H	2	10" x 29-5/8"	Drawer front
J	2	8" x 29-5/8"	Drawer front
K	2	4" x 29-5/8"	Drawer front
L	2	3" x 29-5/8"	Drawer front
M	2	1-1/2" x 29-5/8"	Drawer front
N	2	3-1/8" x 28"	Toe-kick
1/2" plywood			
P	4	8-1/2" x 27-3/8"	Drawer box front and back
Q	4	8-1/2" x 24"	Drawer box side
R	4	7-1/4" x 27-3/8"	Drawer box front and back
S	4	7-1/4" x 24"	Drawer box side
T	4	3-1/4" x 27-3/8"	Drawer box front and back
U	4	3-1/4" x 24"	Drawer box side
V	4	2-1/4" x 27-3/8"	Drawer box front and back
W	4	2-1/4" x 24"	Drawer box side
X	4	1-9/16" x 27-3/8"	Drawer box front and back
Y	4	1-9/16" x 24"	Drawer box side
1/4" plywood			
Z	2	30" x 44"	Upper back
AA	2	30" x 35-1/4"	Lower back
BB	10	24" x 28-3/8"	Drawer bottom
Solid wood			
CC	1	3/4" x 1" x 61-1/2"	Top edging
DD	2	3/4" x 1" x 25-1/4"	Top edging
EE	10	1/2" x 1-1/4" x 30"	Drawer pull
FF	10	3/4" x 1-1/4" x 30"	Drawer pull
GG	16	3/4" x 3/4" x 23-3/4"	Drawer cleat
HH	4	3/4" x 3/4" x 21-1/4"	Bottom shelf cleat
JJ	20	3/4" x 3/4" x 2"	Drawer stop
KK	20	1/2" x 1/4"– 3/4" x 2"	Drawer kicker
LL	1	3/4" x 3/16" x 100'	Edging

5 Mount the drawer cleats. Position the drawer-support cleats with scrap wood spacers. Use the same set of spacers on all four cabinet sides to ensure identical spacing.

6 Assemble the cabinets. No need for glue—just use screws. The bottom shelf is attached to the bottom cleat. Use trim-head screws for the top shelf. The small holes are easy to fill and will be virtually invisible below the top edging.

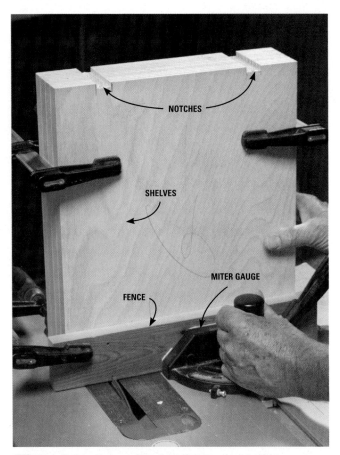

NOTCHES

SHELVES

MITER GAUGE

FENCE

7 Notch the shelves. Notches fit over the shelf supports and prevent the shelves from slipping out of the cabinet. To cut notches, mount a fence on your miter gauge and clamp the shelves to it. Make several passes to complete each notch.

edge facing forward. The shims ensure the drawer shuts in the same position each time. This will help maintain an even margin on the drawer fronts when the drawers are closed.

Cut your drawer fronts (H-M), leaving them a little oversize. Add edging to the bottom of each drawer front. Flush-trim the edging. Cut the drawer fronts to final length on the table saw. Add the trim to the sides, flush-trim and rip the drawer front to the final width.

Now it's time to build the handles. Cut the drawer handle parts (EE, FF). Cut a 45-degree bevel on part EE **(Photo 8)**. Glue and clamp the parts to form the handle. When the glue has set, sand the handles smooth and attach to the drawer fronts. We used glue and nails, but you could use trim-head screws to attach the handles as well.

With the drawers in their openings, hold the top drawer front in place so the bottom of the drawer front is flush with the bottom of the drawer box and even with the outside edge of the cabinet. Pin the drawer front in place with a brad nailer or a 23-gauge pin nailer. Carefully open the drawer by pushing on it from behind. Clamp the drawer front in place and secure it with No. 10 x 1-in. washer head screws. Use a 3/32-in.-thick strip of wood to space the other drawer fronts as you work your way down.

We finished our cabinets with a penetrating oil finish, then added part JJ, the drawer stops **(Photo 9)**. You can add dividers or line the drawer bottoms with nonslip mats so your hand tools don't rattle around. Best of all, you'll know right where to find your tools—that is, if you remember to put them away. But that's not something we can help you with.

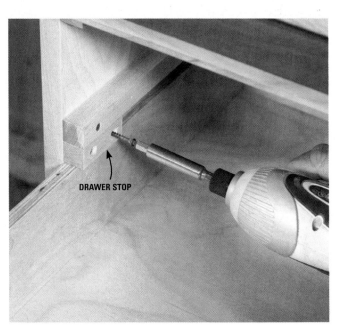

FEATHER-BOARD

HANDLE STOCK

DRAWER STOP

8 Bevel the handle stock. Set the table saw blade to 45 degrees and mount featherboards on the table to hold the stock tight against the fence. As you reach the end of the cut, drive the stock with a push stick to keep your fingers away from the blade.

9 Attach stop blocks with screws. Stop blocks add a measure of safety so the drawer can't be pulled all the way out and crash to the floor.

Roll-Around Tool Caddy

This simple workstation rolls right up to the job—anywhere in the work area.

by Brad Neumann

With specialty tools organized and within easy reach, there's no more wandering around the shop gathering materials.

As shown here, the caddy is configured for woodturning and is ready to roll up to the lathe. Gearheads could build it with a flat top with bins for sockets and wrenches and add shelves below for car supplies. Woodworkers could outfit it with planes, mallets and chisels. However it's used, just roll it out of the way at the end of the job.

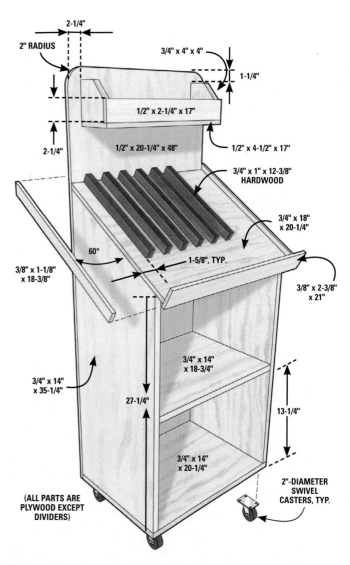

2-1/4"

2" RADIUS

3/4" x 4" x 4"

1-1/4"

1/2" x 2-1/4" x 17"

2-1/4"

1/2" x 20-1/4" x 48"

1/2" x 4-1/2" x 17"

3/4" x 1" x 12-3/8" HARDWOOD

3/4" x 18" x 20-1/4"

60°

1-5/8", TYP.

3/8" x 1-1/8" x 18-3/8"

3/8" x 2-3/8" x 21"

3/4" x 14" x 35-1/4"

3/4" x 14" x 18-3/4"

27-1/4"

13-1/4"

3/4" x 14" x 20-1/4"

2"-DIAMETER SWIVEL CASTERS, TYP.

(ALL PARTS ARE PLYWOOD EXCEPT DIVIDERS)

WHAT IT TAKES	
TIME 3 - 4 hours	**SKILL LEVEL** Beginner
TOOLS & MATERIALS Circular saw, driver/drill	

French Cleat Tool Wall

A wall easy to build and easy to reconfigure as your tool collection grows.

Just think of it—a storage system for your garage or shop that you can endlessly reconfigure to accommodate all your tools. They'll be right at your fingertips whenever you need them. And when it's time to straighten up at the end of the

What is a French Cleat?

French cleats are an ingenious means of hanging just about anything. Mating 45-degree bevels—one on the wall, the other on the tool holder—interlock to form a rock-solid connection. You just drop the tool holder over the cleat and it's done—perfectly level, perfectly solid. No fasteners!

WHAT IT TAKES

TIME
2 weekends as shown

SKILL LEVEL
Intermediate

TOOLS & MATERIALS
Table saw, miter saw, drill/driver, stepladder, level

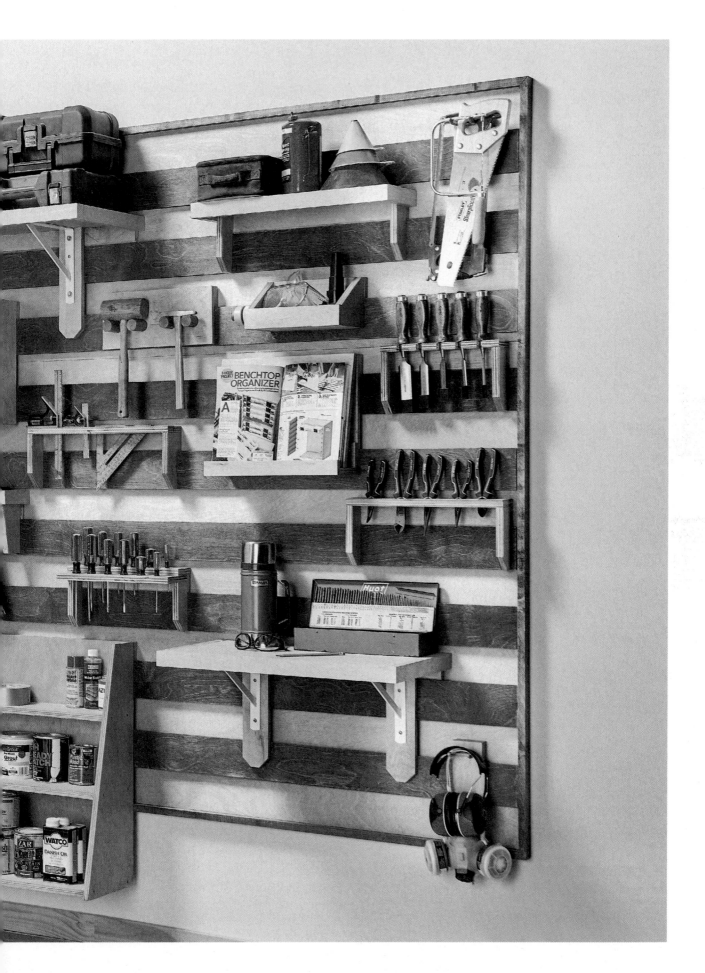

1 Mount a temporary ledger. Cut one of the wall cleats to width (Photo 4), then level it and screw it to the wall studs.

2 Hang the plywood. Rest the first sheet on the temporary ledger and screw it to the studs with 2-in. screws spaced every 12 in. Rest the second sheet on top of the first; screw it to the studs as well. Remove the temporary ledger.

day, you'll know right where everything goes, making cleanup quick and easy.

How much you spend depends not only on the size of your storage wall but also on the level of finish you're after. We spent about $500 on the materials for our wall, but you could build it for about half the price by using 3/4-in. CDX construction plywood.

SIZE IT TO FIT YOUR NEEDS

Placed above a temporary ledger **(Photo 1)**, our wall is two horizontal sheets of 3/4-in. birch plywood (a 4 x 8-ft. sheet and a 2 x 8-ft. sheet; **Photo 2**), with 1x2 maple trim **(Photo 3)**. The size of your wall depends on how much you want to store and how much space you have. The construction techniques are the same for any size wall.

APPLY THE FINISH TO FULL SHEETS BEFORE CUTTING

We prefinished the plywood and trim boards. You should too; it saves lots of time and gives you a smoother finish. You'll still have to coat the cut edges, but that's a lot easier than finishing the entire wall after it's built.

We used Varathane Summer Oak and American Walnut stains to create the light and dark parts. We rolled on the stain with 4-in. foam rollers and then wiped it off with cotton rags. Topcoat with a water-based polyurethane.

A TABLE SAW MAKES THE PROJECT MUCH EASIER

The best tool for ripping the parts and cleats is a table saw. However, if you don't have access to one, you can also make the cuts with a straightedge and a circular saw. If you go that route, it's worth building a dedicated straightedge. To find out how, search for "create circular saw cutting guides" at familyhandyman.com.

A miter saw works well for cutting miters on edge banding and the 45-degree angles on many of the components. Flatten the point of each bevel **(Photo 4)** so they won't cut you or splinter off when you hang your tool holders. You can assemble your tool holders with either glue and 2-in. brads, or 2-in. and 1-1/4-in. trim-head screws.

PLAN FOR OUTLETS

If you have existing outlets near the floor, you can tap into those outlets to feed new outlets in the slat wall itself. These new outlets can be at workbench level to feed battery chargers or higher up to power lights.

You can cut holes in the drywall and feed cable to those locations. No need to patch those holes because they will be covered by the wall. Leave the cables coiled behind the plywood and note their locations. Then you can cut outlet holes in the plywood and insert "remodeling" junction boxes.

3 Add the border. Cut the 1x2 to fit around the perimeter and nail it into place with 2-in. 18-gauge brads.

1x2 TRIM

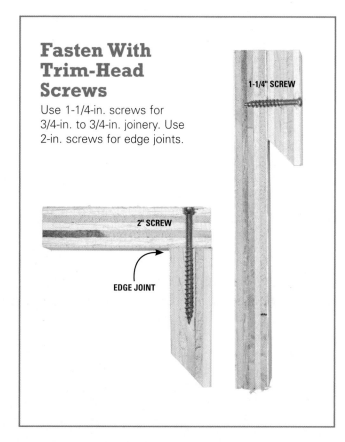

Fasten With Trim-Head Screws

Use 1-1/4-in. screws for 3/4-in. to 3/4-in. joinery. Use 2-in. screws for edge joints.

1-1/4" SCREW

2" SCREW

EDGE JOINT

1/8" FLAT SPOT

4 Cut the wall cleats. Rip the French cleat strips for the wall to 4 in. wide. Then reset the saw to 45 degrees and adjust the fence to leave about a 1/8-in. flat area at the point of the bevels. Cut the 45-degree bevels on the strips. Repeat the process for the accessory cleats, but be sure to rip them to 2-1/2 in. wide.

2x4 SPACER

5 Mount the wall cleats. Space the cleats with a 2x4 block and secure them with a pair of 1-1/4-in. trim-head screws spaced every 16 in. Keep the screws 1 in. from the tops and bottoms of the cleats.

FRENCH CLEAT TOOL WALL BUILDING TIPS

Most of the tool holders take less than 20 minutes to build. Have fun and don't be afraid to toss your failures and try again. Here are tips to help you build your wall and make custom holders for your tools and gear.

A. SMALL SUPPORT

Small shelves can get by with minimal support. They'll need only vertical supports that cover one wall cleat.

B. PLYWOOD OPTIONAL

If your garage or shop wall has exposed studs, you'll find the plywood in our plan ideal for finishing the wall. But you could also screw the wall cleats right through existing plywood or drywall, or even directly to the studs.

C. MEDIUM SUPPORT

Medium-size shelves, depending on their design and the weight of their contents, may need to span more than one cleat.

D. LARGE SUPPORT

Support large, heavy units with double cleats. Screw the top cleat to the tool holder, then hang it on the wall with the bottom cleat already nested in the wall cleat. That way you can screw the tool holder to the bottom cleat from the front, in exactly the right position.

E. PLAN YOUR TOOL HOLDERS

Lay out the tools or other items to help you decide what type and size holder will work the best.

F. FIND THE BEST HARDWARE

Take advantage of the hardware aisle—this is what it's there for! Stroll through the hardware section at your favorite home center. Choose hooks, racks and shelf brackets, and build components to suit them.

A.

B.

C.

D.

E.

F.

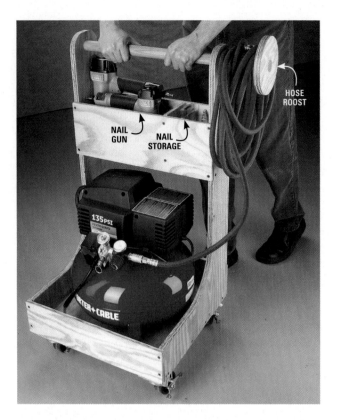

NAIL GUN

NAIL STORAGE

HOSE ROOST

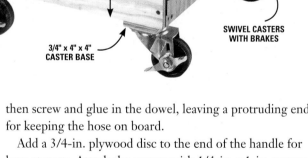

1-1/4" x 25-1/2" DOWEL

3/4" x 6"-DIA. PLYWOOD

PARTITION

1/2" x 7"

5"

34" RISER HEIGHT

CUT A GENTLE CURVE

3/4" x 18" x 18" FLOOR

19-1/2"

3/4" x 18"

1/2" x 5"

SWIVEL CASTERS WITH BRAKES

3/4" x 4" x 4" CASTER BASE

Compressor Cart

Here's a smart way to mobilize your air compressor, and you can neatly store air nailers, nails and air hoses on board. Our cart's dimensions fit a pancake-style compressor, but you can easily adapt the dimensions for another style.

To build one like ours, you'll need:

- Two 2 x 4-ft. sheets of 3/4-in. plywood
- Scraps of 1/2-in. plywood
- 1-1/4-in. x 3-ft. dowel
- Four 3-in. casters with brakes and miscellaneous hardware

Cut the floor from 3/4-in. plywood, and then screw four square pieces of 3/4-in. plywood under it where you will attach the casters. Cut the side risers from 3/4-in. plywood and screw them to the floor. Then cut the front and back pieces from 1/2-in. plywood and screw them together to form a box for the compressor.

Build the tool storage box on the risers with a 3/4-in. floor and 1/2-in. sides, adding a plywood partition to organize the storage space. Drill 1-1/4-in. holes in the ends of the risers,

then screw and glue in the dowel, leaving a protruding end for keeping the hose on board.

Add a 3/4-in. plywood disc to the end of the handle for hose storage. Attach the casters with 1/4-in. x 1-in. screws. Finally, load up your cart and head for your next project!

WHAT IT TAKES	
TIME 1 - 2 hours	**SKILL LEVEL** Beginner
TOOLS & MATERIALS Circular saw, driver/drill	

Tool Tray Tower

It can be hard to keep hand tools organized—this nifty tool tray fixes that.

Because most hand tools are relatively flat, piling them in deep drawers wastes a lot of space and makes them hard to find or dig out. This rather fetching cabinet separates and organizes all those tools. Best of all, you can remove the tray containing, say, the open-end wrenches and take the whole collection to wherever you're wrenching.

There are several plain versions of this design: a few drawers made from MDF with utilitarian handles. We opted to bump it up a notch and build a 10-tray unit out of cabinet-grade birch plywood. And rather than use handles, we made the tray bases with built-in "paddle pulls."

Shaping the paddle pulls is the trickiest part of the whole project. You'll get the best results by clamping the tray bottoms together and "gang-cutting" the paddle pulls all at once with a band saw. Sanding them all at once also saves lots of time and ensures that the parts are identical **(Photo 5)**. (Then get the alternating paddle pulls by flipping over half of the tray bottoms.) If you don't have a band saw, a jigsaw will do. If you're jigsawing, mark one paddle pull

on a tray bottom, and use it to scribe and gang-cut five at a time. You could also just skip the paddle pulls and add the drawer pulls of your choice.

To do that, cut the tray bottoms to 15-1/2 x 12 in., but "gang-sand" them all as shown in **Photo 5**.

WHAT IT TAKES	
TIME 1 day	**SKILL LEVEL** Intermediate

TOOLS & MATERIALS
Table saw (optional: dado blade), jigsaw (or band saw), brad nailer, belt sander

This project calls for a table saw and a dado blade. The good news is that absolutely no hardware is needed, which means no fussy, expensive drawer slides to mess around with.

This project is a real plywood eater. You'll need a full sheet of both 1/4-in. and 3/4-in. plywood to build the tower. Build it with more or fewer trays; it's up to you. If you choose to make a wider or taller cabinet with more trays, fine. But it'll take more than two sheets of plywood!

CUT THE BACK AND SIDES A LITTLE OVERSIZE

Cut the 1/4-in. back first. Take a notch out of a corner of the sheet rather than ripping a whole strip or you won't have enough leftover plywood to make the drawer bases.

Cut the back 1/8 in. larger than the illustration calls for. After the cabinet is assembled, you can get extremely accurate measurements by either cutting the back to fit or using a flush-trim router bit after it's attached. Cut the sides a full 24 in. tall and cut them to length after the dadoes are cut. (You don't need to cut a dado in the center where the stretcher goes. We forgot and cut one there, but it's no big deal—it's hidden anyway.)

Gang-sand the exposed tops of the tray sides before assembly. After you get the cabinet box and trays assembled, finish sanding and apply the clear coat. A nice finishing touch is to line the tray bottoms with squares of indoor/outdoor carpeting. Then load up your hand tools—you'll never have to worry about keeping them organized again.

FIGURE A.
TOOL TRAY TOWER

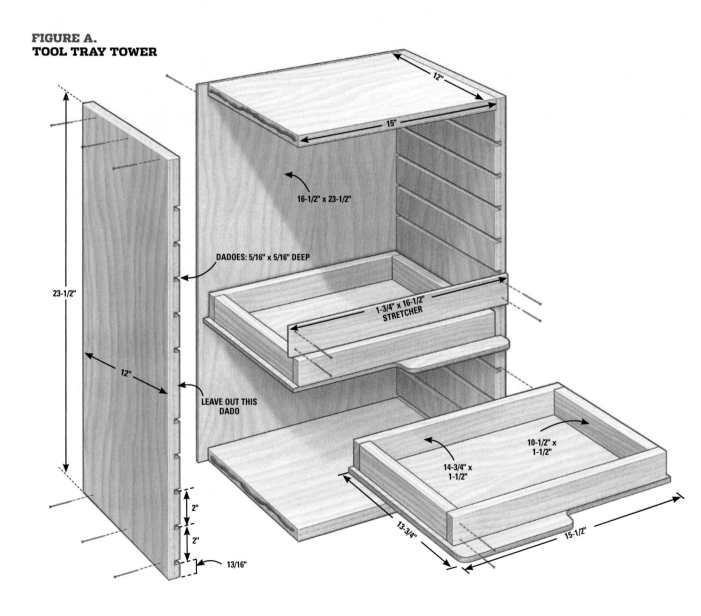

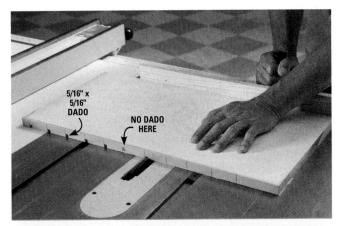

1 Mark and cut the dadoes for the drawers. Mark the dado bottoms on the edges beginning at 13/16 in. up from the bottom and then every 2 in. Don't cut a dado in the center—that's where the stretcher goes. After cutting all 10 dadoes, cut off the top, 2-3/4 in. above the last dado bottom.

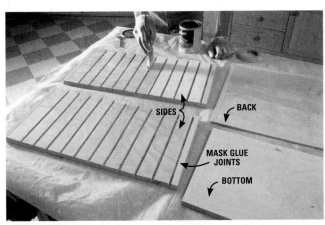

2 Prefinish the interior surfaces. Protect the gluing areas with masking tape and varnish surfaces on the cabinet interior. It's much easier to do now than later. For smooth tray operation, be sure to brush out any varnish pools or drips inside the dadoes.

3 Assemble the box. Glue and nail the box together with 1-1/2-in. brads. Then mark the dadoes to avoid misses when you nail on the back with 1-in. brads. Glue the perimeter, then nail one edge flush with the box side. Square up the box with the back to nail the second side. Then finish nailing the remaining two sides.

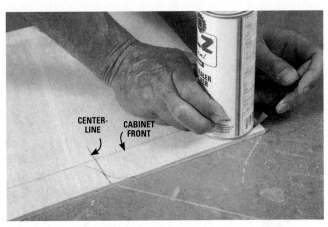

4 Mark the paddle pulls. Cut the tray bottoms into 15-1/2 x 13-3/4-in. rectangles. Draw a line 12 in. from the back edge of the trays and mark a centerline. Use the centerline and one of the corners as a guide while you trace around a spray paint can to mark the curves. Then cut the shapes with a band saw or jigsaw.

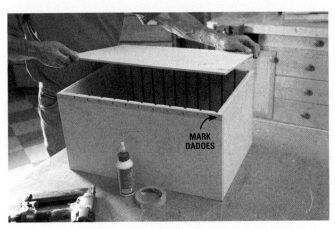

5 Gang-sand the tray bottoms. Clamp the tray bottoms together and sand the fronts of them all at once. Get them roughed out and then finish up with a random orbital sander. (If you have a dedicated drum sander or drum sander accessory for your drill press, use that for the inside curves.)

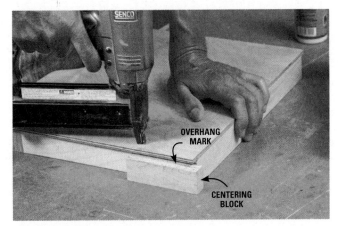

6 Build the trays. Glue and nail the tray sides together. Center one of the bottoms with equal overhangs, then mark a centering block to guide you while you glue and nail on the bottoms. You'll need to use the block on just one side for each tray.

Flip-Top Bench

A space-saving workshop on wheels!

Over the years, we've had a variety of workshops and workbenches. When we were young apartment dwellers, our workshops were often a 3 x 3-ft. broom closet (for real!). Today, many of us are lucky enough to have shops with plenty of elbow room. But in between, most of our workshops consisted of a workbench loaded with tools, tucked into the corner of a garage or basement. If this sounds like you, check out this flip-top workbench. The revolving center section gives you a double platform for your benchtop tools.

START LEVEL AND SQUARE

For the flip-top workbench to "flip," the base, side cabinets and revolving work surface must be flat and square. This means starting with flat plywood, making square cuts, installing components square to one another and checking your accuracy along the way.

Start by ripping three sheets of 3/4-in. plywood into 28-1/2-in.-wide panels using either a table saw or a circular saw and guide. To see how to build a guide, search for

WHAT IT TAKES	
TIME	**SKILL LEVEL**
2 weekends	Intermediate

TOOLS & MATERIALS
Table saw (or circular saw with cutting guide), driver/drill, jigsaw, miter saw, clamps

"circular saw guide" at familyhandyman.com. Set the long cutoffs aside; you'll put them to good use later. Cut parts C, D, E, F, G and N to length.

Build the 1x4 base (A and B) and sheathe it with 3/4-in. plywood **(Photo 1)**. Build the two side support cabinets as shown in **Photo 2**. Note that one of the vertical supports is longer than the other so it can extend down alongside the base to add rigidity to the cabinet. Make certain each cabinet box is square. Secure the 3/4-in. x 3/4-in. cleats (H, J), insetting them 3 in. from the back of the box. Cut the pegboard panels (K) to size, and glue and nail them into place. These panels help keep the cabinet boxes square and rigid.

Position the cabinets **(Photo 3)** and secure them to the base with a couple of drywall screws. Measure to make sure the cabinets are equidistant from each other at the top, bottom, front and back. If you need to adjust the cabinets, remove the screws, adjust them, then resecure them with a couple more screws. Use a square to ensure the front of the cabinet is square to the platform, then secure the 10-in. L-brackets (L) with a few screws.

Note: You'll firmly fasten the cabinets and L-brackets in place once the revolving platform is in place.

1 Build the base. Assemble the base frame from 1x4s, check for square, then install the 3/4-in. plywood sheathing and secure it with 2-in. screws.

2 Build the side cabinets. Assemble the two side cabinets. Make sure the parts are square to one another; cabinets built at an angle tend to stay at an angle.

3 Install the cabinets. Secure the side cabinets to the base with a couple of temporary screws. Make sure the distance between the two cabinets is equal at the front, back, top and bottom. Install the L-brackets.

Loaded with Features

1. The wheels make it mobile (and the simple lock wedges make it immobile).
2. The drawers and recessed pegboard cabinet backs give you convenient places to stash tools, supplies and accessories.
3. The open side cabinet gives you space to store a small drill press or other slim benchtop tool.
4. The outfeed roller lends a helping hand for handling long materials.
5. The power strip allows you to plug in multiple tools. Of course, you could configure the workbench so one side holds benchtop tools while the other serves as a wide-open work surface.

INSTALL THE TOOL PLATFORM

Measure and mark the exact centers of both cabinets on both sides. Measure down 3/8 in. from the bottom of each top piece of plywood (G) to establish crosshairs. Drill a 3/4-in. hole (**Photo 4**); the top should just kiss the bottom of the cabinet top. Use a jigsaw to square off the top edges of the holes so each hole is U-shaped.

Feed the 6-ft. threaded rod (M) through the holes in the first cabinet, slide two 3/4-in. washers over the rod as shown in **Photo 5**, then finish sliding the rod through the holes in the second cabinet. Allow the end to protrude about 2 in. past the cabinet on one side, slide a temporary spacer block (**seen in Photo 6**) over the end, then install a 3/4-in. washer and locknut. Add a spacer block, washer and locknut to the other "long" end too. Leave the nuts a little loose for now.

Install a pair of temporary horizontal cleats 3/4 in. below the threaded rod. Slide one of the platform panels (N) into place so the front and back edges are exactly even with the front and back edges of the cabinets (**Photo 6**). Check to make sure the gaps between the panel and cabinets are equal. If not, adjust the cabinets and L-brackets until the gaps are equal. Now permanently install the L-bracket and cabinet screws.

The center layer of the platform consists of four strips (P). Apply glue to the backs of two of these strips. Position them on each side of the threaded rod, making sure to leave a gap slightly less than the thickness of a credit card between them, then secure them with 1-1/4-in. drywall screws. Next, install the two outer strips (**Photo 7**) even with the outside edges of the platforms.

Apply glue to the center strips (**Photo 8**), position the final full platform panel (N) and secure that in place with 2-in. drywall screws. This top panel should be flush with the tops of the side cabinets. Give your top a 180-degree test spin to ensure it aligns with the edges of the cabinets in both positions.

4 Drill the pivot holes. Find the exact center of both sides of both cabinets, and drill 3/4-in. holes so the top of the hole is just kissing the bottom of the cabinet top. Use a jigsaw to square off the top edges of the holes so you can insert the threaded rod easily.

5 Insert the threaded rod. Wiggle and slide the threaded rod through the two holes in the first cabinet, slip a pair of washers over the end of the rod, then fit the rod through the holes in the second cabinet. Slide a temporary spacer block over each end of the rod (see Photo 6), then loosely install the outer washers.

Drawers and Roller Stand Cutting List

KEY	QTY.	DIMENSIONS	DESCRIPTION
AA	2	3/4" x 8" x 22"	Large drawer sides
BB	2	3/4" x 8" x 10-1/4"	Large drawer ends
CC	6	3/4" x 3-1/2" x 22"	Small drawer sides
DD	6	3/4" x 3-1/2" x 10-1/4"	Small drawer ends
EE	1	3/4" x 10" 13-3/8"	Large drawer front
FF	3	3/4" x 4-1/2" x 13-3/8"	Small drawer fronts
GG	1	1/4" x 3-1/2" x 28"	Roller stand spacer
HH	1	3/4" x 3-1/2" x 28"	Roller stand leg
JJ	1	3/4" x 11" x 26" *	Roller stand arm
KK	1	3/4" x 1-1/2" x 12"	Roller horizontal support
LL	4	1/4" x 11-3/4" x 22"	Drawer bottoms

* At wide top section
Note: The roller, tee nuts and wing nuts are available online.

FIGURE A.
FLIP-TOP WORKBENCH

Overall dimensions: 69" wide x 30" deep x 30-3/4" tall (not including casters)

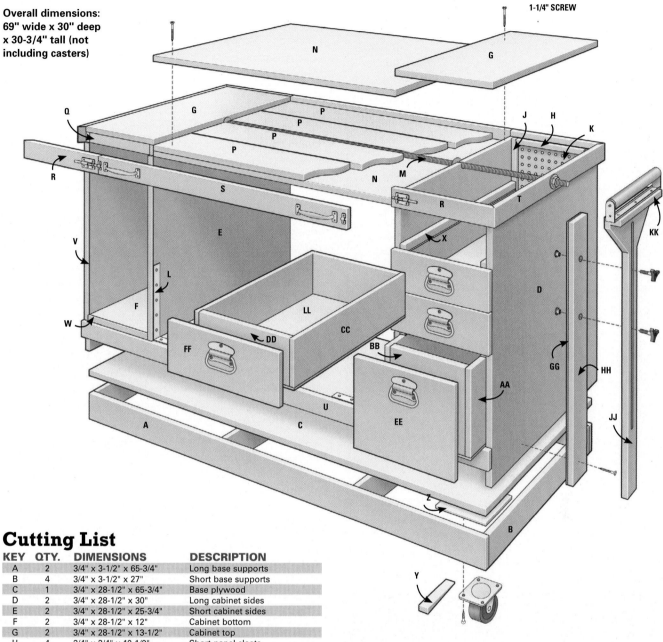

Cutting List

KEY	QTY.	DIMENSIONS	DESCRIPTION
A	2	3/4" x 3-1/2" x 65-3/4"	Long base supports
B	4	3/4" x 3-1/2" x 27"	Short base supports
C	1	3/4" x 28-1/2" x 65-3/4"	Base plywood
D	2	3/4" x 28-1/2" x 30"	Long cabinet sides
E	2	3/4" x 28-1/2" x 25-3/4"	Short cabinet sides
F	2	3/4" x 28-1/2" x 12"	Cabinet bottom
G	2	3/4" x 28-1/2" x 13-1/2"	Cabinet top
H	4	3/4" x 3/4" x 10-1/2"	Short panel cleats
J	4	3/4" x 3/4" x 25"	Long panel cleats
K	2	1/4" x 12" x 25"	Pegboard back
L	2	1" x 10" x 10"	L-brackets
M	1	3/4" x 72" *	Threaded rod
N	2	3/4" x 28-1/2" x 40"	Top & bottom platforms
P	4	3/4" x 6-3/4" x 40"	Middle platform strips
Q	4	3/4" x 1-1/2" x 12"	Cabinet backer boards
R	4	3/4" x 2-1/8" x 14-1/4" **	Front cabinet banding
S	2	3/4" x 2-1/8" x 40"	Platform banding
T	2	3/4" x 2-1/8" x 30" ***	Top side banding
U	2	3/4" x 2-1/2" x 67-1/4"	Bottom banding
V	6	1/4" x 3/4" x 24-1/2"	Side cabinet edging
W	3	1/4" x 3/4" x 12"	Bottom cabinet edging
X	6	3/4" x 3/4" x 24"	Drawer runner
Y	2	1-1/2" x 3/4" x 6" ****	Platform lock wedges
Z	4	1/4" x 8" x 8" plywood	Caster shims

*Cut to length once cabinet is fully assembled (optional)
**Flat to long end (45-degree angle)
***Long end to long end (45-degree angles)
****Tapered from 3/8" to 3/4"

Materials List

ITEM	QTY.
3/4" x 4' x 8' AC plywood	3
1x4 x 8'	3
1x3 x 8'	4
1/4" x 3/4" x 8'	2
1/4" x 4' x 4' pegboard	1
1/4" x 4 x 4' plywood	1
3/4" x 72" threaded rod	1
3/4" washers	4
3/4" locknuts	2
Barrel bolts	4
Fixed handles	4
Drawer D-handles	4
Casters	4
1-1/4" screws	1 lb.
2" screws	1 lb.

6 Slide in the first layer of the platform. Secure temporary cleats to both cabinets, keeping them 3/4 in. below the rod; slide the first platform layer in place. Even up the front and back edges with those of the cabinets on each side.

7 Install the middle layer of the platform. Glue and screw the four middle panels into place, spacing the inner panels a "shy credit card thickness" away from the rod and holding the outer panels flush with the first layer.

8 Secure the third layer. Apply wood glue to the middle panels, position the third layer and secure it in place with 2-in. drywall screws.

INSTALL THE TRIM AND HARDWARE

Install the backer boards (Q) along the inside top edges of the cabinets. Rip 1x3s to the thickness of your revolving platform (2-1/8 in. to 2-1/4 in. depending on the true thickness of your plywood) and install the banding boards (R, S, T and U). You'll need to drill holes through the side trim boards (T) to accommodate the rod, then remove the nuts, slide the trim boards into place, and secure the washers and locknuts for good. Use locking pliers to prevent the threaded rod from turning as you tighten the nuts; make sure the cabinets are snug to the platform while the platform can still revolve freely.

Install the four barrel bolts—one on each corner of the revolving platform—as shown in **Photo 9**. If the bolts don't slide freely, use a pair of locking pliers to open up the U-shaped part of the catch.

Install the 1/4-in. edging strips (V and W) along the edges of the cabinets (with the exception of the front of the drawer cabinet).

Add the four platform handles. With the help of an assistant, tilt the workbench onto its back and install the four casters. You want a 1/2-in. gap between the floor and bottom of the platform. To create that, install 8-in. squares of 1/4-in. to 1/2-in. plywood (Z), as needed, before you install the casters.

Cut two 1-1/2-in. x 6-in. wedges (Y) that taper from 3/8 in. on one end to 3/4 in. on the other. To lock your workbench into place, tap them into the space under the platform. To remove them, tap them out with a hammer.

BUILD THE DRAWERS

Apply masking tape to one side of the cabinet opening, and mark out the desired number and sizes of drawers you want. Each opening should be 1/2 in. taller than the finished drawer and drawers should be built 1/4 in. narrower than the cabinet opening. We chose to install three shallow drawers for benchtop tool bits and accessories, and a deeper drawer for hand power tools.

Use a scrap piece of plywood as a spacer for installing the lowest drawer runners **(Photo 10)**, then rip the scrap to width and use it as a spacer for installing the other runners (X) as you move upward.

Build the drawer boxes from leftover 3/4-in. plywood (AA-DD), then glue and screw the 1/4-in. plywood bottoms (LL) into place **(Photo 11)**. Determine the heights of the drawer fronts and then cut them from leftover plywood (EE, FF). Use a couple of screws as spacers **(Photo 12)**, clamp the front to the drawer box, then secure the front in place with four screws driven in from the back.

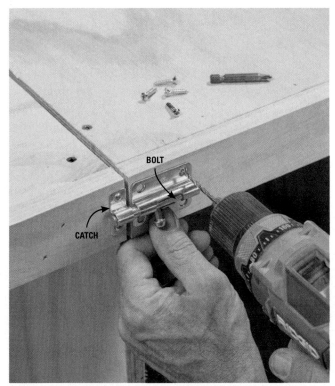

9 Install the barrel bolts. Add the trim using Figure A as a guide. Then predrill holes for the barrel bolts and catches, and secure with screws. Positioning the catch farther away from the bolt will provide more "play" when latching.

10 Install the drawer runners. Lay out the positions of your drawers on masking tape, then use a temporary plywood spacer to hold the runners in place while you attach them. Rip the spacer to width as you install the smaller upper drawers.

11 Install the drawer bottoms. Use the drawer bottom to square up the drawer box. Attach it with glue and finish nails.

12 Install the drawer fronts. Using screws as spacers, clamp the drawer front to the drawer box and secure it in place with four screws driven in from the back side.

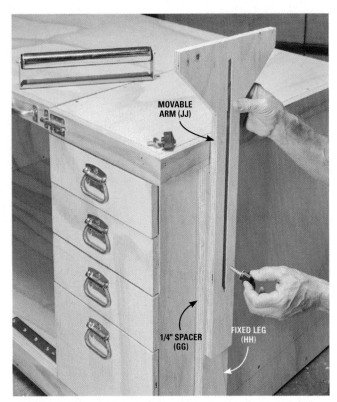

BUILD THE ROLLER STAND

You can build up to four roller stands to help support material as you work. Drill holes and 1-in. counterbores into the back of the fixed leg (HH), then tap the tee nuts in place. Add a 1/4-in. spacer strip (GG) and secure the fixed arm to the cabinet side. Use a jigsaw to cut the movable arm (JJ) to shape and to cut the slot down the center (**Photo 13**). Secure the movable arm to the tee nuts with wing nuts. Glue and nail a 1x2 to the top of the movable arm, then screw the roller carrier into place (**Photo 14**). Secure the tools to the flip-top (**Photo 15**).

USING IT

Your barrel bolts will fit snugly into the U-shaped catches—you want them snug for stability. Take note:

- It may be difficult to latch all four barrel bolts at one time; just make sure to always latch at least three of them for stability.
- If you find the barrel bolts difficult to slide in and out by hand, use a couple taps of the hammer to slide a bolt in and out.
- If the bolts fit really tightly, use pliers to slightly open the U-shaped catch of the barrel bolt.

13 Mount the movable arm. Cut the arm to shape and cut the slot down the center. Secure the movable arm to the underlying tee nuts with wing nuts.

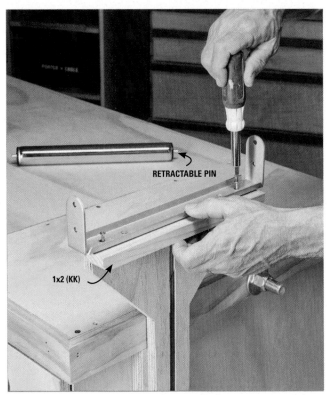

14 Mount the roller. Glue and nail a 1x2 to the top of the arm, then screw the roller carrier into place. A retractable pin in the roller allows you to remove and remount the roller.

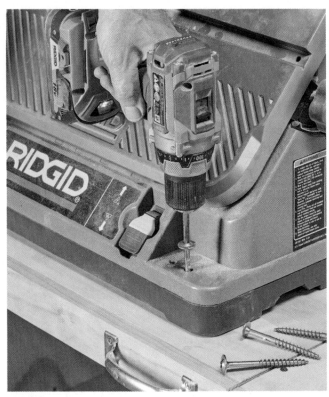

15 Secure the tools. Drive heavy-duty, large-head, coarse-threaded screws through the tool mounting holes into the flip top. Be sure they penetrate 2 in. Keep balance in mind as you select the tools and determine their positions.

STORAGE CONTAINERS

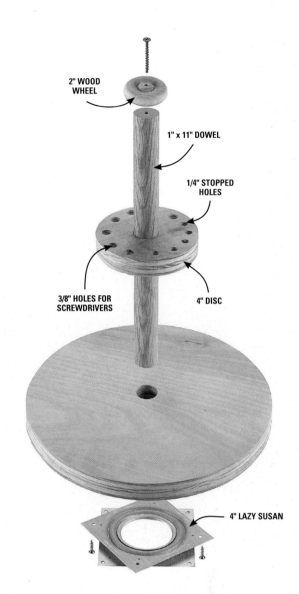

2" WOOD WHEEL

1" x 11" DOWEL

1/4" STOPPED HOLES

3/8" HOLES FOR SCREWDRIVERS

4" DISC

4" LAZY SUSAN

SCREW CONTAINERS TO DISC

Screw Carousel

Screws are one of the easiest things to lose around your workshop—and if you're keeping all of yours together, you can forget about finding the right one when you need it. Thankfully, this super-convenient carousel solves the problem.

Build this spinning screw organizer to dial up the right fastener and tool with a touch of your fingers.

Trace the disc shapes onto the plywood using a compass, and cut them out with a jigsaw or band saw. Sand the edges and drill holes in the center of each disc with a 1-in.-diameter spade bit. Also drill several 3/8-in. holes around the rim of the 4-in. disc for screwdrivers and a few stopped 1/4-in.-diameter holes for driver bits

Secure five containers to the 11-in. disc with 1/2-in. screws, using two screws to anchor each container. Here's what you'll need to build it:

- One 11-in.-diameter x 3/4-in. plywood disc
- One 4-in.-diameter x 3/4-in. plywood disc
- One 11-in. x 1-in.-diameter dowel

- One 4-in. low-profile lazy Susan (rockler.com; part No. 28969)
- One 2-in.-diameter wood wheel
- One package of Ziploc 8-oz. food containers (grocery stores or online)

Glue the dowel in the 11-in. disc, then run a bead of glue around the dowel 4 or 5 in. up from the bottom and glue on the 4-in. disc, sliding it down from the top. When the glue is dry, screw the lazy Susan under the base with 1/2-in. screws and the wood wheel on top of the dowel. Load it with screws and give it a whirl!

P.S. Add stick-on labels to the lids.

WHAT IT TAKES	
TIME 1 hour	**SKILL LEVEL** Beginner
TOOLS & MATERIALS Jigsaw or band saw, driver/drill	

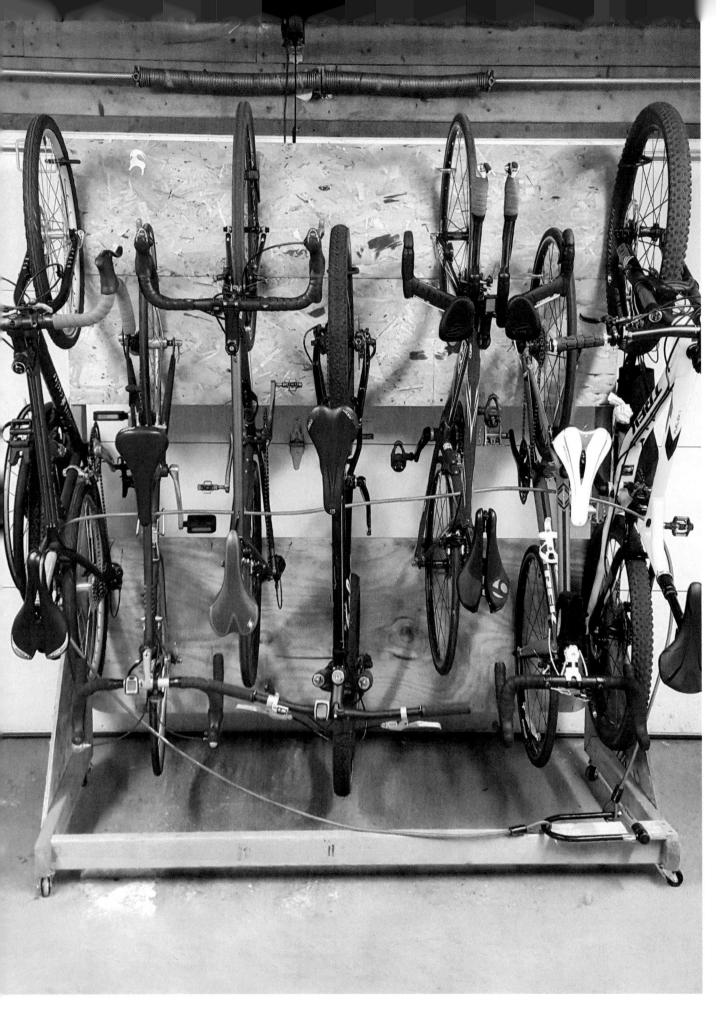

SPECIAL SECTION

STORING SPORTS GEAR

Door-Track Bike Rack

We attached a box rail to a well-braced shelf. Each machine-threaded bike hook hangs from a box-rail hanger, using a nut and thread locker. (The box rail and box-rail hangers are from Home Depot; the bike hooks from parktool.com.)

Bikes slide both ways for easy access, and the hooks rotate, allowing bikes to hug the wall.

The rail and hangers hold 450 lbs.

NUT

BOX RAIL

BOX RAIL HANGER

Fishing Rod Catcher

Cut an 8-ft. 1x4 in half and use 1-in. screws to mount 1-1/4-in. PVC caps 4 in. apart on one 1x4 piece. On the second 1x4 piece, equally space 1-1/4-in. PVC couplings. Screw the 1x4 with caps to the wall a foot from the floor, and the one with couplings 6 ft. off the floor directly above the first. The rod tips slide up through the couplings and the handles rest in the caps.

Fishing Rod Saver

When you go on fishing trips, it's easy to be careless with your rods—just tossing them into the truck bed. But there's an easy way to keep them organized: Cover rods with pool noodles to avoid breakage. Cut a slot down the length of the noodle and slip it over the rod. No more damaged or broken rods, thanks to a pool noodle.

Rolling Bike Storage

A rolling bike rack offers easy access and efficient storage for your family's bikes. To build the rack, make a 2x4 lower frame with 2x4 uprights on each end. Large triangular plywood braces support the uprights. Plywood panels span the uprights, adding strength and rigidity. Staggering their heights and alternating their orientation, you can hang seven bikes on this 6-ft.-wide rack. Casters make it easy to roll the rack away for storage.

For security, run a long steel cable through the bike frames and connect the looped ends with a hefty lock. All the biking essentials—helmets, shoes, pumps, spare wheels and tires—can hang on the back of the rack.

Ski and Pole Organizer

Keep skis up and easy to find with this simple 2x4 rack. Drill 3/4-in.-diameter holes spaced 3/4 in. apart. Glue 4-1/2-in. lengths of 3/4-in. dowel into the holes and then mount the 2x4 to the wall studs. Space the groupings about 8 in. apart to make room for ski bindings. Now you'll spend less time looking for skis and more time on the trails.

All-in-One Ball Storage

This sports storage rack holds a lot of equipment. Toss large balls into a round hole at the top; bungee cords span the front to keep them from falling out. Two baskets on the bottom half of the rack hold baseballs, hockey pucks and more. And the storage hooks on the side of the rack hold baseball bats and hockey sticks.

Sports Rack

A wall-mounted rack will keep bats and balls from getting lost in the recesses of the garage or basement. Just cut 6-in.-diameter holes in the top 1x10 shelf and 3-in. holes in the bottom 1x6 shelf. Then screw the bottom shelf to the top shelf from below. Attach a 1x2 cleat to the back and screw it to the wall studs. Customize the size and shape to fit your needs.

6" HOLES

SLOT FOR BATS
OR RACKETS

1x6 BOTTOM
AND SIDES

3" HOLES